How Long O Lord?

COWLEY PUBLICATIONS is a ministry of the Society of Saint John the Evangelist, a religious community of men in the Episcopal Church. Emerging from the Society's tradition of prayer, theological reflection, and diversity of mission, the press is centered in the rich heritage of the Anglican Communion.

Cowley Publications seeks to provide books, audio cassettes, CDs, and other resources for the ongoing theological exploration and spiritual development of the Episcopal Church and others in the body of Christ. To this end, it is dedicated to developing a new generation of theological writers, encouraging them to produce timely, creative, and stimulating publications of excellence, and making these publications available widely, reaching both clergy and lay persons.

"How Long O Lord?"

Voices from the Ground
and Visions for the Future
in Israel/Palestine

Maurine and Robert Tobin, editors

Published in the United States of America by Cowley Publications, a division
of the Society of Saint John the Evangelist. No portion of this book may be
reproduced, stored in or introduced into a retrieval system, or transmitted, in
any form or by any means—including photocopying—without the prior
written permission of Cowley Publications, except in the case of brief
quotations embedded in critical articles and reviews..

Library of Congress Cataloging-in-Publication Data:
    How long O Lord? : Christian, Jewish, and Muslim voices from the ground
    and visions for the future in Israel–Palestine / Maurine and Robert Tobin,
    editors.
        p. cm.
    Includes bibliographical references
    ISBN 1-56101-214-9 (pbk. : alk. paper)
    1. Arab-Israeli conflict. 2. Arab-Israeli conflict—Causes. 3. Arab-Israeli
    conflict—1993—Peace. 4. Zionism—History. 5. Palestinian Arabs—Social
    conditions—20th century. 6. Palestinian Arabs—Ethnic identity. 7. Israel—
    Ethnic relations. I. Tobin, Maurine, 1938– II. Tobin, Robert, 1936– III. Title.
    DS119.6.H69 2003
    956.05'3—dc21
                                2003001097

Scripture quotations are taken are taken from the following:
The New Revised Standard Version of the Bible, copyright 1989, by the
Division of Christian Education of the National Council of the Churches
of Christ in the United States of America. Used by permission. All rights
reserved.
The Revised Standard Version of the Bible, copyright 1952 (2nd edition, 1971)
by the Division of Christian Education of the National Council of the Churches
of Christ in the United States of America. Used by permission. All rights
reserved.
TANAKH, copyright 1985, Jewish Publication Society of America, Philadelphia,
PA. www.jewishpub.org.

Cover design: Gary Ragaglia

This book was printed in the United States of America on acid-free paper.

COWLEY PUBLICATIONS
907 Massachusetts Ave.
Cambridge, Massachusetts 02139
800-225-1534 • www.cowley.org

Table of Contents

Part Two: Voices from the Ground

Part Three: Visions for the Future

Appendices

Acknowledgments

We wish to thank the Right Reverend M. Thomas Shaw SSJE for his courageous stand for peace founded upon justice and security for both Israelis and Palestinians and for his prayerful guidance in all we've undertaken; Mark Brown SSJE, who initially proposed that we edit such a book; Kevin R. Hackett SSJE for his wise editorial counsel; Dr. Elaine Hagopian for her vast knowledge and willingness to verify detail; Dr. Shukri and Mrs. Randa Khuri for introducing us to significant voices within the Palestinian community and for providing invaluable historical materials; the many American Jewish Peace activists with whom we work whose dedication inspires us to continue speaking on this issue; and, of course, to the authors who have shared so willingly their expertise, experiences, emotions, and dreams of a better future for all who call the Holy Land home. Many of these writers have devoted their lives to the search for a just peace in keeping with the tenets of Judaism, Christianity, and Islam, and we are grateful to them for their generosity in contributing to this book and for waiving their royalties in lieu of contributions to organizations whose missions foster the hard and rewarding work of peacemaking and justice.

We dedicate this book to all the children of Palestine and Israel.

Foreword

The strength of the Anglican Communion at its best is its commitment to a worldview that works for justice and peace and that truly respects the dignity of every human being. That conviction has led many of us to stand with the Palestinian Christians when they called to us. Over the years those who have been part of the support network for the Diocese of Jerusalem and for other Christians in the Holy Land have gained new respect for justice and peace. We have also gained enormous respect for all who dwell in Israel and Palestine.

Many of us have raised our voices against the senseless violence that is common on both sides of the conflict. There is no moral justification for the suicide bombings that target innocent people just because they are Israeli. Likewise, there is no moral justification for the senseless attacks on Palestinian populations, their infrastructures, and their livelihoods. The deaths and wounds suffered offend our sensibilities and our faith.

It is also clear that we as citizens of the United States are complicit in the problem. In so many ways we have turned our backs on the people in the Holy Land even as our government has sent billions of dollars to support the military and to purchase weapons. We have too often remained in denial and too often been misled into thinking that the problem and the conflict are the result of a long and insoluble historical battle between Jews and Arabs. That is simply not the case.

How Long, O Lord? is an attempt to raise our level of understanding by clarifying history and presenting the voices of the people who are directly involved in working for justice. Whether Israeli, Palestinian, or international, these writers seek to present a deeper knowledge and deeper truth that will ultimately contribute to a lasting peace for all the children of Abraham, the peace of God that passes all understanding.

Edmond Browning
Presiding Bishop (retired) of the Episcopal Church

An Unfinished Pilgrimage

Maurine and Robert Tobin

During the last few years we have enjoyed a large number of encounters with remarkable people who are deeply and passionately committed to peace in the Middle East. They are people that we have met along the way of our personal pilgrimage toward understanding the life, culture and conflict in the Holy Land. Some of them have been working for a just resolution of that conflict for more than forty years. This book is our tribute to them.

Our pilgrimage began in 1994 when we attended a month long course called *Jesus and His Setting* at St. George's College in Jerusalem. Our motive was to learn about the Holy Land, to experience the environment in which the spiritual roots of Judaism, Christianity, and Islam are so firmly planted, to re-experience the Bible from the perspective of our spiritual ancestors, and to learn from fine teachers at St. George's, people like The Rev. John Pederson, now Secretary General of the Anglican Communion, and Dr. Henry Carse, who have devoted much of their lives to Jerusalem, the cradle of our religious and spiritual heritage.

We received more than we had bargained for. We learned more than we had anticipated. We prayed regularly at the Church of the Resurrection in Jerusalem, a practice we have repeated each of the four times we have returned to Jerusalem. We walked up Mount Sinai and slept in *wadis* in the desert. We learned archeology at Askelon and Megiddo. We drank water from the cold streams flowing to the Jordan River from Mount Hermon. These experiences were extremely powerful and important. They changed our lives.

Yet the unanticipated experience which changed our understanding of what the Holy Land is now was an experience of the

Israeli Occupation of the West Bank and Gaza. The transforming day for us was a day in Ramallah where we visited two schools: the Arab Evangelical Episcopal School of the Diocese of Jerusalem, one of the finest institutions in the West Bank, and the renowned Ramallah Friends' School, run by the Quakers. At the Friends' School we experienced *curfew*, a particularly cruel feature of the Occupation. We arrived at the school about 10 o'clock in the morning. After a tour, the headmistress was explaining to us that the children, who were about to finish the spring term, had received fewer than fifty full days of instruction that year. The Israeli Military, who control the Occupied Territories through regulations determined solely by the military establishment, called curfews almost every day. The children and teachers were required to go home and remain there until the curfew was lifted. Businesses were required to close, thus crippling the local economy. As we began to raise questions about the reason for the curfews, the sirens sounded and we were told that we must leave along with the students and staff. We boarded our bus with the intention of traveling to St. Luke's Hospital in Nablus. As we approached a roundabout, the Israeli military blocked our way. No explanation would convince the soldiers that we were international students simply trying to leave town. The driver calmly backed the bus several blocks in order to turn around and head to another exit. Shocking as the event was to us, this was not an unusual experience for him! We were again blocked and told that the curfew prevented our passing. For nearly an hour we waited for higher ranking military officers to arrive and grant us permission to leave Ramallah. Of course, Palestinians would not have been allowed to pass at all.

There was no apparent reason for the curfew or the minor ill treatment we received. The Olso Peace Accords had been recently signed and implementation begun. In fact, our St. George's group had been the first delegation to enter Jericho after the Palestinian Authority took charge. We found this treatment deeply troubling. We were informed that this was a small example of what the general population experienced every day. When we returned home and told this story, we encountered disbelief.

The second phase of our pilgrimage was a visit to Israel/Palestine in May, 2000. We volunteered to work in the Mar Elias Educational Institutions (MEEI) in the upper Galilee. Both of us have devoted a good portion of our lives to education and the Ramallah Friends' School experience had continued to trouble us. Because of that event, we wanted an in-depth experience with Palestinian children and their educational opportunities. MEEI is the creation of Abuna Elias Chacour, a Melkite priest, who is one of the most dynamic leaders in the Christian Palestinian community. Beginning with a preschool started more than 30 years ago, he has built institutions ranging through college level programs for more than 3500 students. An Israeli citizen, Abuna Chacour has become a worldwide spokesperson for peace in the Middle East and in 2001 was awarded the Japanese equivalent of the Nobel Peace Prize, the Niwano Peace Prize. Author of several books, among them *Blood Brothers* and *We Belong to the Land*, he works tirelessly for the day when Jews and Arabs can live together in peace, sharing the land that is the inheritance of both. When Abuna Chacour speaks about the plight of the Palestinians, he always says, "I want you on our side, but I don't want you to be one-sided." Our common humanity comes first. Both Jews and Palestinians are first of all human beings.

During a trip to Gaza after leaving MEEI, we experienced the next deepening of our concern for those who are suffering under the Occupation. We went to Gaza with Paul Beren, then a staff member of World Vision in Jerusalem, a faith based organization that works worldwide with the poor, with refugees and with the disenfran- chised. Under the leadership of Tom Getman, the Jerusalem office played a wonderful and significant role ministering to and assisting refugees in the Gaza and West Bank camps. We learned that more than one quarter of the world's refugees are Palestinian, many of whom have lived for three generations in the UN Gaza refugee camps, which are now more than 50 years old. These camps in one of the most densely populated region on earth offer little hope of improvement for the inhabitants or their children. World Vision and other relief groups, however, struggled there to create training programs and schools for deaf children and adults, medical programs and facilities, and some housing programs.

As we drove into Gaza on a recently built super highway that June morning, we were surprised to see lush green fields being irrigated by vast sprinkler systems. This was not what we had expected in Gaza. Paul informed us that we were looking at the land taken by Israeli settlers. We were told that the settlements, created in violation of the Fourth Geneva Convention, control 40% of the tiny Gaza Strip. The settlements use 80% of the available water for rich irrigated farmland, swimming pools, and other amenities for about 6000 Israeli settlers. The Palestinian population of 1.2 million must live on

60% of the land and rely on the remaining 20% of the water, placing them well below the international standard for water and space required for basic health. Most of the Palestinian population has to draw water from common wells and carry it home by donkey cart, by bicycle or on foot. The impressions of masses of people trying to live under such severe restriction and in such squalid conditions burned into our memories. Again, when we returned home, we found much disbelief or denial when we told our stories.

The third phase of our pilgrimage led us to the International SABEEL Conference in 2001. SABEEL is an ecumenical Christian liberation theology center based in Jerusalem with chapters around the world. The *Al Aqsa Intifada* had begun between our visits. More than 300 concerned people from the international community spent five days together hearing from Israeli, Palestinian, South African, American, and other experienced advocates for peace. We listened to members of the Knesset, journalists, lawyers, and people involved in direct non-violent action. We heard from those who lived daily with the Occupation amid rising violence on both sides. Among the most impressive were those who put themselves forward to prevent violence. The Christian Peacemakers Team, a non-violent activist group started by the Mennonites and the Brethren, works in Hebron, literally placing their bodies between the Palestinians and the military, the bulldozers, and the settlers when violent actions are anticipated. Their courage is absolutely remarkable. We met Rabbis for Human Rights and Gila Svirsky, the Israeli coordinator of nine Jewish women's peace groups. We walked at the Bethlehem check point with Neta Golan, a remarkable young Israeli woman who is co-founder of the International Solidarity Movement, a group of volunteers from around the world who are committed to non-violence and who monitor the events in the Occupied Territories and accompany the farmers who are often subject to attack by settlers or military while they attempt to farm their land or pick their olives. We heard from the Rev. Naim Ateek, the founder of SABEEL, who forcefully and compassionately speaks the truth in love about the extremely complex and dire results of the Occupation. Our visits to Ramallah, Bethlehem, and Hebron revealed the deteriorating situation as abject poverty crept into the lives of almost every Palestinian family and unemployment soared to 75% and above. However, a ray of hope was the growing number of Jewish Israelis who were appalled by their own government's treatment of Palestinians, their fellow human beings.

The next phase of our journey began in Boston at a vigil in front of the Israeli Consulate in Boston on October 30, 2001. We had been joining local Jewish, Christian and Muslim peace activists and others who were concerned about the Israeli/Palestinian conflict for demonstrations and prayer vigils for several months. Very few paid attention. We expected the same lack of response to the vigil in front of the Consulate. However, on the preceding Sunday, Bishop Tom Shaw had made his official visit to our parish, Christ Church, Cambridge. During the announcements, we cited the vigil to be held the following Tuesday. After the service, Bishop Shaw asked us for more information and said that he might like to come. He had been praying about the plight of Palestinians and the conflict for several years since he too had been exposed to the violence when he spent three months in Jerusalem at St. George's College and had seen a young man shot dead on the street in East Jerusalem. On Tuesday, Bishop Shaw, along with Bishop Barbara Harris and Bishop Bud Cederholm attended the vigil, holding posters and candles with us. For the first time, the press was interested. The pictures and articles over the next two days in the *Boston Globe* caused a firestorm primarily in the local Jewish community. However, the Bishops' participation precipitated new dialogue with members of the Jewish community and with other Christian leaders. Hard questions about the policies of the Israeli government surfaced. As a result, Bishop Shaw decided that the Episcopal Diocese had a responsibility to follow up by providing education and further dialogue. Bishop Shaw called for a series entitled *Praying for the Peace of Jerusalem.* The series included co-sponsoring with SABEEL North America a major conference at which South Africa's Archbishop Desmond Tutu spoke, along with the Rev. Naim Ateek and others. More than 600 attended; Bishop Tutu's remarks are part of this book. Also from the conference we have included a brilliant essay presented by Dr. Sara Roy from the Middle East Studies program at Harvard University. Three additional prayer and lecture programs were held at St. Paul's Cathedral in Boston during which Dr. Shurki Khuri, a Palestinian American Episcopalian; Charles Sennott, Middle East correspondent for the *Boston Globe;* Dr. Nasir Aruri; and Yehezkel Landau from Open House in Ramle, Israel, made presentations to which Bishop Shaw responded. The final part of the series was a pilgrimage of Diocesan laypeople and clergy led by Bishop Shaw to Israel, the West Bank and Gaza.

Twenty-four participants traveled to the major cities in Israel and Palestine, talked with Israeli and Palestinian officials as well as with leaders of Jewish, Christian and Muslim peace organizations. We listened to stories from those living under the Occupation and heard from Israelis who had suffered from the results of suicide bombers. Once again we were acutely aware of the deterioration of a region wracked by violence and near hopelessness. This visit was harder for us because of memories of our first visit in 1994. In 2002, we saw the dramatic and rapid decline of economic conditions, the demolition of Palestinian homes and olive trees, the destruction of Palestinian infrastructure, and the rapid increase of Israeli settlements and by-pass roads. We decided that the reality of the Occupation must be told.

Upon our return to the United States we once again encountered a high degree of disbelief and misunderstanding. The common discourse and categories for understanding this devastating conflict are incomplete and often distorted in our country. Media reports and current political debate are far from adequate. However, this time we sensed a growing willingness to listen and to learn, at least in some quarters, especially in faith communities.

How might we define the conflict in terms that rise above the usual political and stereotypical categories that prevail in the press and in the minds of many? We have found hope among those speaking in this book. We also found in the Parents' Circle an icon for what must happen before a just peace can be achieved. Made up of families in Israel and Palestine who have lost family members to the violence that dominates the current landscape, members of the Parents' Circle travel the world calling for an end to the violence that cost them their loved ones. They do not forfeit their identity as Israeli Jews or Palestinian Arabs, but they do give up the hatred and bitterness that perpetuates violence. They have risen above the historical hatred that has developed since 1948 and above the fear that leads to more and more estrangement between the peoples who dwell on the small bit of land they both call home. When challenged to debate the virtues of one side or the other, they refuse. There are two sides, they believe— but the sides are not Israeli or Palestinian. The sides are those who strive for and wish to live in peace with each other and those who do not. They claim more in common with each other, their common humanity and their common suffering, than with those who create and commit the violence that has shredded the land, culture, and future of their homeland. Like the prophet Habakkuk, they survey the injustice and devastation that grip their land and cry out, "How long, Lord, how long?"

We hope this book will honor their shared vision of a better way. Our attempt is to gather information not widely reported, to allow voices not often heard in the United States to find an audience, and to present visions and options for a peaceful future in a most extraordinary and strategic land. You will hear Christians and Jews and Muslims. You will hear voices of people who live in the midst of chaos and voices of women and men laboring to bring about godly order and peace from other parts of the globe.

We have come to love the Holy Land more and more each time we visit. In spite of all, it is a place where one can enter into the holy not only through the stones of historical sites but more often through the "living stones" who dwell there. Often with tears and a torn heart one can still find the roots of the faith we share—Jewish, Christian and Muslim. Our hope is that you, the reader, will gain greater appreciation of the complexity of the history and present reality of Israel/Palestine, experience the depth of the conflict with those who live it, and share the visions for peace and reconciliation of those who are working so hard to change a brutal and oft times heartless situation.

We understand the limitations of our efforts. We have not tried to present all points of view. There are certainly many more voices we could have included. However, the writers are people we know personally or know to be people of great integrity.

Franklin Roosevelt said near the end of World War II:

> **Unless the peace that follows recognizes that the whole world is one neighborhood and does justice to the whole human race, the germs of another world war will remain as a constant threat to mankind.**

Our writers know that. The Middle East crisis contains the germs of larger conflicts. We believe that justice and security for both Palestinians and Israelis are essential to our common welfare. Thus, the voices you will hear are wide in range, passionate in tone, and totally committed to genuine justice and peace in the Holy Land and, indeed, in all the world.

Part One:

Perspectives on the Past

CHAPTER ONE

Why Peace Failed— An Oslo Autopsy

Sara Roy

This essay was originally published in
Current History, vol. 100, number 651, January 8, 2002.

The tragedy of September 11 and the increasingly violent struggle between Palestinians and Israelis have refocused attention on the continuing Palestinian-Israeli conflict as a primary concern of the Arab world. The Palestinian problem, perhaps more than any other, resonates deeply with Arab and Muslim peoples. According to a recent survey quoted by journalist David Hirst, nearly 60 percent of the people of Saudi Arabia, Kuwait, the gulf emirates, and Lebanon regard Palestine as the "single most important issue to them personally"; for Egyptians this figure rises to 79 percent. Not surprisingly, Osama bin Laden, for whom the Palestinian issue had not appeared primary, stated that Americans will not be safe until Palestinians are safe. Soon after, President George W. Bush and British Prime Minister Tony Blair acknowledged the centrality of the Palestinian question in the current crisis and the need for a viable Palestinian state (although the Bush administration's hardening toward the Palestinians following the suicide bombings in December 2001 may change this).

It is commonly believed that the failure of the Middle East peace process to resolve the Palestinian-Israeli conflict occurred at the Camp David II summit in July 2000, when Israeli, Palestinian, and American delegates met to reach a final settlement. It was at Camp

David that Israel supposedly offered the Palestinians an exceedingly generous compromise that came close to an agreement—but which the Palestinians selfishly and foolishly rejected. This perception was reinforced by President Bill Clinton, who publicly blamed Palestinian Authority President Yasir Arafat for the summit's failure. Others have since argued that the summit's failure was not due to the Palestinians alone but to the Israelis and Americans as well, and that the failure of the Oslo peace process was due largely to faulty negotiating styles, poor management of the implementation process, and the unwillingness of right-wing Israeli Prime Minister Benjamin Netanyahu to honor negotiated agreements. Hence, it was the inability to negotiate the terms of the Oslo peace agreements that was the problem rather than the terms themselves.

But the ongoing crisis among Israelis and Palestinians is not primarily the result of a failed summit, poor implementation, or Netanyahu's intransigence: it is instead the result of a "peace" process that by design altered the political, economic, and physical landscape of the Palestinian territories in a manner that intensified rather than mitigated Palestinian dispossession, deprivation, and oppression, and so precluded a fair and workable settlement of the Palestinian-Israeli conflict (irrespective of what might have been agreed to at Camp David II). The egregious outcomes imposed by the Oslo process were not an unfortunate by-product of a fundamentally fair set of agreements but largely a direct result of the terms of those agreements themselves (and Israeli closure policy, a defining feature of the Oslo period), which were fundamentally unfair. Rather than coming close to an agreement, the parties had never been farther apart.

Oslo: Key Terms and Outcomes

The initiation of the Oslo peace process in September 1993 brought with it the hope and expectation among Palestinians and Israelis that a resolution to the conflict was attainable. Yet, in the years between Oslo's inception and its unofficial end in September 2000, when the Al Aqsa uprising began, conditions in the West Bank and Gaza steadily and dramatically deteriorated to a point far worse than during any other period of Israeli occupation, providing the context for the current uprising. Illustrations of this decline include the influx of almost 100,000 new Israeli settlers into the West Bank and Gaza— which doubled the settler population—and the addition of at least 30 new Israeli settlements and settlement-related infrastructure since

1993. During this time, the government of Israel confiscated over 40,000 acres of Palestinian land—much of it viable agricultural land worth more than $1 billion—for Israeli settlement expansion and road building. (The latter refers to the paving of 250 miles of settler bypass roads onto expropriated Arab lands designed to connect Jewish settlements and divide Palestinian population centers.)

Palestinian decline is also seen in the institutionalization of closure policy, the measure that had the single most damaging effect on the Palestinian economy and the free movement of people during the Oslo period; closure resulted in significantly heightened unemployment and increased poverty and child-labor rates between 1992 and mid-2000. Perhaps the most striking indicator of Palestinian weakness during this period was the dissection of the West Bank and the Gaza Strip into territorially noncontiguous enclaves that directly resulted from Oslo's terms. According to Amnesty International, by December 1999 the Oslo agreements had created 227 separate areas in the West Bank under the full or partial control of the Palestinian Authority (PA). The overwhelming majority of these areas were less than 2 square kilometers in size with entry and exit controlled by Israeli military checkpoints. The Gaza Strip was divided into three enclaves and surrounded by an electric fence.

The last seven years of the Oslo peace process were shaped primarily by the policy imperatives of the Israeli government with the explicit support of the United States government, and secondarily by those of the Palestinian Authority. Israeli imperatives were three: the solidification of Israeli control over the Palestinian population and resources (notably land and water); the preclusion of Palestinian geographic continuity; and the institutionalization of policies of economic integration with political, social, and demographic separation with the Palestinian people. PA imperatives were also three and fundamentally no different from those of Israel: the demobilization and repression of the Palestinian people and the disempowerment of their institutions; the elimination of all forms of dissent and opposition, particularly to the Oslo accords; and security cooperation with Israel.

The Oslo agreements and the process to which they gave shape were not about peace or reconciliation but about security and Israel's continued control of Palestinian resources. In the words of one Israeli official, "Both sides gained from this [security] cooperation. After all, Israel and the PA have one thing in common. Both want stability, not democracy, in the territories...."[1] Indeed, Prime Minister Yitzhak

Rabin's decision to allow Arafat to return and establish a governing authority was not based on Israel's desire to see democracy flourish in the West Bank and Gaza, but on the need to devolve responsibility for controlling Palestinians to a body wholly dependent on and accountable to Israel. Just days before the signing of the first Oslo agreement on the White House lawn, Rabin told the political council of the Labor Party that "I prefer the Palestinians to cope with the problems of enforcing order in the Gaza [Strip]. The Palestinians will be better at it than we are because they allow no appeals to the Supreme Court and will prevent the [Israeli] Association for Civil Rights from criticizing the conditions there by denying it access to the area. They will rule there by their own methods, freeing—and this is important—the Israeli army soldiers from having to do what they will do."[2]

The Oslo process, therefore, did not represent the end of Israeli occupation but its continuation, albeit in a less direct form. The structural relationship between occupier and occupied, and the gross asymmetries in power that attend it, were not dismantled by the accords but reinforced and strengthened. The Oslo agreements formalized and institutionalized the occupation in a manner that was altogether new.

Oslo I: Legalizing Israeli Control

The first Oslo agreement, the Declaration of Principles (DOP), was signed September 13, 1993. It contained several noteworthy features: the removal of international law as the basis for resolving the Palestinian-Israeli conflict, the redeployment of Israeli forces from within circumscribed areas of the Gaza Strip and West Bank (beginning with the West Bank town of Jericho), the delinking of interim and final status issues (whose linkage was a major obstacle for both sides at the 1991 Madrid peace talks), the establishment of the PA, and mutual recognition.

Perhaps the most critical feature of the Oslo process was the abandonment of the entire body of international law and resolutions pertaining to the conflict that had evolved over the last 53 years in favor of bilateral negotiations between two actors of grossly unequal power. The only legal underpinning of the Oslo agreements was un Security Council Resolution 242 (and 338, reaffirming 242), which calls for the withdrawal of Israeli troops from territories occupied in the 1967 war. Israel's interpretation of UN Resolution 242 differed from that of the PLO and the international community. Israel viewed 242 as not requiring it to withdraw from all occupied Arab territories, given that the accepted English version of the resolution refers only to "territories" occupied in 1967, but not to *the* territories as is stated in the French version. This ambiguity was deliberate. The Palestine Liberation Organization (PLO) and the majority of the international community regarded Israel as an occupying power and understood 242 as requiring Israel to withdraw from all the Palestinian areas occupied in June 1967.

Given the United States position that negotiations would be based on "land for peace," Israel understood that it would have to relinquish some land. Its implicit objective was to assure that its interpretation of 242 would be the framework for negotiations. When Arafat signed the DOP and the subsequent interim agreements, he de facto affirmed the Israeli position, which has prevailed and is reflected in all the Oslo accords, none of which contains the word "occupation" or acknowledges Israel as an occupying power. (The agreements also do not recognize the right of Palestinian statehood, borders, or full equality).

A review of the various Oslo agreements clearly demonstrates that Israel successfully established itself as the sole authority that would determine which land areas it would yield to the Palestinian Authority. The major confirmation of the Israeli position was the Hebron Protocol. When Arafat signed the protocol in 1997 he conceded the Palestinian interpretation of 242 forever since the protocol gave Israel the right, supported explicitly by the United States, to decide for itself from which of the occupied territories it would withdraw and from which it would not. Furthermore, the final status issues, such as borders, refugees, Jerusalem, and settlements, which lie at the core of the conflict, were not subject to the provisions of the DOP but were instead relegated to a later phase set to begin in May 1996. However, not until Camp David II did Israel actually agree to make some commitments regarding key Palestinian national demands (for example, the status of Jerusalem and the return of Palestinian refugees). In the interim, both the Labor and Likud governments created many "facts on the ground"—the construction and expansion of settlements and the vast network of bypass roads, for example—that compromised negotiations greatly. (Settlement expansion and land confiscation were not expressly prohibited by the DOP.)

Contrary to accepted belief, the PA had no legal power to stop Israeli measures. In fact, under the terms of the 1995 Oslo II agreement, which extended limited self-rule to the West Bank, the Palestinian Authority gave its legal seal of approval to the confiscation of certain Palestinian lands for the paving of Israeli bypass roads. In this and many other ways, the Oslo agreements did not aim to end the occupation but to normalize it. Thus, under the DOP's terms, the primary task of the new Palestinian Authority was to implement rather than to negotiate interim arrangements, and to manage the occupation for Israel.[3] That the PA quickly revealed itself to be repressive and corrupt was not unwelcome by Israel or the United States.

Although Israel and the PLO traded "mutual" recognition by signing the Oslo I agreement, no power symmetry exists between them. Israel, a fully sovereign state, possesses total power, and the PLO–PA, the acknowledged representative of the Palestinian people, possesses virtually none. By reducing the conflict to power negotiations between two such unequal parties, the Oslo agreements reflected Israeli strength and Palestinian weakness, and not the application of accepted international law or universal standards of justice. In this regard and far less known is the fact that under the terms of Oslo I, Israeli military law—including the Israeli military government and approximately 2,000 military orders in effect before Oslo during direct Israeli occupation—remained the legal framework for governing the West Bank and Gaza after Oslo. Thus, although the PA was assigned responsibility for various sectors of activity such as education and health, final authority over the territories, particularly regarding security and the economy, remained wholly with Israel. Furthermore, by agreeing to Israeli military government control over the West Bank and Gaza Strip, the PA, ipso facto, accepted both the existence and legitimacy of Israeli occupation.

Oslo II: Territorial Bifurcation

The second Oslo agreement, the "Interim Agreement," was signed September 28, 1995. A key feature of Oslo II was the division of the West Bank into three areas, each under varying degrees of Palestinian or Israeli control.

The territorial division of the West Bank legalized in the Oslo II agreement was first carried out in the Gaza Strip just one month after the famous handshake between Rabin and Arafat on the White House lawn. In the Taba negotiations that took place in October 1993, Israel presented and eventually implemented a plan that grouped Jewish settlements in Gaza into three blocs that included the lands between the individual settlements. These blocs, combined with a network of bypass roads and military bases, comprise around a third of Gaza's land, now home to 6,000 Israeli settlers. The remaining two-thirds of Gaza, cut into cantons, was left to 1.1 million Palestinians, leaving roughly 128 Israelis per square mile in Gaza compared to 11,702 Palestinians per square mile.

With Oslo II, the Gaza arrangement was extended to the West Bank in the form of Areas A, B, and C. Area A, which initially consisted of seven major Palestinian towns, is under the total civilian and security control of the PA. Area B comprises the remaining Palestinian population centers (excluding some refugee camps) where civilian control resides with the PA and security control with Israel, which effectively places Area B under Israeli jurisdiction. Area C, which incorporates all Israeli settlements, "state lands," and Israeli military bases, remains under the total control of Israel. By mid-2000, Area A comprised 17.2 percent and Area B 23.8 percent of the West Bank; Area C incorporated the remaining 59 percent. In practical terms, therefore, by the time of the Camp David summit, Israel actually controlled almost 83 percent of the West Bank according to the terms of the Oslo agreement. Critically, all Palestinians in the West Bank presently live within six kilometers of Area C lands.[4]

Thus, while the absolute area under full or partial Palestinian control had increased, these areas were noncontiguous and remained isolated cantons separated by areas under the complete jurisdiction of Israel. Under this scenario, even if Palestinians had been given authority over 90 to 95 percent of the West Bank—as allegedly proposed by Israeli Prime Minister Ehud Barak at Camp David II—they would have had five enclaves isolated from each other by several Israeli settlement blocs, along with highways, industrial infrastructure, and army checkpoints. Additionally, many individual settlements are in the midst of these Palestinian enclaves themselves. Under Barak's offer, therefore, the Palestinian state would consist of the northern, central, and southern West Bank enclaves, some isolated areas of East Jerusalem under autonomous or sovereign control by Palestinians, and at least two-thirds of the Gaza Strip.

Crucially, Palestinians would not have control over borders— internal or external—to the West Bank or Gaza. That control would remain with Israel; Palestine's only borders would be with Israel.

Thus, Barak's supposedly generous offer at the Camp David summit basically aimed to enlarge the geographic areas under Palestinian authority while maintaining their geographic fragmentation and isolation. In this way, the division of the West Bank into territorial sections, itself inconceivable in other national contexts and illegal under international law, would give Israel a new mechanism with which to ensure control over Palestinians and their resources even if a Palestinian state is declared. The question remains: Under these conditions, what kind of state could it be?

Settlement expansion has been a key factor in fragmenting Palestinian lands. By 2000, Palestinian built-up areas in the West Bank (including East Jerusalem) comprised no more than 5 percent of the territory, while the built-up area of the settlements (including East Jerusalem) covered 1.8 percent. This reflects the scale and rapidity of Israeli settlement construction since 1967 and the myriad restrictions on Palestinian development. Despite promises to reduce and even halt the expansion of settlements as part of his commitment to the Oslo peace process, Prime Minister Barak engaged in policies that did just the opposite. Barak's 2001 budget earmarked $500 million for settlements and, according to official data from Israel's housing ministry, Barak's government began construction of 1,943 housing units in the West Bank and Gaza in 2000, the largest number in any year since 1992.[5] The Palestinian Authority, corrupt and mismanaged, conceded to and approved these and other Israeli policies from 1994 on, facilitating the status quo.

With the Oslo II agreement, Israel gained legal control over a majority of the West Bank, something it had sought since 1967. The territorial divisions agreed to in the second Oslo accord established the framework for a final settlement in the West Bank that would preclude any territorial continuum for a future Palestinian state and ensure the continued presence of the Israeli occupation in some form. Moreover, by accepting the division of the West Bank according to the provisions of the accord, Yasir Arafat accepted the legitimacy of Israeli settlements in the occupied territories.

The Hebron Protocol: Defining New Precedents

The first Oslo accord brokered by Israeli Prime Minister Benjamin Netanyahu's government—the Hebron Protocol—was signed on January 15, 1997. It introduced some important departures from earlier accords and set new precedents for future negotiations.

According to the protocol, the city of Hebron was divided into two parts: H1 and H2. Israel redeployed from 80 percent of Hebron or H1, home to 100,000 Palestinians, and retained full control over the remaining 20 percent or H2, where approximately 250 to 400 Israeli settlers, protected by the Israeli army, live among 30,000 Palestinians. H2 is the downtown, commercial area.

The Hebron Protocol contains no reference to UN Resolutions 242 or 338 as the legal framework for negotiations. Furthermore, in a letter appended to the document from former United States Secretary of State Warren Christopher, the United States explicitly pledged its full support for Israel's interpretation of its obligations under these accords, which stipulate that Israel alone will decide the timing and scope of any future redeployments. Furthermore, such redeployments are to be conditioned on Palestinians meeting their responsibilities as defined by Israel.[6]

Hebron's division into two parts created an important precedent for the further division of Palestinian lands into isolated enclaves on territories where Palestinians expect to achieve statehood. The PA's acceptance of an armed Israeli settler presence in a predominantly Arab population center also established another precedent for the permanence of Israeli settlements throughout the West Bank and Gaza and, by extension, for the bifurcation of Palestinian lands that results from the presence of those settlements. The protocol also makes clear and concrete the right of Israel to decide unilaterally, and not through negotiations, when and how it will fulfill its obligations.

Closure Policy

The Oslo peace process and the conditions it imposed were directly linked to, and shaped by, Israeli closure policy, which has had a devastating impact on the Palestinian economy and people. The period between the start of the peace process in September 1993 and the beginning of the Al Aqsa uprising in September 2000 was a time of increasing and virtually uninterrupted economic decline for the majority of Palestinians living in the West Bank and Gaza Strip.[7] Arguably, not since the beginning of Israeli occupation in 1967 had the Palestinian economy been so weak and its people so vulnerable. In fact, when measured against advances made by other states in the region, the Palestinian economy is weaker today than it was 33 years ago. The economic reality of the Oslo period is defined by the continuation of preexisting structures of dependency and de-development and by the introduction of new structures, particularly closure, that have exacerbated an already weakened economic base.

Although the Israeli government first imposed closure in early 1991, it was in March 1993, in response to heightened violence by Palestinians against Israelis inside Israel, that closure became a permanent administrative measure. Closure has since become an institutionalized system in the Gaza Strip and West Bank and, almost nine years after it was introduced, has never been lifted, although its intensity is subject to change.

Initially and most harshly imposed by Labor governments, closure restricts the movement of people, labor, and goods, and has produced a double dissection of the occupied territories: one, demographic, and the other, economic. Demographically, closure has severed most movement between the West Bank and Gaza. By 1998, virtually all demographic (and commercial) interaction between the territories had ceased. Furthermore, closure prohibits Palestinian access to Jerusalem. By early 1998, less than 4 percent of Palestinians living in the West Bank and Gaza Strip had permission to enter Jerusalem (and hence, Israel). As a result, Israel's closure policy physically has separated the northern and southern regions of the West Bank, whose primary road connections pass through Jerusalem.

Closure has three forms: general, total, and internal. General closure refers to the overall restrictions placed on the movement of people, labor, goods, and the factors of production between the areas described earlier; it is typically accompanied by long delays at border crossings and by prolonged searches. Total closure refers to the complete banning of any movement between the West Bank-Gaza Strip and Israel and other foreign markets, and between the West Bank and Gaza; it is typically imposed in anticipation of or after a terrorist attack in Israel. Internal closure refers to restrictions on movement between Palestinian localities within the West Bank (and Gaza Strip) itself, and was made possible by the geographical cantonization of the West Bank formalized in the Oslo II agreement. Thus, although closure was imposed several months before the implementation of Oslo, the accords, in effect, legalized and institutionalized closure as a policy measure.

Between 1993 and 1996 (considered the euphoric height of the Oslo process), the Israeli government imposed 342 days of total closure in the Gaza Strip and 291 days of total closure in the West Bank. Thus, for almost one-third of each year between 1993 and 1996, Palestinians were prohibited from any physical or economic movement outside the West Bank and Gaza, and on the remaining days were subject to closure in a less extreme form.

The economic effects of closure have been enormous. In 1996, for example, losses derived from closure amounted to 39.6 percent of Gaza's GNP and 18.2 percent of the West Bank's GNP. Furthermore, the World Bank estimated the economic damage caused by closure policy to be between 11 and 18 percent of gross national income in the West Bank and between 31 and 40 percent in the Gaza Strip annually between 1994 and 1996. More recently, the World Bank stated that with the sealing of the Palestinian borders that followed the outbreak of the Al Aqsa uprising, "the Palestinian economy has been decimated."[8] In the first four months of the uprising, the Palestinian economy lost more than $1.15 billion primarily in production and income in an economy that produces only $5 billion annually; by June 2001, that loss had reached $5.2 billion.

Perhaps the most immediate and dramatic effect of closure has been the high and fluctuating unemployment rates and declining income levels among Palestinian workers in Israel. Between 1992 and 1996, the average unemployment rate among Palestinians increased from 3 percent to 28 percent. The highest levels occurred during total closures. Following the total closure of March–April 1996, for example, 66 percent of the Palestinian labor force was either unemployed or severely underemployed. As the closure was eased, unemployment levels decreased but still remained high, standing at 10 to 20 percent in the West Bank and 18 to 30 percent in the Gaza Strip between 1997 and 1999. By mid-2000, unemployment stood at a striking 25 percent among Gazans and 10 percent among West Bankers. With the current intensification of closure policy, Palestinian unemployment levels have risen to between 35 and 50 percent, according to the World Bank and official Palestinian sources.

Rising poverty rates among Palestinians is another painful expression of closure's effect and a stark illustration of economic life during Oslo. The number of poor living below the poverty line (defined as a household of two adults and four children with a per capita consumption of less than $2.10 per day), comprised around 21 percent of the total Palestinian population in mid-2000, a decrease from almost 25 percent in 1997. However, since the start of the intifada, poverty levels have risen dramatically and quickly: between October 2000 and April 2001, the number of Palestinians living in poverty increased from 650,000 to 2,100,000, or from 21 percent to 64 percent of the population.[9] Palestinian families have responded to economic distress in several ways. One has been an increase in child-labor rates, particularly among children 12 to 16 years old. In 1999 the Palestinian Central Bureau of Statistics found that 74 percent of working children under 18 years of age were not enrolled in school, and 73 percent worked in excess of 35 hours per week. Given that children below 18 years of age make up just over 53 percent of the population, the long-term social implications of an increasingly uneducated population are overwhelming.

People also spend a greater percentage of their income on food, deplete savings, incur greater debt, and sell personal possessions to maintain family consumption levels. With the current uprising, economic conditions have deteriorated even further, creating, for the first time in the history of Israeli occupation, a looming humanitarian crisis in the occupied territories. According to the Gaza Community Mental Health Program, 15 percent of all children in the Gaza Strip presently suffer from chronic malnutrition. A survey conducted by the Palestinian Central Bureau of Statistics in May–June 2001 found that 14.2 percent of Palestinian households (or 74,200 people) completely lost their sources of income during the current uprising and approximately 47.4 percent of households reported losing more than 50 percent of their income.

Closure, in effect, is the method by which the Israeli policy of separation has been implemented (a policy that has historical antecedents in the British Mandate period). The idea of separating from the Palestinians—physically and politically (linked only economically in the form of cheap labor and captive export markets)—was revived by, and underlines the substance and implementation of, the Oslo agreements. According to Meron Benvenisti,

> The separation…is not only a strategy designed "to remove Gaza from Tel Aviv." It is in fact a complex master plan, which is founded on a dual separation between Palestine in its British Mandate boundaries from the neighboring states; and second, an internal separation between Jewish and Arab demographic blocs within the country. The concrete control (known as "security") of all the international borders, which Israel is succeeding in retaining at the land crossings, the Gaza airport and…seaport, enables it to implement the internal separation….Control of the external wrapper is essential for the Oslo strategy, because if the Palestinians control even one border crossing—and gain the ability to maintain direct

relations with the outside world—the internal lines of separation will become full-fledged international borders, and Israel will lose its control over the passage of people and goods. Puncturing the external system will necessitate the establishment of a vast array of physical obstacles, crossing points, and customs barriers between the enclaves of the "internal separation," and will expose the absurdity of the tortuous and non-contiguous borders of the ethnic cantons on which all the ideas of the permanent settlement are based.[10]

Israel currently operates 97 Israeli military checkpoints in the West Bank and 32 in the Gaza Strip. Shlomo Ben Ami, who was Barak's minister of internal security and chief negotiator at Camp David, maintains that "in practice" the Oslo agreements "were founded on a neo-colonialist basis, on a life of dependence of one on the other forever."[11] There should be no doubt that as long as Oslo and closure remain the defining policy framework for achieving a settlement, Israeli control over the Palestinians is assured.

On the Eve of Camp David II . . .

By the time the Camp David summit was held, several processes had become permanent features of the Palestinian landscape: 1) the steady confiscation of Arab lands in the West Bank and Gaza; 2) the accelerated expansion of existing Israeli settlements and the construction of new settlements on confiscated lands, bisecting them; 3) the near doubling of the settler population to 200,000 in 10 years; 4) the division of the West Bank and Gaza Strip into cantons disconnected from each other by territories under the control of Israel; 5) the paving of 250 miles of bypass roads onto confiscated lands that further bisect, truncate, and encircle Palestinian areas; 6) the institutionalization of closure policy, restricting movement, locking Palestinians into the enclave structure created by the Oslo accords, and wreaking havoc on their economy; and 7) the construction of myriad checkpoints and barricades throughout the West Bank and Gaza Strip designed to control and further restrict Arab movement. In these policies, Israel relied on the Palestinian Authority and its vast security apparatus to maintain control of the population, suppress any visible forms of opposition, and provide protection for Israeli actions.

By July 2000, the fundamentals of occupation had remained unaltered and the structure of occupation had become more entrenched. Separation—internal and external—also was becoming a demographic and political reality. Thus, by that July, the establishment of an adequately sovereign, resourced state was impossible. During the Oslo period, like the one preceding it, Palestinians had little recourse against Israeli measures. After Oslo, however, Israeli actions were defined as the price of peace rather than as a cause for conflict. Within this construct, legitimacy for Palestinians no longer derived from resisting Israeli occupation but from their willingness to accede to it. At Camp David, for the first time since the Oslo process began, the Palestinians refused any further concession.

...And Barak's "Generous" Offer

Through the Oslo process and finally at Camp David, Prime Minister Barak sought international recognition and legal ratification for a form of ethnic separation that extended to all final status issues, including Palestinian statehood, the disposition of land, Jerusalem, and refugees. At the summit, Barak moved directly to final status talks rather than implement a third redeployment of Israeli troops as was mandated under previous agreements. Thus, the PA was placed in a position of discussing permanent-status issues when it controlled only 17.2 percent of the West Bank and between 66 and 80 percent of the Gaza Strip in isolated, encircled enclaves. "Barak's strategy sharpened Oslo's fundamental imbalance of power: whereas final status talks had been contingent on withdrawal from almost all the Occupied Territories, the third (and final) redeployment was now contingent on major Palestinian concessions on final status issues."[12]

Although Barak did go further than any other Israeli leader in breaking the taboo on talking about Jerusalem and the Temple Mount/Haram al Sharif, refugees, and the "return" of territory, his vision of a final settlement—neither generous nor a compromise—did not depart from the one described earlier and consisted of the following general terms:

- Passing reference to UN Resolution 242 and its mandate of full Israeli withdrawal to the borders of June 4, 1967, which effectively transformed a basic legal reference into a nonbinding Palestinian demand.
- The annexation of three large settlement blocs (80 percent of the settlers) and other areas of the West Bank to Israel (although Israel did not specify how it would handle all the settlements), which equaled roughly 10 percent of the West Bank. The

annexed settlement blocs include around 160,000 settlers who would retain their Israeli citizenship, in addition to 80,000 to 100,000 Palestinians who would likely be disenfranchised. The integration of these three settlement blocs would split the West Bank into four cantons: northern, central, and southern (with the passages between them under full Israeli control), and an encircled and divided East Jerusalem cut off from its Palestinian hinterlands. Under this scenario, Palestinians were denied control over borders with the outside world and over Arab East Jerusalem. Their only borders were with Israel.

In exchange for annexed lands, Israel would "return" around 90 percent of the West Bank in addition to a swapping of land to compensate Palestinians for any additional West Bank lands taken. At least two-thirds, if not more, of the Gaza Strip, the fifth enclave, also would remain under Palestinian control but isolated from the West Bank and Jerusalem. Critically, therefore, Palestinians were offered around 90 percent of the West Bank (which did not include annexed East Jerusalem) and the majority of the Gaza Strip in separated, encircled cantons.[13] In addition, a sizeable portion of the Jordan Valley would remain under Israeli control.

- Some form of Palestinian administrative autonomy or sovereignty over Arab neighborhoods in East Jerusalem (outlying Arab communities—the outer ring—would have full Palestinian sovereignty, and an inner ring of Arab neighborhoods would have autonomy only), Palestinian sovereignty over the Muslim and Christian quarters of the Old City, and some form of Muslim control over the Temple Mount/Haram al Sharif, with Israel retaining ultimate sovereignty.

The Israeli solution for Jerusalem also included the annexation of the main bloc of settlements in East Jerusalem: the Adumim bloc, 120 square kilometers around Ma'aleh Adumim, and the Etzion bloc. Under this scenario, the borders of Greater Jerusalem would have extended as far south as Gush Etzion near Hebron, dividing the northern part of the Palestinian state from the southern. Hence, despite the lack of specifics regarding the disposition of Arab and Jewish neighborhoods in Jerusalem and the Old City, the formulation for Jerusalem proposed by Israel would preclude territorial contiguity and functional economic borders between Jerusalem and the West Bank and between regions within the West Bank.

- A "satisfactory solution" for the refugees, which included no right of return for Palestinian refugees (that is, no choice for refugees and no acknowledgment by Israel of its role in creating the refugee problem) except perhaps to the Palestinian state. Barak, however, did discuss the possibility of allowing the return to Israel of several thousand refugee families from Lebanon (out of a total Palestinian refugee population in Lebanon now estimated to be 250,000 to 300,000, itself a small percentage of the 4.9 million Palestinian refugees worldwide) under the family reunification laws. In exchange, Israel wanted Palestinian negotiators to sign an end-of-conflict statement releasing Israel from all further responsibilities for the refugee problem.

- Israel's continued control over the Palestinian economy through the imposition of an Israeli import and indirect taxation regime, which would make it impossible for a Palestinian state to implement external trade or fiscal policies different from Israel's. Israel further insisted on maintaining control over indigenous groundwater resources in the West Bank and Gaza and all economic borders.

Despite their lack of specificity, the Israeli proposals put forth at Camp David, which clearly reflected the terms and parameters of the Oslo agreements, precluded contiguous territory, defined and functional borders, political and economic sovereignty, and basic Palestinian national rights. Israel made it clear that it would not withdraw completely from the occupied territories (that is, withdraw from settlements and from the grid of bypass roads connecting them) or relinquish fully its control over vital areas of Palestinian life, which it deemed important to its own security.

Palestinians, who had already compromised by conceding 78 percent of Mandatory Palestine to Israel, were now being asked to compromise further on the remaining 22 percent that was the West Bank and Gaza Strip. Yet, the actual amount of land returned to the Palestinians was less important than the disposition of that land and who would control it. And there was little if any doubt that such control would remain with Israel. By the time of Ariel Sharon's visit to the Temple Mount/Haram al Sharif, the situation among Palestinians had become untenable. The Al Aqsa *Intifada* was the tragic but inevitable result.

A Concluding Thought

Even if both sides had been able to reach an agreement based on the policy parameters put forth at Camp David, that agreement would have failed for one fundamental reason: control over Palestinian life would have remained with Israel and the occupation would have remained structurally intact—two features that underpinned the Oslo agreements. Palestinians seek their own state, which must consist of a contiguous West Bank and Gaza, a connection between them, and only minor adjustments to 1967 borders. Palestinians will no longer tolerate occupation in any form. Yet, occupation remains the structural and policy cornerstone of Oslo, and Oslo, tragically, remains the official framework for future negotiations.

Clearly, a new negotiating framework is needed that must consist of certain elements that were absent in Oslo: dismantling Israel's matrix of control; incorporating the issues of control, sovereignty, and viability as formal elements in the negotiation process; integrating a political solution with current realities on the ground, particularly with regard to land, settlements, Jerusalem, refugees, and borders rather than deferring these issues to the future; incorporating international law and UN resolutions into the negotiating framework to provide Palestinians with greater leverage and protection; eliminating bilateral (power) negotiations in favor of an international framework involving a constellation of nations that includes the United States and the European Union; and addressing the Palestinian refugee issue both in principle and practice.[14]

Future negotiations must bring a complete end to Israeli occupation and yield two viable and sovereign states. Anything short of this will fail, and failure will bring greater violence and instability to the Middle East and beyond.

---

1 Judy Dempsey, "Move to Stop Israel's Policy of Liquidation," *The Financial Times*, January 9, 2001.

2 Yediot Aharanot, September 7, 1993.

3 Dr. Souad Dajani, "What Are the Terms of the Oslo Peace Process?" *Fact Sheet* No. 3 (Boston, Mass.: Grassroots International, Fall 2000).

4 Geoffrey Aronson, "Recapitulating the Redeployments: The Israel–PLO Interim Agreements," *Information Brief* No. 32 (Washington, D.C.: Center for Policy Analysis on Palestine, April 27, 2000).

5 Nadav Shragai, "Barak Was Biggest Settlement Builder Since '92," *Ha'aretz,* February 27, 2001.

6 Dajani, op cit.

7 This section draws on Sara Roy, "Postscript," *The Gaza Strip: The Political Economy of De-development,* 2d ed. (Washington, D.C.: Institute of Palestine Studies, 2001), pp. 345–348, which contains the original citations for the data in this section; and idem., "Palestinian Economy and Society: The Continued Denial of Possibility," *Journal of Palestine Studies* (Summer 2001), pp. 5–20.

8 World Bank, *Economic Crisis in the West Bank and Gaza,* Internal Document, August 19, 2001.

9 United Nations, *The Impact on the Palestinian Economy of Confrontations, Mobility Restrictions and Border Closures, 1 October 2000–31 January 2001,* Summary (Gaza Strip: Office of the United Nations Special Coordinator in the Occupied Territories [UNSCO], February 2001); and *Palestinian Central Bureau of Statistics, Impact of the Israeli Measures on the Economic Conditions of Palestinian Households,* Press Conference on the Survey Results, Ramallah, West Bank, April 2001.

10 Meron Benvenisti, "The Illusion of Soft Borders," *Ha'aretz,* October 14, 1999.

11 Cited in Noam Chomsky, "Introduction," in Roane Carey, ed., *The New Intifada: Resisting Israel's Apartheid* (London: Verso, 2001), p. 20.

12 Rema Hamami and Salim Tamari, "Anatomy of Another Rebellion," *Middle East Report 217* (Winter 2000), p. 9.

13 See Jan de Jong and Geoffrey Aronson, "The Final Status Maps—A Territorial Analysis," *Report on Israeli Settlement* (Washington, D.C.: Foundation for Middle East Peace, January–February 2001), p. 6.

14 Jeff Halper, "No Return to Oslo," *Information Brief No. 83* (Washington, D.C.: Center for Policy Analysis on Palestine, October 5, 2001.).

CHAPTER TWO

Palestinian Refugees: Victims of Zionist Ideology

Elaine C. Hagopian

Tent #50, on the left, that is my present,
But it is too cramped to contain a future!
And – "Forget!" they say, but how can I?

Teach the night to forget to bring
Dreams showing me my village
And teach the wind to forget to carry to me
The aroma of apricots in my fields!
And teach the sky, too, to forget to rain.

Only then, I may forget my country.

Rashid Hussein

"All schemes for establishing a Jewish State in Palestine...came up against the major problem of the existence of a large Arab minority [numerically, the majority]..."[1] The Zionist goal of establishing a demographically Jewish State in Palestine inherently required the removal of all, or a major portion of the indigenous Palestinian population. In 1917—the year of the infamous Balfour Declaration—Palestinian Arabs constituted more than 90% of the population of Palestine. This chapter recounts the unswerving Zionist pursuit and plots for the removal of the Palestinian population from Palestine, leading ultimately to the 1948 Nakba (catastrophe), the 1967 "displacement," and the present refurbished Israeli preoccupation with modalities for cleansing the Occupied Territories. The line of Zionist demographic transformation thinking begins before and during the British Mandate period [officially 1923–1948] in the form of "transfer," i.e., resettlement of Palestinians elsewhere. It develops into forcible expulsion before, during and after the 1948 war, during the 1967 war, and reaffirms itself today still under the heading of "transfer" aimed at cleansing Palestinians from the land.

The Concept of "Transfer" In Zionist Thought

Nur Masalha pioneered the historical study of the concept of "transfer" in Zionist political thought.[2] He demonstrates that early on, Zionist leaders were contemplating the need for removal of the Palestinian population. Two examples beyond the well-known Herzl pronouncement in June 1895 "to spirit the penniless population across the border" suffice to illustrate the latter. First, Masalha quotes Socialist Zionist leader, Nahman Syrkin from his 1898 pamphlet, The Jewish Question and the Socialist Jewish State. In that pamphlet, Syrkin "called for the liberation of Palestine from Turkish rule...and for the subsequent evacuation of Palestine's Arab inhabitants. 'Palestine,' Syrkin wrote, '...in which the Jews constitute today 10 per cent of the population, must be evacuated for the Jews.'"[3] Second, Masalha reproduces U.S. Mission member [to the 1919 Peace Conference] William K. Bullitt's recollection of conversations with Aaron Aaronsohn, member of the Zionist Executive, as follows:

> Aaronsohn's proposal was the following: While Palestine must be made a Jewish state, the vast valley of Iraq, which is irrigated by the Euphrates and Tigris, should be restored, through the use of planned irrigation, to be the paradise of the world...and furthermore the Arabs of Palestine should be offered lands there...to which as many Arabs as possible should be persuaded to emigrate.[4]

These early declarations laid the foundation for schemes of "transfer." The specific planning for "transfer" took coherent form after the British Peel Commission Report was issued on July 8, 1937. It concluded that Arab and Jewish nationalisms were not reconcilable and recommended partition of Palestine. The report also recommended what it euphemistically called an "exchange" of Arab and Jewish populations. Some 225,000 Palestinian Arabs would be "transferred" out of the area designated as the Jewish State, and 1,250 Jews would move out of the territory designated as the Arab

[Palestinian] state. In the last resort, the report stated, "the exchange should be compulsory."[5]

The Commission's "transfer" plan was preceded by secretive proposals offered by leaders such as Weizmann, Baron de Rothschild, Ben-Gurion, Yosef Weitz, and Menahem Ussishkin. Weizmann, Ben-Gurion and others felt that the British would have to carry out the expulsion. However, a number of British ministers had reservations about "transferring" Arabs, even as they favored partition. The British Government appointed a second commission in January 1938 to examine the mechanics of partition. However, the British Secretary of State made it clear that there was no possibility that Britain would carry out compulsory "transfer." Moreover, the Palestinian Arabs were not likely to leave voluntarily. Nonetheless, the Zionists were determined to execute "transfer": "David Ben-Gurion...believed that the Zionists had to exert pressure to force the British to act. But if necessary, he wrote in his diary, 'we must ourselves prepare to carry out' the removal of the Palestinians."[6]

In anticipation of British withdrawal from Palestine on the heels of the Peel Report, Ben-Gurion ordered the commander of the Haganah [the mainstream Zionist paramilitary organization that was a precursor to the Israeli Defense Force, i.e. the regular army] to develop a plan for the takeover of Palestine. This plan was known as the Avnir plan, and it was the forerunner of the March 10, 1948, Plan Dalet, also developed in anticipation of the British withdrawal announced for May 1948.[7] The 1937 Partition Plan was shelved, as war clouds loomed heavily over Europe. Great Britain remained the Mandatory Power in Palestine. Nonetheless, Zionist leadership continued to elaborate plans for "transfer."

"Transfer" and the Making of the Refugee Catastrophe: The 1937 Peel Commission and Beyond

The leadership of the Mapai Party, the most influential Party among Jews in Palestine, convened a congress of supporters in Zurich from July 29 to August 7, 1937, shortly after the Peel Commission Report was issued. It was at this meeting that "transfer" became official policy, "planned and supported by most of the highest-ranking leaders and opposed on moral grounds by none."[8] The Zionist leadership had actually moved beyond the Peel Commission recommendations for "exchange" to a broader conceptualization of "transfer" of Palestinians to other Arab States, e.g., Syria and Iraq, as was articulated earlier by individuals such as Aaronsohn. This was in keeping with the Zionist goal of establishing a Jewish State in all of Palestine even though in 1937, and again in 1947, Ben-Gurion and his colleagues accepted the idea of partition. Partition was viewed as a tactical step to be followed by expansion in stages into all of Palestine.[9]

Yosef Weitz, Director of the Jewish National Fund and later the head of the post-1948 "Transfer" Committee appointed by the Israeli Cabinet, stated quite clearly in June 1941 that the State of Israel would only come about by "transferring the Arabs from here to the neighboring countries, to transfer them all....And the transfer must be directed to Iraq, to Syria, and even to Trans-Jordan. For that purpose we will find money, a lot of money."[10] In September 1941, Weitz traveled to Syria to explore the actual feasibility of population "transfer." He focused on the Jazirah region of Syria in the northeast. "On 18 September he arrived in the region and recorded that 'this Jazirah will become a huge absorbing home' for the Palestinians to be expelled...[and] he also felt the Iraqi part of the Jazirah would be needed...."[11]

When Weitz returned to Jerusalem, he formed a permanent council to prepare for "transfer." The members proceeded to plan carefully for the implementation of "transfer," but their efforts were interrupted by W.W. II. Nonetheless, the committee did not cease to exist.

Plans C (May 1946) and D (March 1948) and the Expulsion of Palestinians

In October 1945, Great Britain, searching for a way to resolve the issue of Palestine, convinced President Truman to have the two countries study the problem. An Anglo-American Committee of Inquiry was established. They visited both Palestine and Jewish refugee camps in Europe, where they were deeply affected by the sight of the survivors of the Holocaust. They recorded testimony from all sides and released a report on May 1, 1946. Among the recommendations made were that 100,000 Jews be issued permits to enter Palestine in 1946; that Palestine should be bi-national with equal representation for both groups; and that Palestine should become a trust area under the U.N. to prepare the communities for independence on a bi-national basis. Ben-Gurion rejected all of the recommendations. He was not interested in a bi-national state. "In fact, Ben-Gurion had already asserted before the committee that in his eyes 'statehood was now more necessary than the 100,000 refugees.'"[12]

Ben-Gurion and his colleagues focused on the timetable for British withdrawal from Palestine. They feared that the British might withdraw all at once, bringing an end to its Mandate. However, the British decided to withdraw from successive areas over a period of time while maintaining *de jure* authority over the whole. In this way, Britain protected the Zionist forces from possible incursions by regular Arab army forces. It allowed Zionist forces time "to dislodge the Arabs of Palestine and to create by 15 May [1948] a new status quo in the country which would be beyond the means of the regular Arab armies to reverse."[13] Given the British timetable, Zionist strategy was formulated in two-phases: Plan Gimmel (Plan C, 1946) and Plan Dalet (Plan D, 1948).

Plan C provided directives for strong retaliatory strikes against Arab outbreaks challenging Zionist implantation advances in Palestine. Among the "countermeasures" delineated were strikes against Palestinian political leadership, those who provided shelter to Palestinians carrying out operations, Arab transportation, vital economic targets, villages, neighborhoods, and farms, and places of assembly. The goals of the strikes included damaging property of political leaders, expelling or doing physical harm to the leaders and to those who carried out operations, damaging Arab printing presses, and holding Palestinian political leaders as hostages and/or preventing them from undertaking other operations. Part and parcel of this plan was a terror campaign to publicize Zionist retaliatory actions by radio, leaflets, and whispering campaigns in order to make the population fearful and thus encourage flight. The plan was also designed to "unite [Jewish forces] with the [Jewish] settlements that had been cut off."[14]

Plan D (March 1948) was formalized after the U.N. General Assembly passed Resolution 181 (II) [November 29, 1947] calling for partition of Palestine and served as the second phase of Zionist strategy, i.e., building on Plan C, the first stage. U.N.G.A. Resolution 181 (II) designated 55% of Palestine for the Jewish State, although Jews owned less than 7% of the land, and 45% of Palestine to Palestinians who owned most of the land of Palestine. Jerusalem and environs were to become an International *corpus separatim* under the United Nations. Within the proposed borders of the Jewish state, the Palestinian population was almost equal to the Jewish population. Given the terms of 181 (II), the "Jewish" state would have been a *de facto* bi-national state, an outcome the Zionist leadership had already rejected. Hence, it was clear that "transfer," i.e., ethnic cleansing, continued to be a Zionist imperative if a Jewish State was to be a reality.

Building on previous Plans, but especially Plan C, Plan D was aimed at securing the areas designated as the Jewish State under U.N.G.A.181 (II) as well as to secure areas beyond those borders. Plan D continued the measures included in Plan C.[15] On April 9, 1948, Zionist terror groups, including the Irgun, commanded by Menahem Begin, and Lehi (Stern Gang), co-commanded by Yitzhak Shamir, committed the notorious massacre in the Palestinian village of Deir Yassin. The Deir Yassin massacre was committed in spite of the fact that the village leaders had signed a non-aggression agreement with the Haganah, Ben-Gurion's para-military group. The assault on Deir Yassin had the support of the Jerusalem Haganah commander. It was the single greatest contributory factor among the many factors that led to the Palestinian exodus. Word of the massacre was publicized so as to terrorize Palestinians into leaving.[16] During April and early May atrocities were committed in other Palestinian villages, followed by more massacres after the May 14, 1948, Zionist declaration of the State of Israel.

The period before the official declaration of the State of Israel in May 1948 is described in the literature as a civil war. Palestinians understood it as an anti-colonial struggle. During this period, as the British were withdrawing, the Zionists were deploying their forces throughout the country and consolidating their military position. The first wave of expulsions of Palestinians occurred between December 1947 and March 1948. The British Mandate ended on May 14, 1948, and the Zionist Movement declared Israeli statehood on that same day. Up to this point and before the Arab Armies moved into the Palestinian theatre, some 200,000 Palestinians had already become refugees.[17] Included in this period was the expulsion of West Jerusalem Palestinian Arabs, some 28,000 souls owning 33.69% of the land in what was to become West Jerusalem. As Palestinians were expelled, Zionists forces settled Jews in Arab homes—which were simultaneously looted of furnishings, paintings, personal items and musical instruments—and consolidated their hold on that part of Jerusalem.[18]

Declaration of the State of Israel (May 14, 1948) and the Arab-Israeli War

Although some sources say May 15, May 14 marked the end of the British Mandate over Palestine and is the official date of the declaration of the establishment of the State of Israel by the Jewish People's Council as representatives of the Jewish Community in Palestine and of the Zionist Movement. Popular belief, fostered by Zionist leaders, has it that the "Arab invasion of Palestine on May 15...made the 1948 war inevitable. [However] the documents show that the war was not inevitable. The Arabs had agreed to a last-minute American proposal for a three-month truce on the condition that Israel temporarily postpone its Declaration of Independence."[19] That is, given the documents affirming Arab agreement to a truce and the fact that a number of Palestinian leaders sought an accommodation with the Zionists, the 1948 war could have been averted. However, Ben Gurion feared that acceptance of these initiatives would lead to a Palestinian State within historic Palestine, and hence he rejected them. The Jerusalem Mufti's call to launch a war against the Zionist forces could no longer be resisted: "It was only Ben-Gurion's profound opposition to the creation of a Palestinian state that undermined the Palestinian resistance to the Mufti's call."[20]

War did ensue. And while initially the Israeli forces appeared at a disadvantage, in fact, they came to outnumber and outgun the Arab forces.[21] At best, the Arab forces reached areas designated in U.N.G.A. 181 (II) as part of the proposed Palestinian Arab State. The Israeli Provisional Government built on the foundations of Plans C and D and became emboldened to elaborate them further. After all, the dream of a Jewish state was becoming a reality. The Zionist imperative for a demographically Jewish state required Israeli forces to defeat Arab forces and expel sufficient numbers of Palestinians. Hence, more massacres were committed by Israeli forces in 1948–49, which precipitated and accelerated the Palestinian exodus. Israeli military historian Arieh Yitzhaki confirms the massacres. In fact, "Another Israeli historian, Uri Milstein, corroborates Yitzhaki's estimate of the extent of massacres and goes even further to suggest that each battle in 1948 ended with a massacre: 'In all Israel's wars massacres were committed but I have no doubt that the war of Independence [1948] was the dirtiest of them all.'"[22]

Benny Morris, Simha Flapan, Michael Palumbo, Meron Benvinisti,[23] Ilan Pappe,[24] Nafez Nazzal,[25] Salman Abu-Sitta,[26] Audeh G. Rantisi and Charles Amash,[27] and Walid Khalidi,[28] are among the researchers and eyewitnesses who have documented the methods and process of expulsion of the Palestinians. A few examples will suffice here to portray the Palestinian **Nakba.**

The Arab-Israeli war lasted from May 15, 1948 to July 20, 1949. It was interspersed by truce periods that allowed the Israeli forces to consolidate and strengthen their positions. Emboldened by their success, the Israeli Provisional Government prolonged the war in order to gain more land area not originally designated as part of the Jewish State in U.N.G.A. 181 and to effect the removal of the Palestinians from the controlled and conquered areas.

One of the most notorious episodes of expulsion took place in Lydda [now known as Lod] on July 13, 1948. Yitzhak Rabin is quoted in his service diary [later part of his biography in the English version] as saying:

> Yigal Allon asked Ben-Gurion what was to be done with the civilian population. Ben-Gurion waved his hand in a gesture of 'drive them out.' 'Driving out' is a term with a harsh ring. Psychologically, this was one of the most difficult actions we undertook. The population of Lydda did not leave willingly. There was no way of avoiding the use of force and warning shots in order to make the inhabitants march the ten or fifteen miles to the point where they met up with the Arab Legion [Jordanian].[29]

Audeh Rantisi recounts how Israeli soldiers came to his family's home and ordered the family to go out. The soldiers directed his parents, three brothers, two sisters and two grandparents to a road that led into the mountains. There, they were joined by a growing number of people. Panic set in as word spread that the Israelis had assembled 136 men in a local mosque and machine-gunned them. No one survived. The people were forced to walk over rough terrain with the heat surpassing 100 degrees fahrenheit. Forced through a gate to a vegetable farm, the soldiers ordered everyone to put their money, jewelry, watches, pens, etc., on a spread blanket. One man refused to give up his money, and one of the soldiers shot him. Rantisi goes on to describe their trek across barren areas without water. Scores died [an estimated 4000], pregnant women miscarried leaving their babies for jackals to consume. Among those expelled was George Habash, later the head of the Popular Front for the Liberation of Palestine. The same fate befell Ramle. Some 60,000 Palestinians were expelled from Lydda and Ramle under the cruelest conditions.[30]

The village of al-Dawayma, located in the western Hebron hills, was conquered by Israeli forces on October 29, 1948. The villagers were unarmed. Eighty to one hundred people were massacred for no reason of war, and their bodies were thrown into pits. Children were killed by cracking their skulls. Others were sealed in houses while the village was systematically destroyed. At least two women were blown up in a house; another was raped and then shot. A U.N. Special Investigative Team requested that the Israelis allow them to visit Dawayma. After three tries, two of the team's members were allowed to visit the village. Some of the houses were still smoking and gave off a peculiar smell as if bones were burning. Then they asked to see the Dawayma village mosque but were told it was culturally inappropriate to enter the mosque. Still, when the Team got a brief look inside, they saw Israeli soldiers there and saw that the place had been desecrated. When asked about the evacuation of inhabitants from the village, the Israelis told them that they had fled when Arab forces retreated. The Israelis denied they expelled the villagers. Nonetheless, the U.N. team understood well what had happened at Dawayma.[31]

In all, 750,000 Palestinians were expelled from the 78% of Palestine that Israel conquered in the war. There were originally some 900,000 plus Palestinians in 1948 in that conquered 78% of the land. This meant that approximately 83–85% of the Palestinian population was expelled directly and/or under threat of death. Some 531 Palestinian villages were destroyed. Today, refugee land and villages constitute 92% of Israel proper today.[32]

"Transfer" fused with forced expulsion, an opportunity afforded by the superior Israeli forces. In June 1948, more than a year before the Arab-Israeli war officially ended, Weitz gave a proposal by the still extant "Transfer" Committee to Prime Minister Ben Gurion of the Israeli Provisional Government, entitled a "Scheme for the Solution of the Arab Problem in the State of Israel." The Scheme called for preventing expelled Palestinians from returning to their homes; destroying Arab villages; preventing cultivation of Palestinian lands; settling Jews in Palestinian towns and villages; passing legislation to bar the return of refugees; launching a campaign to discourage refugee return; and working to resettle refugees elsewhere.[33] Hence, "transfer" efforts continued. Among some of the proposed projects were "transfer" of Christian Arabs of the upper Galilee [in Israel] in

1951 to South America [Argentina]; in 1955–56, a proposal to settle Palestinian refugees in Libya [then under a pro-West monarchy] with American assistance; and a stillborn plan in July 1956 to expel Israeli Palestinians from a northern area to Lebanon. Then "transfer" receded from 1957 to 1967 while Israel consolidated its power, economy and society.

However, simultaneous with the post-state efforts of the 1950s to "transfer" more Palestinians were efforts undertaken through UNRWA [United Nations Relief and Works Agency] to permanently resettle Palestinians through large-scale job-creating projects [see below], the history of which begins with the U.N.G.A. Resolution 194 (111). That resolution, popularly known as the "right of return" of Palestinians resolution (Article 11)—though it has other directives within it—was submitted to the General Assembly by the United States and the United Kingdom. It was adopted on December 11, 1948. The United States had supported and helped to push through the November 29, 1947, partition plan, U.N.G.A. 181 (II), thus favoring the Zionist push for a Jewish state. Submission of resolution 194 (111) seemed a somewhat contradictory American action, but it wasn't.

President Truman faced a post-WW II transformation of the world from a multi-polar world to a bi-polar world. He was anxious to inherit the British strategic map in the Middle East but was also concerned about placating various Arab regimes and preventing Soviet intrusion and influence in the area. U.S. member of the U.N. Palestine Conciliation Commission, Mark Ethridge, reported to Truman on April 13, 1949: "Israel does not intend to take back one refugee...and does not intend to compensate any directly if she can avoid it [,]"[34] nor does Israel accept responsibility for the creation of the refugee problem. Ethridge further noted that he told Ben Gurion flat out "that I could not for [a] moment accept that statement in face of [what happened in] Jaffa, Deir Yassin, Haifa and all reports that come to us from refugee organizations that new refugees are being created every day by repression and terrorism..."[35] On April 29, 1949, Truman cabled Ethridge saying, "I am rather disgusted with the manner in which the Jews are approaching the refugee problem."[36] Even so, Truman refused to apply the kind of pressure on Israeli leaders that was needed to implement the right of return.

On December 8, 1949, U.N.G.A. Resolution 302 was adopted establishing the UNRWA to provide relief and assistance to the refugees until such time as the conflict would be resolved. Benjamin Schiff points out in a comprehensive history and analysis of UNRWA that the United States and Great Britain were the dominant donors in the early years (72% and 19% respectively from 1952–1962). The U.S. and British goal was to work through UNRWA to facilitate major development projects that would employ Palestinian refugees and lead to their resettlement in their countries of refuge. Hence, *de facto*, repatriation would no longer be necessary or an option. The U.S. and Britain thought this would be a way out of their cold war dilemma, and help solve the refugee part of Israel's "Arab Problem." Various schemes were tried and failed, leading eventually to American and British reduction of donations. Thereafter, UNRWA emphasized education of refugees and relief. After the 1967 war, and especially during the first *intifada*, UNRWA attempted to assist Palestinians suffering from Israeli excesses in the Occupied Territories.[37]

"Transfer" Efforts after the 1967 War

The 1967 war reinvigorated "transfer" planning. Israel conquered the remaining 22% of Palestine (Gaza, the West Bank and East Jerusalem), territories it considered part of Eretz Israel. Israel did not want to give up the territories, but it faced a new demographic problem resulting from the conquest. Shahak identifies three kinds of "transfers" Israel carried out after the June 1967 war: 1) 320,000 Palestinians were expelled by force from Gaza and the West Bank during and after the war period; 2) others left when ordered to do so by collaborating Palestinian local mayors who received bribes from the Israelis; and 3) after discussions of pushing the refugees into the Sinai [Egyptian territory adjacent to Gaza], a "secret unit" was formed to "encourage" the departure of Palestinians. The secret unit set up an office in Gaza, which gave Palestinians one-way tickets to South American countries, mainly Paraguay. The Palestinians were promised that further financial help would follow, but the promise was never kept. Some 1000 Palestinians were "transferred" by this method.[38]

In spite of the new "transfer" efforts, the majority of the Palestinians in the 1967 Occupied Territories managed to stay put, including both the original residents and the refugees from 1948 who were pushed out at that time to the remaining territories of Palestine as well as surrounding Arab countries. Given the fact that Israel ultimately intended to keep the Occupied Territories, the existence of a large Palestinian population there recreated Israel's original demographic problem. A Whole Land of Israel Movement issued a

Manifesto in 1967 affirming that "no government in Israel is entitled to give up [the conquered territories which Zionists define as part of the whole of Israel, i.e., *Eretz Israel*] this entirety, which represents the inherent and inalienable right to our people from the beginning of its history."[39] The dimension of the demographic issue for Israel is revealed by the population figures. Today, there are 3.2 million Palestinians in the Occupied Territories, and over 1 million [the descendants of those 150,000 who managed to stay in Israel in 1948–49] within Israel proper. The Jewish population numbers some 5 million. Hence the ratio is approximately 4 Palestinians to every 5 Israeli Jews in Israel and the Occupied Territories.

A post-1967 debate ensued in Israel with regard to resolving its dilemma: keeping the territories but not absorbing the Palestinians into the Israeli State. The immediate "transfer" schemes that were initiated after 1967 were insufficient to remove significant numbers of Palestinians from the Occupied Territories. Therefore, the debate yielded "solutions" that ranged from dependent autonomy for Palestinians while Israel retained control over the land, to one favored by Sharon and Shamir, i.e., engineered emigration [meaning "transfer," meaning ethnic cleansing] and *de facto* annexation. These alternative "solutions" remained in the Israeli political discourse over the years. Israel was able and content to occupy and benefit from the territories and seek no "solution" until Camp David I (1978–79) raised the question of Palestinian rights.[40]

Complicating Israel's end game was the fact that the Palestine Liberation Organization (PLO) began to change its position from liberation of all of Palestine to a two-state solution that focused on the Occupied Territories as the site of the Palestinian State. While the PLO began to focus on self-determination, the leadership did not abandon the Palestinian Refugee Right of Return. Israel was confronted with the possibility of not only having to give up the territories but additionally not being "relieved" of the legal obligation of refugee right to return to their homes and properties within Israel proper, two things on which the Israeli leadership were bound and determined not to yield.

With the Egyptian President Anwar Sadat's peace initiative trip to Jerusalem to address the Israel Knesset in November 1977, the Israelis had to face the challenge of a two-state solution and how to continue ignoring refugee return rights. The Israelis, under the leadership of Prime Minister Begin, rejected the idea of a Palestinian State and rejected any acknowledgement of refugee rights. Sadat insisted that

Palestinian Rights be discussed as part and parcel of the Egyptian/ Israeli peace talks. Begin responded with a dependent autonomy plan for the residents of the Occupied Territories and totally ignored the refugee issue as well as the PLO's call for self-determination. Begin's plan called for the separation of the fate of the population from the land. The population would have some "self-rule," but the land would remain effectively under Israel's control. That plan became the Framework for Peace agreed upon in Camp David I and would be resuscitated in 1991 as the framework for peace talks initiated in Madrid and culminated in Oslo. While the Camp David 1 Accords were fruitful for Egypt and Israel, they had nothing to offer Palestinians.

Following the 1991 Gulf War, President George Bush Sr. felt the time was opportune to finish off the destabilizing Palestinian problem on terms favorable to Israel. The Madrid/Oslo peace "process" got underway on October 31, 1991. The legal framework for the "process" was the murkily worded U.N.S.C. Resolution 242, which called neither for a Palestinian State, as had previous UN resolutions, nor for the Refugees' right of return, also in previous resolutions and affirmed by refugee conventions. Instead, Prime Minister Yitzahk Shamir insisted on the Framework for Middle East Peace of Camp David 1 in which the Begin plan for dependent autonomy was embedded. While the Madrid "process" failed because the Palestinian delegation from the Occupied Territories refused to accept dependent autonomy in the Occupied Territories with no end result of a viable state, Arafat as head of an emasculated PLO in effect accepted the terms.

Prime Minister Rabin, who signed the Oslo Declaration of Principles with Arafat in 1993, was committed to the dissolution of the Palestinian problem through diplomatic assassination. The outcome anticipated was simply dressed-up autonomy in Palestinian populated areas, even if the word "state" was used. It was also aimed at closing the refugee file by having Arafat sign an agreement robbing the refugees of their full rights. Up to and including Prime Minister Barak's mythical "generous" offer [July 2002], proposed while increasing settlements and confiscating more Palestinian land, the autonomy/"state" solution was intended to dissolve the Palestinian problem by incarcerating Palestinians in enclaves that would encourage them to leave or accept a colonized life. It was the diplomatically acceptable way to sacrifice Palestine and Palestinians, since inherent to the Oslo terms were the structural prods to encourage those in the territories to become "voluntary" emigrants/refugees and join their existing refugee brothers as "expatriates" as well. This was the "slow death" process of dissolution.

With the failure of Oslo, the pendulum swung to Sharon's end of the post-1967 debate, i.e., his direct and outright proposal to "transfer" Palestinians in the Occupied Territories to Jordan, which he claims is really the Palestinian State. With his election as Prime Minister, Sharon began seeking ways to destroy the edifice of autonomy created in the Territories during the Oslo years by destroying Palestinian institutions and structures and by fragmenting Palestinian society physically, economically, politically and socially as well as seeking ways to make Palestinians accountable to the whim of Israeli military authorities. Simultaneously, Sharon continues seeking means to expel the Palestinian population from the Territories by various mechanisms of "transfer" that are made to appear legitimate under the "war on terrorism." For example, Israel is directing an attack against UNRWA in the Territories, which is now providing food for Palestinians in the camps, towns and villages besieged by Israeli forces. The intent appears to be to make conditions unbearable for Palestinians so that they will leave "voluntarily." Already, some 200,000 have departed, primarily to Jordan although Jordan has now made it next to impossible for Palestinians to enter that state. "'Transfer Now,' a placard that is now posted on every empty wall throughout the country—is the...answer from one side."[41]

To date [August 28, 2002] President George Bush Jr. has approved of Sharon's assault on the Palestinians as part of the "war on terrorism." Sharon's thinking is that if Arafat is removed from the scene, the Palestinian issue will get off the international agenda, so that forced evacuation and migration can continue undisturbed. Israel's alliance with the Bush Jr. Doctrine of reordering the Middle East and Central Asia provides Israel with a cover for expelling Palestinians, especially if there is a U.S. attack on Iraq. As for the Refugees, Sharon doesn't even mention them. In any case, the majority of Israelis of all political persuasions reject the right of return of Palestinians because they fear it would further complicate Israeli's demographic struggle to maintain a strong Jewish majority in the State and keep it forever a Jewish State. The emphasis is on ridding Israel and the Territories of Palestinians, not on having them stay or others return.

Palestinian Refugee Individual Rights and Palestinian Collective National Self-Determination Right in International Law[42]

Today, there are some five million Palestinian refugees, of which 3.6 million are registered with UNRWA. The remainder non-camp refugees are scattered throughout the world, including within Israel [internal refugees] and the Arab region. Those registered with UNRWA are registered for aid. The UNRWA registration does not include the full count of refugees as is so often assumed mistakenly. The Refugees make up two-thirds of the Palestinian people, and as such, no durable peace can be had without addressing their rights. All of the Refugees are individually entitled by international law, the U.N. Declaration of Human rights and applicable U.N. resolutions to return to their homes and property and to be fully compensated for damage done thereto and income lost therefrom, or to choose compensation in full instead. Israel refuses to acknowledge responsibility for their expulsion and rejects their "right of return," fearing the possible demographic challenge they would be to the Jewish state.

Recognizing its special responsibility for the Palestinian Refugees, whose plight resulted from the November 1947 UNGA 181(II) partition plan and the subsequent 1948 war, the United Nations General Assembly enacted Resolution number 194 (III), December 11, 1948. This resolution called for "Establishing a U.N. Conciliation Commission, Resolving that Jerusalem Should Be Placed Under a Permanent International Regime, and Resolving That the Refugees Should Be Permitted to Return to Their Homes." Paragraph 11 specifically

> *Resolves* that the refugees wishing to return to their homes and live at peace with their neighbours, should be permitted to do so at the earliest practicable date, and that compensation should be paid for the property of those choosing not to return and for loss of or damage to property which, under principles of international law or in equity, should be made good by the Governments or authorities responsible.[43]

There are several factors embodied in Paragraph 11 of UNGA 194 (III), which require elaboration. First, the U.N. General Assembly called for the return of refugees specifically to their original homes. Other options were not suggested such as resettlement or absorption in countries of refuge. Second, compensation should be paid to those not wanting to return, but also to those returning "for loss of or damage to property which, under principles of international law or in equity, should be made good by the Governments or authorities responsible." It is not either return or compensation as so many mistakenly read this Paragraph. Third, UNGA 194 (III) is tied into existing "principles of international law" regarding refugee rights, and reaffirms them regarding the case of Palestinians. Fourth, a special U.N. agency was created by UNGA 194 (III), i.e., the U.N. Conciliation Commission for Palestine, not only to resolve the issue of Jerusalem, but also

> [2nd paragraph]....to facilitate the repatriation, resettlement and economic and social rehabilitation of the refugees and the payment of compensation, and to maintain close relations with the Director of the United Nations Relief for Palestine Refugees...[44]

By 1952, it was clear that the U.N. Conciliation Commission was unable to fulfill its mandate, and hence, it retreated from its office in Jerusalem to New York. This action robbed the Palestinians refugees of the political protective function, which included representing refugee interests in various national and international venues that the UNCCP had previously provided. As such, that protective function should have automatically gone to the United Nations High Commissioner for Refugees. It did not, solely because of a contested interpretation of Article 1D of the 1951 Refugee convention.[45] UNRWA, as an aid agency, was/is not mandated to provide such protection.

Nonetheless, the deprivation of UNHCR's legal protection in no way negates the absolute legal and inalienable right of each Palestinian refugee to return to his/her home/property in Israel proper and to full compensation/restitution under U.N.G.A. Resolution 194 (III) and all of the refugee conventions and laws to which it is tied. The issue is representation. The PLO [a non-state] has claimed to represent the interests of all Palestinians. The latter served to complicate the problem further for the Refugees during the Oslo process. Israel and its U.S. partner tried to fold Palestinian individual refugee rights into the contrived "state" collective right. That is, the Palestinian struggle to achieve self-determination (collective right) was legitimated not only by the original U.N partition plan, but also by U.N.G.A. Resolution 2787, December 6 1971, affirming the right of Palestinian self-determination,[46] which was reaffirmed in U.N.G.A. 2955 (XXVII), December 12, 1972,[47] and U.N.G.A. Resolution 3236 (XXIX), November 22, 1974, which not only reaffirmed the right of self-determination without external interference and national independence and sovereignty, but also reaffirmed the "inalienable right of the Palestinians to return to their homes and property [individual refugee rights] from which they have been displaced and uprooted, and calls for their return."[48]

It is important to note that the United Nations recognized that Palestinian Refugee Right of Return is an individual right separate from the collective right of self-determination. Israel and the United States worked hard during the Oslo process to convince the PLO headed by Arafat that 1) the proposed "dependent autonomy," cloaked by the sometime use of the word "state," met the collective right of Palestinians, and that 2) the individual right of the refugees could be folded into the collective right. In essence, this meant that Refugees might be able to "return" to the Palestinian "state," subject still to Israeli approval of numbers and means, and that an international fund would assist their resettlement in various areas. Israeli culpability for the *Nakba* would not be acknowledged. What Oslo boiled down to for the Refugees was that their right of return under international law was to be denied under the umbrella of the emasculated Palestinian "state" with no guarantee that they would even be allowed to "return" there. The Israeli/American plan failed because, in the end, Arafat knew he could not sign away Refugee rights, among other issues, and expect a durable peace. The Israelis and Americans attempted to create symbolic solutions, which could only fail no matter the public relations theatre.

Conclusion

The conflict has now come full circle. It has returned to its original form: Israel's determination to keep all of Palestine as Eretz Israel has reverted to its consistent policy of "transfer." Sharon and his ultra-right wing colleagues would welcome the opportunity of chaos and declarations of war against terrorism that an American war against Iraq would afford Israel to expel the Palestinians. On the other hand, others are simultaneously employing earlier tactics of resettling Palestinians elsewhere. For example, Haim Shapiro notes in the *Jerusalem Post* that Meir Kihan, president of Hamotzi-Assisted Emigration Services wants to "help" Arabs [Palestinians] leave the country. His organization's web site [www.emigrations.net] "offers help in financing...legal services, travel arrangements, and social services. Three countries are listed as possible destinations: the U.S., Argentina, and Brazil."[49] The *Post* articles states further that

> ...the organization's goal is to help 200,000 Palestinians emigrate from the West Bank by 2004 and then another 200,000 every year after that....Kihan...says that he cannot reveal who else is involved in the organization....he admits that practically all those involved are on the right of the political spectrum, although...at least one leftist has joined...
> ...Kihan makes no secret of the fact that his aim is to change the demographic balance of the country. When asked whether this was not an unrealistic goal, he says that 60 years ago the demographic situation made it seem unrealistic to establish the State of Israel.
> 'Our aim is to empty the state of Arabs,' he says.[50]

Kihan's organization is not alone. There are others even further to the right, such as Gamla, founded by Israeli military officers. Its web site is: www.gamla.org.il/english. Among other things they advocate getting the international community to establish a Palestinian state in Iraq or Saudi Arabia. If not, then Israel should expel them by force into Jordan and the Sinai.[51]

What are we to think of a world in which the majority of States support Palestinian National and Refugee rights, but one in which two countries, Israel and the United States, not only work to deny those rights but also work aggressively to sacrifice Palestine and Palestinians to U.S. global and Israeli regional hegemonic and imperial interests? At the beginning of the Zionist project to gain Palestine, Zionists and their British supporters assumed that Palestinians were of little consequence and that they would accede to whatever fate was planned for them. History has proven them wrong. But there is a lesson here. Israel cannot defeat Palestinians conclusively nor can Palestinians defeat Israelis conclusively. The conclusion to draw therefore is a humane one: democracy, equality and justice for both people in the land of Palestine/Israel.

---

1   Benny Morris, *The Birth of the Palestinian Refugee Problem, 1947–1949.* Cambridge, Cambridge University Press, 1987, p. 25.

2 Nur Masalha, *Expulsion of the Palestinians: The Concept of "Transfer" in Zionist Political Thought, 1882–1948*. Washington, D.C., Institute of Palestine Studies, 1992.

3 Masalha, *Expulsion*, p. 11.

4 Masalha, *Expulsion*, p. 13.

5 Peel Commission Report, Cmd. 5479, pp. 389–91, reproduced in Masalha, *Expulsion*, p. 61.

6 Michael Palumbo, *The Palestinian Catastrophe: The 1948 Expulsion of a People from Their Homeland*. London, Faber & Faber, 1987, pp. 3–4.

7 Walid Khalidi, "Revisiting the UN Partition Resolution," *Journal of Palestine Studies*, #105, Vol. XXVII, No. 1, Autumn 1997, p. 7.

8 Israel Shahak, "A History of the Concept of 'Transfer' in Zionism," *Journal of Palestine Studies*, # 71, Vol. XVIII, No. 3, Spring 1989, p. 23.

9 Khalidi, "Revisiting," pp. 16–17.

10 Shahak, "Concept", p. 26.

11 Shahak, "Concept", p. 27.

12 Fred J. Khouri, *The Arab-Israeli Dilemma*, Syracuse: Syracuse University Press, 1968, p. 35.

13 Walid Khalidi, "Plan Dalet: Master Plan for the Conquest of Palestine," *Journal of Palestine Studies*, #69, Vol. XVIII, No. 1, Autumn 1988, p. 15.

14 Khalidi, "Plan Dalet", Appendix A of this article: *Text of Plan Gimmel (Plan C), May 1946: Section on Countermeasures*, pp 20–23, and p. 15.

15 Khalidi, "Plan Dalet," *Appendix B, Text of Plan Dalet (Plan D)*, 10 March 1948: General Section, pp. 24–33 and *Appendix C, Text of Plan Dalet: Operational Orders to the Brigades*, pp. 34–37.

16 Nur Masalha, "The Historical Roots of the Palestinian Refugee Question," in Naseer Aruri (Editor), *Palestinian Refugees: The Right of Return*, London: Pluto Press, 2001, pp. 46–47.

17 Khouri, *Arab-Israeli*, p. 124. Also see, Wm. Roger Louis & Robert W. Stookey (Editors), *The End of the Palestine Mandate*, Austin: University of Texas Press, 1986, pp. 10–27.

18 Nathan Krystall, "The De-Arabization of West Jerusalem 1947–50," *Journal of Palestine Studies*, #106, Vol. XXVII, No. 2, Winter 1998, pp. 5–22.

19 Simha Flapan, *The Birth of Israel: Myths and Realities*, New York: Pantheon Books, 1987, p. 9 & pp. 155–186.

20 Flapan, *Birth*, p. 9.

21 Flapan, *Birth*, pp. 189–199; and Khouri, *Arab-Israeli*, pp. 70–95

22 Masalha, "Historical Roots," p. 46.

23 Meron Benvenisti, *Sacred Landscape: The Buried History of the Holy Land Since 1948*, Berkeley: University of California, 2000.

24 Ilan Pappe, *The Making of the Arab-Israeli Conflict, 1947–1951*, London: I.B. Tauris, 1994; and "Israeli Perceptions of the Refugee Question," in Aruri (Editor), *Palestinian Refugees*, pp. 70–76.

25 Nafez Nazzal, *The Palestinian Exodus from Galilee, 1948*, Beirut: Institute for Palestine Studies, 1978.

26 Salman H. Abu-Sitta, *The End of the Palestinian-Israeli Conflict: From Refugees to Citizens at Home*, London: Palestine Land Society and Palestinian Return Centre, 2001.

27 Audeh G. Rantisi and Charles Amash, "The Lydda Death March," *The Link*, New York: AMEU, Vol. 33, Issue 3, July–August 2000.

28 Walid Khalidi, *Before Their Diaspora: A Photographic History of the Palestinians 1876–1948*, Washington, D.C.: Institute of Palestine Studies, 1991; and (Editor), *All That Remains: The Palestinian Villages Occupied and Depopulated by Israel in 1948*, Washington, D.C.: Institute of Palestine Studies, c. 1992.

29 Yitzhak Rabin, *Service Diary*, quoted by David Shipler, *The New York Times*, October 22, 1979 and reproduced in Flapan, *Birth*, p. 81.

30 Rantisi and Amash, "Lydda Death March," pp. 3–9; and Masalha, "Historical Roots," p. 45.

31 Palumbo, Palestinian Catastrophe, pp. xii–xvii; and Masalha, "Historical Roots," p. 47.

32 Khalidi, *Remains*, identifies 418 destroyed villages in his book but notes that there were many more, p. xvi; Abu-Sitta, *End of the Palestinian-Israeli Conflict*, lists 531 villages destroyed, and a higher number of refugees by the end of the war, over 800,000. The land ownership figures come from Abu-Sitta, p. 11.

33 Masalha, *Expulsion*, p. 189.

34 Donald Neff, "U.S. Policy and the Palestinian Refugees," *Journal of Palestine Studies*, #69, Vol. XVIII, No. 1, Autumn 1988, p. 105.

35 Neff, "U.S. Policy," p. 105.

36 Neff, "U.S. Policy," p. 105.

37 Benjamin N. Schiff, *Refugees unto the Third Generation: UN Aid to Palestinians*, Syracuse: Syracuse University Press, 1995, passim, but especially Chapter 2, pp. 13–47, and p. 114 for percentage figures on donors and how U.S. contributions declined as resettlement projects failed; and Benjamin N. Schiff, "Between Occupier and Occupied: UNRWA in the West Bank and Gaza," *Journal of Palestine Studies*, #71, Vol. XVII, No. 3, Spring 1989, pp. 60–75. Also see, Edward H. Buehrig, *The UN and the Palestinian Refugees: A Study in Nonterritorial Administration*, Bloomington: Indiana University Press, 1971, especially Chapter V, pp. 113–125.

38 Shahak, "Concept of Transfer," pp. 28–33. The figure of 320,000 expelled Palestinians during and after the 1967 war is noted in Masalha, "Historical Roots," p. 61. In his footnote on p. 67 regarding this figure, Masalha notes "Israeli estimates range from 173,000 to 200,000 while Jordanian and Palestinian estimates range from 250,000 to 408,000 (from June 1967 to the end of 1968). Cited in Walid Salim, 'The [Palestinians] Displaced in 1967: The Problem of Definition and Figures,' in The Palestinians Displaced and the Peace Negotiations (Ramallah, West Bank: Palestinian Diaspora and Refugee Centre, 1996), p. 21. The real figure is probably somewhere around 300,000."

39 Nur Masalha, *Imperial Israel and the Palestinians*, London: Pluto Press, 2000, pp. 28–29.

40 Sheila Ryan, "Plans to Regularize the Occupation," in Naseer Aruri (Editor), *Occupation: Israel Over Palestine*, Belmont, MA: AAUG, 1983, pp. 339–375.

41 Lily Galili, "A Jewish Demographic State," *Ha'aretz*, June 28, 2002 (internet English edition, page undetermined)

42 Most of this section is based on the legal analysis of Professor Susan Akram. For a summary of her analysis, see Susan M. Akram, "Palestinian Refugees and Their Legal Status," *Journal of Palestine Studies*, #123, Vol. XXXI, No. 3, Spring 2002, pp. 36–51. Also see her chapter, "Reinterpreting Palestinian Refugee Rights under international Law," in Aruri, Palestinian Refugees, pp 165–194. Additionally, see Susan M. Akram & Guy Goodwin Gill, *United States Department of Justice, Executive Office for Immigration Review (Board of Immigration Appeals): Brief Amicus Curiae (Palestinian Refugee Rights Under International Law)*, 1999. For a set of comprehensive studies on the Palestinian Refugees, go to the Badil Resource Center for Palestinian Residency and Refugee Rights website: www.badil.org.

43 United Nations General Assembly Resolution No. 194 (III) of 11 December 1948, reproduced in George J. Tomeh (Editor), *United Nations Resolutions on Palestine and the Arab-Israeli Conflict 1947–1974*, Washington, D.C.: Institute for Palestine Studies, 1975, pp. 15–17, specific article, p. 16.

44 Tomeh (Editor), *United Nations Resolutions*, p. 16.

45 See Akram as in endnote 42 and Lex Takkenberg, *The Status of Palestinian Refugees in International Law*, Oxford: Clarendon Press, 1998 for a discussion of this contested article.

46 Tomeh (Editor), *United Nations Resolutions*, pp. 83–84.

47 Tomeh (Editor), *United Nations Resolutions*, pp. 92–93.

48 Tomeh (Editor), *United Nations Resolutions*, pp. 111–112.

49 Haim Shapiro, "Meir Kihan says that, in the present situation, thousands of Palestinians want to leave the country. He wants to help them," *Jerusalem Post*, August 26, 2000. Internet copy, page undetermined.

50 Shapiro, "Meir Kihan."

51 Ali Abunimah, "The Growing Clamor for Ethnic Cleansing," August 29, 2002, Abunimah news analysis email list.

CHAPTER THREE

The Problem of Peace in the Middle East—A Role for the Democratic World

Haidar Abdel-Shafi

Historical Background

It is difficult, if not impossible, for Europe and the West to play a fair and objective role in the Middle East conflict without knowing the roots and evolution of the problem from the time Britain assumed mandate over Palestine in 1922. The following brief account enumerates the facts and factors bearing on the problem.

Palestinian Rights

Palestine has been settled by Semitic tribes from the Arabian peninsula since the earliest recorded history. Later on, successive invasions took place by other tribes including the Hebrews, Assyrians, Persians, Romans, Philistines and Turks. The early Semitic tribes sustained their presence and preserved their Arab affiliations, including language and general orientation, in the face of these invasions. As the indigenous residents of the land, they are entitled to the right of self-determination and independence as are other people. The question then arises: why do the Palestinians continue to be denied their right to self determination and to be condemned to statelessness with all its difficulties and hazards?

Zionist Claims

The Zionists started and activated their claims to Palestine and other Arab territory in the latter half of the 19th century, exploiting circumstances of Eastern European persecution of Jews to propagate falsehood and distortions and to earn sympathy in Western Europe. Initially the Zionists were tempted to say that Palestine was empty territory, as in the famous slogan: "A land without a people for a people without a land." Soon, however, they abandoned this obviously false statement and claimed instead that the Palestinians do not constitute a stable society but are simply migrant groups not ready for or entitled to self-determination. Unfortunately these absurd claims met readily believing ears for several reasons. First is the cosmopolitan character of Diaspora Jews that has allowed easy communication with people all over the world, playing on the gullibility and sympathy of international audiences to Jewish persecution, underscored dramatically in the 20th century by the Holocaust and its aftermath. The effective use of worldwide media by sophisticated Jews overshadowed the primitive and ineffective use of such facilities to reflect the truth of Arabs, who were effectively absent from the world stage.

At the first Zionist Congress, held in Switzerland in 1897, Theodore Herzl promoted a platform that was adopted and has been consistently expanded. One key idea is that the Zionist program can be implemented only through force; hence, it has been crucial to develop and expand strong military and economic entities to support the political program of a Jewish state: "Peace through strength." Another fundamental posture is the rejection of any recognition of a Palestinian national entity. Practically, this has led to adoption of a strategy of presenting the world with facts on the ground. A Jewish homeland without a Palestinian homeland is a *fait accompli.*

The British Role

The Zionist claims suited the British colonialist designs on having a friendly base close to the Suez Canal on the long route to their colonies in the Far East and in helping maintain their mandate over the region: Iraq, the Persian Gulf, Syria, Lebanon and Jordan. So the British government promised in the Balfour Declaration of November 2, 1917, to help the Zionist program in spite of promises to its Arab allies in the war against Turkey.

During the British Mandate of Palestine, which began with the 1917 defeat of the Ottoman Empire in World War I, British conduct was biased, favoring the Zionist program in violation of the innate Palestinian rights. As the governing entity, Britain, under the protection of arms, supported Jewish immigration against Palestinian opposition, a matter that represented a stark violation of the Palestinian right to self-determination. The extent of this violation is evident in the shift of the demographic ratio from one Jew to eleven Palestinians to one Jew to two Palestinians over the 25 year span of the British Mandate (1923–1948).

The British adopted a biased and discriminatory attitude, favoring the Jewish community by giving them a measure of self-rule and permitting military training and possession of arms, while denying the same rights to Palestinians. In fact, Arabs suffered severe punishment for possession of arms. Therefore, by the end of the Mandate, there were two conflicting societies claiming the same territory, one well organized and well armed while the other was the reverse. Given these realities, what took place 1948 in Palestine need not be much of a surprise to anybody as the Zionists claimed control at the end of the British Mandate.

Zionist Tactics of Falsification and Deception

Israel often accuses the Palestinians of being responsible for the absence of peace in the Middle East because they rejected partition in 1948, implying that the Israelis themselves have sincerely accepted partition. Facts, however, contradict this claim:

- Israeli troops occupied the Gaza Strip in 1956 for no valid reason and refused to implement the UN resolution to withdraw until subjected to pressure by President Eisenhower, who threatened sanctions.
- In 1967 Israeli aggression produced the Occupation of the rest of Palestine. Immediate engagement in settlement activity implemented the *fait accompli* strategy in spite of condemnation by UN General Assembly Resolutions.
- The Israeli government exploited peace with Egypt, the biggest and strongest neighboring Arab state, for further aggression rather than for peace as desired and expected by everybody. An active settlement program in the West Bank accelerated in the summer of 1982, and all sorts of atrocities followed, culminating in the massacres at Sabra and Shatila Palestinian refugee camps in Lebanon.

Israeli rejection of all Palestinian conciliatory moves, including the acceptance of the two state principle, indicates that to all intents and purposes, Israel remains committed to all that Zionism claimed in the first Zionist Congress 1897. It is notable that since its establishment in 1948, Israel has never defined its final borders. When Ben Gurion, the first prime minister of Israel, was asked about the ultimate border, he replied that Israel's borders are where Israeli soldiers stand!

The Peace Process of Madrid

In spite of its conviction that Israel had not abandoned any of the declared Zionist claims asserted in Switzerland in 1897, the Palestinian leadership decided to participate in the Madrid Peace conference promoted by the US government in the spring of 1991 for two reasons:

1) They did not wish to afford the Zionists another chance to smear and distort the Palestinian attitude towards peace.

2) They hoped that the American sponsors would adopt a fair and balanced position, especially after waging a war in the Persian Gulf under the banner of liberating Kuwait from Iraqi occupation.

Since the US forcibly opposed an occupation that had lasted only few months, Palestinians felt it was legitimate to seek an end to the Israeli Occupation of the West Bank and Gaza that had lasted over 20 years with many documented violations of and aggressions counter to international law.

This hope was frustrated at the inception of negotiations in Washington D.C. because Israel refused to suspend its settlement activity in the Occupied Territories of the West Bank and Gaza, thus violating the terms of reference for the Peace Process spelled out in UN Resolution 242, and thereby depriving the Process of any real content. The American sponsor failed its duty to preserve the integrity of the Peace Process. The Palestinians' ill-advised continuing participation in negotiations provided a cover for further Israeli violations as well as an excuse for the American failure to respect the integrity of the negotiating process.

The Declaration of the Oslo Agreement, which was reached secretly in 1993, did not add any hope to the prospects of a genuine peace. Surprisingly, the agreement came void of any reference to the settlement issue, which was the cause of the impasse in the Washington negotiations. Under cover of negotiations to implement the Oslo Agreement, Israel doubled its settlement presence in the Occupied Territories and simultaneously established a network of bypass roads for the benefit of the settlers and military. These roads destroyed the demographic continuity of the Arab habitat and turned it into a series of disconnected *bantustans*.

Palestinian and General Arab Failures

The Zionist program, which has enjoyed support by Western colonial powers, has been viewed as an Arab national challenge, for Palestine and Palestinians are part and parcel of the Arab world. While this understanding has been accepted in principle, it has not been translated into serious and organized action. In the absence of an organization to utilize appropriately the available potential of the Arab world, a state of disarray and paralysis has prevailed and continues to prevail. This reality, especially among Palestinians, is actively exploited by Israel. The management of the Al Aqsa *Intifada* is a clear example. Failure on the part of the Palestinian leadership to organize and control the *Intifada* by limiting its spontaneity and emotionalism, restraining its military action to a defensive style, and properly attending to the basic needs of the population under the emergent situation has played into the hands of Israel, providing a pretext for Sharon's exaggerated violence and brutality. Unfortunately the Arab world, in the absence of democracy, could neither provide a better example to the Palestinian leadership nor honor its responsibility in defense of general Arab legitimate rights.

Failure of the Democratic World

At the end of World War II leaders of the democratic world decided to get together and find ways and means to prevent a repeat of the suffering and loss of life and property caused by that war. After due deliberation a world body was established in 1945 and named the United Nations Organization, later simply the United Nations. A detailed Charter was drawn up emphasizing rules and principles as well as procedures to find a peaceful way to prevent armed conflict before it started. Specialized bodies and instruments within the UN were set up to enable the organization to achieve its objectives.

The test, however, came too soon. When the Arabs rejected the Partition Plan for Palestine recommended by the UN General Assembly in November, 1947, troubles started and promised to escalate. The British, who were still in charge as the Mandatory Power, decided to end their Mandate without planning to hand over the responsibility of running the country to any other power. Although that could be construed as a dereliction of British responsibility, the UN itself cannot be excused. The British announced that May 15, 1948, would be the last day of the British Mandate in Palestine. Did the British intentionally design to leave the weaker Arabs at the mercy of the far stronger Zionist gangs? Nobody can honestly answer this question with assurance, but anyone with a deep enough knowledge of the situation could have predicted who the winner would be.

Even before the promised withdrawal of the British administration, the Zionists capitalized on the situation and started terrorizing the Arabs. Well-planned massacres in Arab towns and villages were perpetrated in order to intimidate the Arabs into running away. The exodus that followed the destruction of more than 400 Palestinian villages and the confiscation of countless Palestinian properties was the start of the current Palestinian refugee crisis. The Zionists were intent on preventing any Palestinian who left his or her home in terror from returning. That was a definite policy. The infamous massacre of Deir Yassin, a village near Jerusalem, is only one of countless such atrocities. Before the end of 1948, the Palestinian refugees numbered around 800,000. Because of these events, when Israel applied soon after the declaration of statehood to be accepted as a member of the United Nations, her acceptance was contingent upon her promise to allow the refugees back. Although Israel made that promise, she has yet to honor it, and the largest refugee population in the world is Palestinian.

In May, 1948, the UN Secretary General sent a special envoy to Palestine, Count Folke Bernadotte of Sweden, as a mediator. The envoy arrived and became active in studying the situation to see what he could do. He formulated certain ideas, some of which were published. The Zionists obviously didn't like that kind of activity; the man was dispatched with a bullet in a busy street in Jerusalem. He paid for his honesty with his life, and the world watched helplessly!

The Role of the Democratic World

The crisis for Palestinians has continued throughout the past 54 years and increased markedly after the 1967 Occupation. All conciliatory moves by the Palestinian Authority have been rejected and peace efforts such as the treaty with Egypt have been exploited for further aggression. The Peace Process of Madrid has been abused and again used for further aggression. Israel took advantage of the hopeful mood of the Oslo Peace Process to double its settlement presence in the Occupied Territories, violating explicit UN Resolutions. The "generous final offer" at Camp David offered nothing more than *bantustans* in place of a viable Palestinian state. Naked force stands supreme in opposition to legal and human rights principles.

In the face of Israel's intransigence, the inaction of the democratic world is incomprehensible. There are legions of peaceful punitive measures that the democratic world could adopt to force Israel to respect and implement UN resolutions in the commercial, diplomatic, cultural, scientific and other fields. Europe and the United States can and must play a crucial role in implementing such measures for the sake of peace. It is time to end the ongoing tragedy in Palestine.

References

Flapan, Simha. *The Birth of Israel: Myths and Realities* (New York: Pantheon Books), 1987.

_____. *Zionism and the Palestinians* (London:Groom Helm, Ltd.), 1979.

Masalha, Nur. *Expulsion of the Palestinians*, Institute for Palestine Studies, 1992.

CHAPTER FOUR

Chosenness, Zionism, and the Implications for Occupation

Martin Federman

I begin—as all good writers know they should not—with a disclaimer: the topic at hand is virtually impossible to address. Each component could be, and indeed has been, discussed, defined, dissected, and defamed almost to death; it would be a colossal act of *hubris* to think that I had some grand insight that would replace what has already been said. I *will* attempt to reflect on the history and traditions of the concepts of chosenness and Zionism and to posit some of the ways in which their interaction sets a rationale for Israel's claim to *Eretz Yisrael* (the "Land of Israel"). Having done that, it is my hope that I can offer some observations about different ways to see these ideas and their historical uses, exposing a complex set of relationships—the relationships of words, ideas, and beliefs as well as the relationships between the peoples who use, hold on to, and believe in them—so that they cease being unbreachable barriers to an equitable resolution of the current situation.

Chosenness

Let me begin with the obvious: Judaism includes a clear belief, seen in the *Torah* (Hebrew Bible) and later Rabbinic commentaries, that there exists a special relationship between God and the Jewish People. The text is clear about this, as is the Rabbis' awareness of it. I

would argue, however, that the precise sources, nature, or implications of this relationship are not so universally established, nor are
the ramifications for Israel's place among the nations.[1]

There has been a common cultural inclination, waning somewhat
in the last generation or so, but still present in the Jewish community,
for us Jews to see ourselves as having certain inherited cultural,
ethnic, and educational characteristics which lift us collectively, in
the jargon of the day, in the gene pool. Phillip Roth reflects on his own
upbringing and sense of Jewish identity this way:

> ...what one received, I think, was a psychology, not a culture
> and not a history in its totality. The simple point here is, I
> think, that what one received of culture, history, learning, law,
> one received in strands, in little bits and pieces. What one
> received whole, however, what one feels whole, is a kind of
> psychology; and the psychology can be translated into three
> words—"Jews are better."

Many of us who grew up in the last century were raised—
sometimes subtly, sometimes not so subtly—with a not fully defined
sense of our tiny community's "better-ness." It's difficult to identify
the nature of this sense of superiority. What *was* clear was that the
rest of the world, through no fault of their own, simply did not have
this quality, and while it did not make them lesser human beings, it
did make them *different*. This difference was reflected in our use of the
word *goy*—which, in the Bible and common language simply means
"nation" and is a neutral term that refers to *any* nation, *including* Israel.
And yet, over time, it has come to mean "the other nations" and
eventually, especially when said with any of a number of unflattering
tones of voice, *them, the other.*

---

1 It should be pointed out that the "family" name *Yisrael* (Israel) is derived
from the Patriarch *Yaacov* (Jacob), *Avraham's* (Abraham's) grandson, through
whose twelve sons the Jewish people are created. At the end of the profound
encounter (recorded in Genesis 32:23–30) when Yaacov "wrestled a man," he
was given a new name (always a sign of a life transformation)—Yisrael,
roughly: God-wrestler. The first way the people are identified as a group is
B'nai Yisrael, the Children of Israel. It is much later that the name of the people
becomes attached to the land and, while this has significant implications
rooted in tradition, Israel, the people, is not simply synonymous with Israel,
the land or state.

But this is only the cultural manifestation of ideas that have always been part of the Jewish belief system. And, as is always true with cultural manifestations, they have been so transformed and redefined that they become only a dim reflection of the ideas that gave birth to them. In our context, we are more concerned with the basis for the idea of the sense of uniqueness of Israel, the people. As with everything in Jewish tradition, the source lies in the texts: the Torah, and the oral tradition which emanates from it.

A digression—this will resonate far more with some readers than others. If, for instance, one reads the text in an absolutely literal, untextured way, my observations will not be persuasive. If, however, one recognizes the layers inherent in Torah, as I believe the Rabbis did, we will find some interesting messages that we often tend to overlook.

To understand the nature of "chosenness," we need to understand that the whole of the Torah is a story about relationships. Indeed, the very creation of the world is motivated by God's desire[2] to have a being with whom to be in relationship, and, like all relationships, it requires a basis on which the two can freely decide to relate. The Torah sees human beings as living in a potentially covenantal relationship with God, one in which both commit themselves to particular beliefs and behaviors on which the relationship is based. It is impossible to comprehend the nature of chosenness without this idea of the *b'rit*—the covenant. We generally identify Judaism's "gift to the world" as monotheism; what Judaism actually gave to the world was the idea of a single, universal God who, for reasons we cannot begin to fathom, and lack the words to describe, chose to enter into relationship with His[3] creation.

And so, we read in the text a series of covenants that God makes initially with various individuals. Each of these "contracts" contains a

---

2 Language fails us here. Does God "decide" to do this? Or is it something that is in the very nature of the divine, something that God "must" do? What is relevant here is that, in the view of the Torah, the impetus for the creation is the presence of a being which, while emanating from the divine, is separate enough to make choices and to relate to God.

3 I note the use of "His" reluctantly. My God includes all gender, is simultaneously both male and female and yet not either. But use of the neuter "It," is awkward and, in speaking about traditional texts, I choose to echo the original Hebrew which has no neuter. I trust that the flow of the essay will make up for any potential affront to some readers.

traditional legal formula noting that "I give, or do this and in return you promise to give, or do that." God makes covenants with Noah, with each of the patriarchs (Abraham, Isaac, and Jacob) and with Ishmael. And God writes a huge contract—we call it the Torah—with the entire people of Israel at Mount Sinai.

The presence of a special relationship with Abraham and his descendants begins almost as soon as his family story begins.

> I will make a great nations of you, and will make your name great, I will bless those who bless you, and will give you blessing. Be a blessing!
>
> *Genesis 12:2*

> For Avraham is to become, yes, become a great nation and mighty, and all the nations of the earth will find blessing through him.
>
> *Genesis 18:18–19*

Later, after the near-sacrifice of Avraham's beloved son *Yitzhak,* we read:

> Now YHWH's messenger called to Avraham a second time from heaven and said: By myself I swear indeed, because you have done this thing, have not withheld your son, your only-one, indeed, I will bless you, I will make your seed many, yes many, like the stars of the heavens and like the sand that is on the shore of the sea; your seed shall inherit the gate of their enemies, all the nations of the earth shall enjoy blessing through your seed, in consequence of your hearkening to my voice.
>
> *Genesis 22:15–18*

These promises and blessings are repeated over and over again to Avraham, and to his son and grandson. Then, with the great revelation of Sinai, the covenant is broadened to include all of the people of Israel:

> So now, if you will hearken, yes, hearken to my voice and keep my covenant, you shall be to me a special-treasure from among all people. Indeed, all the earth is mine, but you, you shall be to me a kingdom of priests, a holy nation.
>
> *Exodus 19:5–6*

> For you are a people holy to YHWH your God, [it is] you
> [that] YHWH your God chose for him as a treasured people
> from among all peoples that are on the face of the soil.
>
> *Deuteronomy 7:6*

By the time of the prophets, the idea that Israel is the elect of God is firmly set in the psychology of the people. There is no question that there is a special relationship between God and Israel, different from God's relationship with the other nations

> You alone have I known[4] of all the families of the earth;
> therefore I will visit upon you all your iniquities.
>
> *Amos 3:2*

And for prophets like Nehemiah, Israel's special relationship is rooted in the furthest reaches of our shared history:

> You are YHWH God, who chose Avram, and brought him up
> from Ur of the Chaldees; You changed his name to Avraham
> when you discovered his heart was faithful before you. You
> made a covenant with him.
>
> *Nehemiah 9:7*

By the beginning of the Rabbinic period, the idea of Israel's election was assumed:

> The Holy One, blessed be He, said to Israel, I am God over
> all who come into the world, but I have only associated
> My name with you. I am not called the God of idolaters but
> the God of Israel.
>
> *Exod. R. XXXIX. 4*

> Come and see how beloved are the Israelites before the Holy
> One, blessed be He; for wherever they were exiled the
> *Shechinah (the presence of God)* was with them....
>
> *Meg. 29a*

But, to get the full picture, we must examine some interesting aspects of Israel's election. First we must look at *why* God chose Israel. Is the choice based on Israel's innate power, strength, or superiority?

---

4 Note that the Hebrew word for known used here is *ya-dati*, the most profound sense of knowing. It is the word that is used to imply a simple, complete, unfiltered sense of knowledge, and in describing the sexual act between man and wife.

We need only look back to the passage quoted above from Deuteronomy and the verses that follow to find the answer:

> Not because of your being many more than all the peoples has YHWH attached Himself to you and chosen you, for you are the least numerous of all peoples! Rather, because of YHWH's love for you and because of His keeping the sworn oath that he swore to your fathers did YHWH take you out, with a strong hand, and redeem you from a house of serfs…

In other words, election is a product of God's love, and His commitment to the *b'rit*, the covenant with the people. Thus, we must consider the nature and purpose of chosenness. What we learn from the text is that the relationship with God is dependent on Israel's behavior, particularly in connection to the role that Israel is to play in the world, i.e., as a "holy people" and "a kingdom of priests, a holy nation." While God will always continue to love Israel (as He loves all nations), the special relationship exists only when Israel maintains its faith and keeps its part of the covenant by doing God's will. We see this clearly by re-reading the texts above and noting the dialectical nature of God's promises. Avraham is, indeed, promised a great future, but there is a qualification: *"Indeed, I have known him, in order that he may charge his sons and his household after him: they shall keep the way of YHWH, to do what is right and just, in order that YHWH may bring upon Avraham what he spoke concerning him."* Even at the *Akedah* (the binding of *Yitzhak*), God's promise is a response to Avraham's actions: *"in consequence of your hearkening to my voice."*

It becomes clear that there are qualifications to the nature of Israel's election, qualifications that were acknowledged even by that most ethnocentric group of thinkers, the Rabbis. While they were absolutely sure of Israel's special relationship with God, they clearly acknowledged that it called for a special responsibility on Israel's part to fulfill its potential as a "light to the nations," and that Israel therefore bore a greater sense of responsibility for it failures. (See the Amos quotation above.) The Rev. Dr. A. Cohen, author of the classic *Everyman's Talmud*,[5] observes:

> It is therefore evident that, in the opinion of the Rabbis, their people possessed no exceptional inherent superiority for which they merited the distinction conferred upon them by

---

5 Cohen, A., *Everyman's Talmud*, E. P. Dutton & Co., New York.

> God, and the special status would come to an end immediately on the abandonment of the Torah as their exclusive possession. On the contrary it was destined for all mankind, and happy the day when all nations accepted it.(62)

Equally important for us, neither the Torah nor the Rabbinic literature sees chosenness as limited to one person or group. We need only look again at the story of Yitzhak's binding to see the potentials in God's relationship with human beings. This is a pivotal event in Avraham's life—an event with profound implications for our future. Indeed, it is important enough to be chosen as the scriptural reading for the second day of *Rosh Hashannah*, the Jewish New Year. While we are aware of this story of God's testing of Avraham, we know less about the portion that immediately precedes it—and is the reading for the first day. This section relates the story of Avraham's first-born, Ishmael. We are told that this son by Sarah's hand-maiden Hagar is sent out, with God's permission, to assuage Sarah's fears that he will inherit instead of Yitzhak. It appears as if he will die, but at the moment of despair:

> God heard the voice of the lad, God's messenger called to Hagar from heaven and said to her. What ails you, Hagar? Do not be afraid, for God has heard the voice of the lad there where he is. Arise, lift up the lad and grasp him with your hand, for a great nation will I make of him!
>
> *Genesis 21:17–18*

What we have here is acknowledgement, within the text itself, that God can make multiple promises and covenants. And the Rabbis emphasize that: there is a tradition that embellishes the beginning of the Akedah narrative. The text simply says that God decides to test Avraham, and says: *Pray take your son, your only son, the one you love, Yitzhak.*" But the Rabbis tell us that this is only one side of a conversation that took place between Avraham and God:

God	Avraham
Take your son	Which one, I have two
Your only son	Didn't you hear me, I have two sons
The one you love	*(and remember, this is the Rabbis talking)* I love them *both!*
Yitzhak	

What is the text telling us? First, that God can have covenants and special relationships with as many people as He wants. It is not incidental that both Jewish and Muslim traditions hold that *Ishmael* is the progenitor of twelve princes—a direct parallel to the twelve sons of Yaakov. And further, if we think about the flow of the narrative, and this is crucial, the text is telling us that there are many stories. This book (the Torah) is *our* (the Jews) story, but don't forget that there are other stories out there. By juxtaposing God's promise to Hagar with the other story that the Torah will go on to tell, we only learn that our story must happen through Yitzhak.[6]

Finally, we need to acknowledge that part of God's promise includes the land Avraham has been brought to. Again, if one reads selectively and without analysis, there is nothing that can be said to mediate the meaning of this promise. But we must see this in the same way we have looked at the rest of the relationship. First, the exclusive nature of Israel's right to the land is by no means absolute. Many, for instance, use the Torah's account of Avraham's purchase of the Cave of Machpelah to bury his wife Sarah (*Genesis 23:3–18*) as proof that the land belongs only to the Jews—a contention that makes Hebron *the* current flash point of the Israeli/Palestinian conflict. Indeed, for many years I taught this passage, with its oriental bargaining (which Avraham short-circuits by agreeing to an outlandish payment), and the Torah's repetition of the presence of the men of the town and the boundaries of his purchase, as a legal deed. This transaction cannot be questioned—the "deed" precludes the possibility of someone questioning that the payment was unfair, or the borders unclear—and it all happened in front of witnesses. This does not, however, take two things into account: 1) that Avraham had to purchase the land because it *didn't* belong to him, and 2) the boundaries indicate that he owned *only* that parcel. Furthermore, we know that there is some sharing of this place since *both* of Avraham's beloved sons come together to bury their father. This is, of course, a complicated issue, both in biblical tradition and it the implications for the current conflict. But it is complicated precisely because there is not a single, clear answer.

At the same time, the right to the land, like the rest of the promise, is predicated on Israel's behavior. This is confirmed by explaining exile, first to Babylon, later throughout the world, to Israel's lack of constancy. And the core of Israel's responsibility is *tzedek*—justice. The prophets make it clear that Israel's punishment is a result of

---

6 It should be noted that the Qu'ran, Islam's holy scripture, includes a parallel binding narrative—with *Ishmael* as the intended sacrifice!

having forgotten its responsibility—and this responsibility is not so much to the cultic practices (although the prophets supported them) but to the profoundly more important responsibility to those in need like the widow, the orphan, and the homeless:

> Behold, you fast only to quarrel and to fight and to hit with the wicked fist. Fasting like yours this day will not make your voice to be heard on high. Is this not the fast that I have chosen: To share your bread with the hungry, and that you bring the homeless poor who are cast out to your house? And when you see the naked that you cover him?
>
> *Isaiah, 58:5–7*

It should be noted here that, even if we were to accept that the land belongs to us, our responsibility to others living among us is clear:

> Now a sojourner you are not to mistreat, you are not to oppress him, for sojourners were you in the land of Egypt.
>
> *Exodus 22:20*

We rely on the promise that God will never fully abandon us, and we can always return to His ways, but we have no automatic right to His protection in the absence of our own practice of justice.

The implications for the later history of the Jewish people are complex and erratic. Certainly, despite indications otherwise, they create a sense within Judaism that this relationship with God must be based on some special aspect of the character of the people, or, at the very least, a place in the universe merited by the character of our ancestors, who, according to scripture, had a special and very personal relationship with God. After the destruction of the Temple, and as the reality of a long dispersal throughout the world set in, there was a need to reinforce the sense that God had not abandoned us. If we were no longer tied to the land, and God was somehow universal, the only basis on which to support the very existence of the Jewish nation was in the unique relationship we have with God, a relationship which transcends time and place, and must be based either on our distinctive qualities or some indefinable connection that God has with us. Mordechai Kaplan, founder of Reconstructionism, suggests that "the Jews could never have displayed such power of endurance had they not been fortified by the doctrine of election."[7]

---

7 Kaplan, Mordecai, *Judaism as a Civilization.*

This sense of our own distinctiveness, if not superiority, fed into an unfortunate cycle that plagued the Jews for centuries. The sense of superiority, linked with the growing rejection of Jews by the ever-more-powerful Christian community because of the Jews' rejection of both Jesus and his *new* covenant, brought upon us growing persecution. And, as that persecution grew and became more intense and terrifying, so did the isolation, physically and psychologically, of the persecuted. In this situation, the sense of there having to be some reason for our suffering also grew and fed the sense that our very suffering was a proof of the special role we played in history. This is a cycle which has had unfortunate parallels in modern history, especially in some of the ways in which the experience of the Holocaust has influenced the psychology of the founding of the State of Israel.

It is crucial for us Jews to come to grips with the complexity of the idea of our own election. And we must not be obsessed with the conflicting messages from our texts, from our rabbis, or from our history. We know that there are many voices represented in our past, and we need to look for the *tendencies*, the directions to which the composite leads us. And it would appear that certain realities are represented in that composite. First, that there *is*, indeed, a special, covenantal relationship between God and Israel—one that we should not be embarrassed about. At the same time, we need to understand that, while that relationship may be different from God's relationship with other nations, it is neither exclusive nor necessarily better, and this has profound implications for how we view our relationships with other people—and peoples.

Zionism

To begin, a confession: I—to the disappointment of many of my associates and with full awareness of the assumptions that arise when I say this—consider myself a Zionist. Having said that, I must qualify what I mean by this statement. There are so many definitions and manifestations of Zionism, each with countless forms of their own, that in many contexts the word has become almost meaningless. So why hold on to it? I am reminded of the prelude to Martin Buber's *The Eclipse of God*,[8] where he recounts a conversation with "a noble old thinker": "How can you bring yourself to say 'God?'" the acquaintance

---

8 Buber, Martin. *The Eclipse of God*, Harper & Row, New York, 1952.

asks. "What word of human speech is so misused, so defiled, so desecrated as this? All the innocent blood that has been shed for it has robbed it of its radiance. All the injustice that it has been used to cover has effaced its features"(7). I think about this when I think how the term "Zionism" has been used—and misused. But I also cannot escape Buber's response: "Yes, it is the most heavy-laden of all human words. None has become so soiled, so mutilated. Just for this reason I may not abandon it." I do not suggest that Zionism is to be equated to God (God forbid!), but I do think that the idea of Zionism, going back even before the word and certainly the movement even existed, has been used and misused in much the same way.

From the very beginning of the Jewish community, there was a tie to this piece of land given for our use by its ultimate landowner, God. In our exile we mourned and chanted lamentations at the waters of Babylon, and our tradition records our joy at returning. After the destruction of the second Temple, even as the Rabbis were recreating a Judaism that could survive despite our separation from our central place of worship, they were certain that the exile would be temporary. We never stopped praying for our return, and "Next Year in Jerusalem" became a permanent declaration in our liturgy.

These religious roots, however, were not the source of the modern Zionist movement. While there were some religious Zionists, the reality was that in the nineteenth century, after almost 2000 years of exile, for the most staunchly orthodox, hope for a return to Zion was invested substantially in a miraculous event heralded by the arrival of the Messiah. The impetus for return came from predominantly secular communities as a response to widespread anti-Semitism and a desire to find a place where Jews could be safe and have control over their own destiny. There was no question that the assumed location of a new Jewish state would be in Palestine although it should be noted that there were other plans floated, most notably the suggestion of a Jewish state in Uganda. While it was reported that Chaim Weitzman, the first president of Israel, and some of his colleagues, in response to this suggestion, put ashes on their heads and sat in sack-cloth in the halls of their hotel, for others this idea was not out of the realm of possibility.

The reality, however, was that for the overwhelming number of Zionists, Zionism was exactly what it said—a return to *Zion*. Over the next fifty years a cacophony of different Zionist movements grew, including Labor Zionists, Bundists, Communists, and Religious Zionists, united by the commitment of return impelled by a disparate assortment of motivations. One of the coalescing ideas was the comfortable symmetry of the idea of "a land without a people, a people without a land": the belief in a natural return of exiled heirs to their otherwise unused ancestral home. Awareness of the reality of an Arab/Palestinian people living for generations on this land had an effect on the strategies of populating the country with Jewish "pioneers" but did not stem the sense of importance, even necessity, of settling. This is not the place to trace the political intricacies that involved the Ottoman Empire, Great Britain, the League of Nations, the United States, and any number of other entities. Nor is there any benefit to enumerating the countless atrocities perpetrated on all sides. What is pertinent is the fact, in 1947/48, of the partition of Palestine and the creation of the Jewish State of Israel, which was seen overwhelmingly (although not universally) by Jews throughout the world as a miraculous rebirth of historic Israel. The repercussions of that event—not only for Jews, but for Palestinians living in the new state as well as those exiled by choice or force from it—cannot be overstated.

The need to protect the demographics of the new state was obvious from the very beginning, leading to something of a schizophrenic policy. Publicly, Israel invited cooperation and friendship while, as we now know, the private interaction among Israeli leaders was already engaging a perceived need to free Israel from an unwieldy Arab population. Consequently, the state, rooted in socialist and democratic convictions (represented significantly by the *kibbutz* movement) had to begin dealing with the growing realities of security, modernization, and *real-politick*. With a huge influx of immigrants, an expanding and diversifying economy, the growth of cities, and a series of wars with its neighbors, culminating in the acquisition of the West Bank and Gaza in 1967, Israel was a decidedly different place, with very different needs.

Two brands of Zionism, emerging from very different but mutually supportive places, arose. On the one hand was a nationalist Zionism, primarily secular, pragmatic, and committed to the need to protect both the existence of the state and its Jewish identity. On the other was a religious Zionism, ideological, zealous, and rooted in the conviction that all of the biblical land of Israel belongs exclusively to the people of Israel—the Jews. These two views of Zionism reinforced one another in the political world, pressing for a hard-line that claims the freedom to determine the "facts on the ground" that emanate from exclusive rights.

There are many, in Israel and abroad, uncomfortable with these visions of Zionism. Guy Grossman, one of the leaders of the Seruv[9] movement, has suggested that these new forms have "hijacked" the essence of historical Zionism, pressuring Israelis into a with-us-or-against-us paradigm. Grossman, like so many others, emphasizes his love for Israel, his connection to the Jewish people, his commitment to Israel's security—in short, his Zionism. But he also raises, as many others have, the question of the nature of Zionism as a *Jewish* movement of national identity. What is the movement's nature if it is not rooted in basic Jewish values and traditions? This may be the decisive question facing Israel today. In its quest to fulfill the 2000 year old dream of an independent, secure haven for Jews, what identifies the political entity as, in fact, *Jewish*? Most of the current debate defines the Jewishness of the state in demographic terms, focusing on the number of Jews relative to the number of Arabs in the state. Must not Israel restrict the number of non-Jews in order to remain democratic but assure the basic Jewish nature of the state? And, how do we accomplish this if we are committed, ultimately, to control over all of historic Israel?

What is less considered is the core question of what defines a Jewish state. I grew up with the belief that Israel was a different kind of entity than any previous nation-state. Our common beliefs and the basis of our decision making came from different places than anyone else's. Our policies were based on Jewish law, tradition, and, above all, values. We would live in harmony with our neighbors. We would accept higher casualties in war in order not to fire on civilians or even holy places. We hated the Arabs, Golda Meir told the world, not because they killed our children, but because they forced us to kill theirs. It is impossible to evaluate how many of these sensibilities were truly at work in the setting of national priorities over the years. What *is* important is for Zionists of all shades to embrace the question of what makes a Jewish state *Jewish*. At what point does Israel cease to be Jewish not because there are too few Jews, but because too few Jews are acting out of Jewishness? Can we justify the Jewishness of a state that acts in ways that cannot be morally justified?

And so, as uncomfortable as I am with the idea, I confess to being a Zionist. I am convinced of the historical connection between the

---

9 The "Refuser" movement represents hundreds of loyal, patriotic Israeli Army active duty and reserve officers who, while accepting military duty, have refused to serve within the Occupied Territories.

Children of Israel and that particular piece of real estate—a connection that goes back 3500 years and will exist throughout time. And I confess to the inconsistency of being a democrat with the uneasy sense that there needs to be a place that is predominantly Jewish, protecting the history, culture, and existence of our people. And, while in my heart I am a single-statist, imagining an Israel that accommodates all the peoples whose histories are bound up with it, living together without negating one another, in my mind I know that will only happen far in the future, perhaps only when *Moshiach* (Messiah) comes. For now I yearn for an Israel that can exist next-door to a free, viable Palestine, focusing on creating an ethically, morally, spiritually Jewish homeland.

The Implications of Occupation

> Zion shall be redeemed with justice, and they that return of her with righteousness.
>
> *Isaiah 1:27*

The nature of Occupation of the West Bank, Gaza, and East Jerusalem confronts Israelis—and Jews everywhere—with contradicting impulses, raising difficult questions. When we look at the current Israeli policy in the Palestinian territories and the virtual destruction of Palestinian economy, culture, and infrastructure that has resulted, and we recognize the effects on Israelis of Palestinian extremist terror, we cannot avoid engaging these questions. There are really two kinds of questions here: the moral and the practical. On the one hand, what is the *right* thing for Israel to be doing? Can a state which has defined its very existence as being based on a particular set of moral and ethical values, defend actions that betray these values in the name of "security?" It is clear that Israel, like any other national entity, has the right—no, obligation—to protect the security of its citizens. However, as I have suggested earlier, we must question measures that are perceived to be justified for the sake of security when they violate the basic principles expounded by the state: Does the security of one people take precedence over the treatment of another? Jewish law and tradition would seem to at least question the validity of this possibility. As noted above, Israel's professed position in its formative years was to take extraordinary risks in order to avoid behavior seen as being in conflict with basic Jewish values. Whether or not actual behavior matched the ideal historically, it is clear that in recent years the balance has shifted decidedly towards justifying virtually any behavior if it is seen, even indirectly, as protecting security or fighting terrorism. It is impossible, however, to excuse a variety of policies including collective punishment, bombing of civilian neighborhoods, firing live ammunition at stone-throwers, uprooting of trees, and the like, in the name of protecting a *Jewish* state and population.

It is even more complicated. The face of the Occupation is determined to a great extent by the existence of the settlements which require a substantial military presence for protection, drawing more hostile reaction from elements within the Palestinian community, which reinforce the need for protection, and so on. It is clear that not only are a majority of Israelis ready to withdraw from the settlements, but that, indeed, a majority of the *settlers* would be ready to return to Israel-proper if offered the kinds of housing incentives they have received in the settlements. The true challenge is the interaction between the religious/ideological settlers and the nationalists within Israel itself. It is these settlers, claiming exclusive Jewish rights to *all* of the land, supported by a government (and its armed forces) that represent a vocal and powerful minority from diverse communities (religious, nationalist, etc.) that maintain a cycle of violence and (often in witting or unwitting collusion with Palestinian extremists) preclude *any* kind of reasonable resolution. It must be understood that the ideologues will never be convinced that their position is anything but God-given and absolutely right, nor will the nationalists ever allow the existence of anything other than a weak, demilitarized Palestinian entity that is no more than a loose confederation of *bantustans* with limited control over internal administrative affairs.

So what is to be done? The answer begins with our expanded view of what it means to be chosen, and what the nature of Zionism is. I have already indicated my belief that there exists a special relationship between Israel (the people) and its God. Further, the promises perceived by this people include the reliance on God's promise to our rights to the land—an expectation that has historically been manifested in the people's ongoing connection to the place. But we have clearly seen that neither chosenness nor ownership of the land is exclusive. Further, we must recognize both the covenantal and conditional bases of the relationship. We have made a deal with God which imposes responsibilities and expectations: if we do not act justly, we forfeit our rights to God's promises. The paradox is that the behavior espoused by the current Israeli government which is meant to ensure the existence of the state may well be precisely the behavior that abrogates our right to have one.

And there the matter rests. We may consider and learn from past history, but it is irrelevant in resolving the situation. What is relevant is that there now exist two peoples, two cultures, two national entities, each with valid claims to a piece of land. It is not important which has suffered more, which is the greater victim, what the chronology of their suffering has been. What *is* important is the acknowledgement that *both* have suffered, *both* have been victims, and *both* have claims on the land. What *is* important is that we hear the stories on both sides and acknowledge that *neither* of these peoples is going away. The only resolution—and sadly, almost everyone already acknowledges this but somehow can't bring it about—is for the two peoples to share the land, carefully and with mutual suspicion at the beginning, but, with God's help, eventually with a growing sense of trust and mutual support.

How this comes about is significantly in the hands of the Israelis, not because they are any more right or wrong, but because, for better or worse, Israel wields the greater power and therefore has both the greater ability to and responsibility for breaking the horrific cycle that now exists. I suggested that there are two concerns in Israel's position: the moral and the practical. Frequently the moral response is in conflict with what is in one's self-interest. I won't address which takes precedence, since I believe that this is not a situation where the two contradict one another. Evacuating the settlements, ending the Occupation, withdrawing to the 1967 borders, and supporting the rebuilding of Palestinian society and a strong, viable Palestinian state is clearly the moral thing to do—but it is also clearly the ultimate solution to Israel's long-term security. Only in these circumstances can Israel defend itself militarily, reenergize its own economy and redirect energies to internal needs, and, at the same time, renew its sense of what it means to be a *Jewish* state.

Ultimately, like Avraham, Jews in Israel—and the world—are being tested. To prove his commitment to the covenant Avraham is asked to sacrifice not only his beloved son, but the very possibility of God's promise of a future (which for *this* story must be carried out through *Yitzhak*). Today we are being asked to remain true to *our* part of the covenant by doing God's will, acting justly, doing the right thing, even if this appears to endanger the ongoing potential of the promise. If we choose correctly, we may well ensure the survival of the covenant and its special relationship. If we choose incorrectly, we lose everything we are and can be, even if a political entity survives. The choice is ours.

CHAPTER FIVE

Improbable Alliances in Uncertain Times— Christian Zionism and the Israeli Right

Andrea L. Anderson

Introduction: Improbability

> In its fiftieth anniversary year, the State of Israel has no better friends than American evangelicals.
>
> *Timothy Weber*

The year is 1980. Jerry Falwell and Billy Graham receive the Jabotinsky Centennial Medal, a top Zionist honor from the Israeli government, in addition to a "gift" jet from Begin, the Israeli Prime Minister at the time. The year is 1982. As Israel invades Lebanon, Pat Robertson broadcasts continual updates on CBN (Christian Broadcasting Network), interpreting each stage of the attack biblically, according to prophecy. He speaks of Israel's invasion as a "modern Joshua event" and urges viewers to phone (former) President Reagan in support of the attack. The year is 1984. Jerry Falwell and the International Christian Embassy of Jerusalem testify on behalf of AIPAC's interests before the U.S. House of Representatives Foreign Affairs Committee in support of moving the American embassy from Tel Aviv to Jerusalem. The year is 1985. Benjamin Netanyahu speaks to American Evangelicals at the National

Prayer Breakfast of a Likud plan to build an alliance with Christian Zionists that will prove politically advantageous for the former and theologically expeditious for the latter.

Historical anomalies? Two decades and *intifadas* later, Christian Zionists spill over each year, in increasing numbers, into the streets of Jerusalem during Sukkot to demonstrate their support for the State of Israel. Perceived by portions of the Israeli populace as a nuisance, the throngs are nonetheless addressed by the Israeli government, including Jerusalem Mayor Ehud Olmert and Prime Minister Ariel Sharon. Days before this article was finished, thousands of Christian Evangelicals gathered at the annual Christian Coalition convention to hear American and Israeli political figures discuss common priorities. House Majority Whip Tom DeLay joined Knesset member Benny Elon and Jerusalem mayor Ehud Olmert in voicing their opposition to the creation of a Palestinian state. Elon went as far as to openly call for the "relocation" of West Bank Palestinians to Jordan, quoting Numbers 33 as his proof. The crowd's response? Cheers!

Improbable at first blush, the ever-intensifying relationship between Christian Zionists and the Israeli right has fully flourished. Signs of the growing "friendship" between America's evangelical Christian community and the Israeli right are becoming more prevalent in the media, in the political halls, and in the balance sheets of corporations, PAC's, and religious NGO's. Christian Zionism provides the link between the Christian Evangelicals and the Israeli right, providing a shared mythology and ideology, manifest by a common political agenda relating to the overriding goal of the preservation of the state of Israel.

Alliances are not necessarily benevolent, but rather they are made out of mutual self-interest. What are the interests being protected in the alliance between Christian Zionists and the Israeli right? What are the gains for each side? What is the cost of the alliance and to whom?

Defining a Movement: Developing the Myth

> The modern day restoration of the state of Israel is not a political accident, or merely the result of a secular political Zionist plot but rather the fulfillment of God's own word.
>
> *Malcolm Hedding,*
> *International Christian Embassy of Jerusalem*

Christian Zionism is one of the more peculiar religious, political, and social phenomena of the 19th and 20th centuries, involving a complex history and theology. The term "Zionism" was coined by Nathan Birnbaum on April 1, 1890, as "the movement whose goal was the return of the Jewish people to the 'Land of Israel.'" Zionism, although primarily secular and political in its Jewish inception, has always also maintained a religious meaning for both Jews and Christians throughout the centuries. Naturally, Zionism is thought of as a Jewish creation to protect the Jewish people and *Eretz Yisrael* (the "Land of Israel"). Therefore, the term "Christian Zionism" can seem puzzling; can Christians, indeed, be Zionists in these terms? Is there a more appropriate terminology that can be employed to describe Christians who support Israel? Or, indeed, was "Zionism" initially a Christian creation, borne out of a particular Protestant theology, which was only later picked up by Jewish-born secularists like Herzl?

Fisher comments on the innate ambiguity of the term *Christian Zionism*: "Because the term is so confusing, [it] can mean anything from supporting tourism to Israel or general support for the State of Israel to the extremes of Hagee"[1](10). A broad spectrum of Christians easily fall within this wide definition, but the focus of this paper is the approximately 40 million Christian evangelical-fundamentalists in the United States. The International Christian Embassy of Jerusalem (hereafter known as ICEJ), one of the largest Christian Zionist organizations, offers the following distinctions (as well as a view from inside the movement):

Zionism "a movement that sought and achieved the re-establishment of a sovereign Jewish state in the biblical 'Land of Israel' with Jerusalem as its capital"

Zionist "a Jew who is committed to the cause of Zionism either out of religious or political belief"

Christian Zionist "a Christian who believes that the Lord's Covenant tying the Land of Israel to the People of Israel remains in force, and who actively stands on this conviction"

Biblical Zionism "the firm belief that God chose the Jewish people and bequeathed to them as an everlasting possession the Land of Canaan, so that they should give to the world His Word, men of faith, the Messiah and a living example of what it means to follow this one true God and experience His faithfulness and correction."

Christian involvement in Zionism is not so puzzling after all, for a "historical partnership" has been established between certain Christian communities (evangelical fundamentalists) and the Israeli political right. The form of the relationship may appear new, but a strong history of alliance exists that must be uncovered in order to understand the mutual gains in both communities for pursuing the common interest of Zionism.

Reformation, Restoration, and Messianic Expectations: Precursors to Zionism

> For Christian Zionists, then, the restoration of the State of Israel to her ancient soil is evidence that there is hope and redemption for this world. To support Israel (Gen. 12:3), comfort her (Is. 40:1–2) and pray for her peace (Ps. 122:6, Is. 66:6–7) is to work in harmony with God."
>
> *Malcolm Hedding, ICEJ*

The Reformation: Shifting Back

Theodor Herzl has been deemed the father of political Zionism, yet the movement to relocate Jews to Palestine was actually initiated by English Protestant Christians three centuries before Herzl. In fact, for 150 years, Christians were the only advocates of Zionism. Before the Reformation, Western Christians used Augustinian filters to interpret the purpose of Zion and Jerusalem as other-worldly locales, as opposed to earthly realities. This began to change in the 16th and 17th centuries, during which time Christians began to interpret the scriptures for themselves and, "in doing so, they began to elevate the concept of Israel and the Jews as the key factors in Biblical prophecy" (Halsell, 134).

Scholars have debated various interpretations as to the shift in Christian thought after the Reformation with respect to the Jews, "traditionally viewed as enemies of the church" as well as their role in Christian theology. For instance, one theory cites the development of European international law as a mode of developing "tolerance" towards Jews. Other scholars have cited the expanded economic roles of Jews, in addition to the "hebraizing" or "judaizing" renaissance during the Reformation, in which people re-focused on the Hebrew Bible scriptures.[2] The Bible acquired infallibility as Protestants shifted their notions of authority from the Pope to the Word, which was being translated en masse into vernaculars. In other words, people gained access and agency to the stories, histories, traditions, and laws formerly monopolized by religious authorities.

Hence, the history of the Bible became the history of the Middle East. Indeed, "Bible-loving Christians came to regard the Old Testament as the only history that mattered in the Middle East" (Halsell, 135). Hence, the symbolic/mythological came to be equated with the actual reality of the land of Palestine; this merging provided the basis for early Christian Zionism. Finally, it is important to note that various Protestant sects fleeing religious persecution after the Reformation identified with the suffering of the Jews and "modeled their communities on the concept of God's covenant with the Hebrews"("Christian Zionism in the Past," 1).

The Puritans: Colonizing a "New Israel"

The history of the Puritans bespeaks a strong philo-semitism, mixed with a messianic and colonial theology, the combination of which advocates a prototype of Christian Zionism. In the mid-1600's, Oliver Cromwell, Lord Protector of the Puritan Commonwealth, "declared that Jewish presence in Palestine would be the prelude to the Second Coming of Christ"(Halsell, 135). Similarly, Paul Felgenhauever, who wrote *Good News for Israel* in 1655, believed that "the permanent return of Jews to their own country eternally bestowed upon them by God through the unqualified promise to Abraham, Isaac and Jacob [was a sign of the Second Coming of Christ]"(Halsell, 135).

As the Puritans were settling the new lands of America (the "New Israel"), the idea of the Jews being "restored" to Palestine to settle the land for God was both appealing, and something with which they could identify. Messianic expectations helped to maintain a sense of purpose in the harsh living conditions of New England by promising a better future with the Second Coming of Christ, as well as allotting significance to the role of the Puritans as settlers and pioneers (and ipso facto, colonizers).

The 19th Century: Preparing the Movement

The 19th century witnessed the consolidation and organization of the Christian Zionist movement. In 1839, the "Great Reformer, Lord Anthony Ashley Cooper, seventh Earl of Shaftesbury, in "State and

Prospects of the Jews" spoke of the "Hebrew race," urging Jews to return to Palestine as part of the "divine plan" for the Second Coming of Christ. He claimed that Jews, "though admittedly a stiff-necked, dark-hearted people, and sunk in moral degradation, obduracy and ignorance of the Gospel" were "vital to a Christian's hope of salvation" (Halsell, 137). The Lord of Shaftesbury[3] convinced his step-father, Lord Palmerston, who was Britain's Foreign Secretary, to open a British consulate in Jerusalem. William Young, a "devout evangelical," was appointed to the post of first British Vice Consul in 1839. His purpose, as well as that of the Consulate, was to "protect all the Jews residing in Palestine," who at the time included 9,690 Jews who were living under Ottoman rule. "The British action not only was an interference in the internal affairs of a foreign country, it also set a major cornerstone of Zionism: it affirmed the national unity of all Jewish people"(Halsell, 136–7). Another key Christian figure in the genesis of Zionism was William H. Hechler (1845–1931), Chaplain of the British Embassy in Vienna. He worked closely with Herzl and introduced him to the Grand Duke of Baden, the uncle of Kaiser Wilhelm II, popularizing further the early ideas of Zionism.

At this point, the term Christian Restorationism came into popular usage and application, based on the call to "restore" Jews to the "Land of Israel" and then to the "Lord of Israel." The concept of land, in addition to the reality of the land of Palestine, became imperative to the theology of Christian Restorationists, where it had played only a peripheral role previously. John Darby's (1800–82) development of dispensationalism was key in placing the "Land of Israel" back at the center of Christian theology through his conviction that "Israel would replace the Church, which was a mere parenthesis to God's continuing covenantal relationship with Israel"(Prior, 138). Dispensationalist interpretations reintroduced Jews and the Old Testament back into the larger schema of salvation, linking the destiny of the Christians with that of the Jews, as well as the New Testament being reconnected to the Old Testament. Indeed, the biblical "Land of Israel" acquired such importance that Thomas Hummel describes the Restorationists' experience of the emotional power of the "Holy Land" as "the fifth gospel"(Bartholomew, 185).

The "true founder of Zionism"[4] came out of this same time period, not Theodor Herzl, but rather William E. Blackstone. Blackstone (1841–1935) had no formal theological education but was an assiduous student of the Bible. He wrote the bestseller, *Jesus is Coming* (1878), which sold over a million copies, an astounding number at the turn of the century. Blackstone is also renown for the "Memorial" (i.e. "petition") he sent to President Benjamin Harrison and Secretary of State James G. Blanton in 1891. In this memorial entitled, "Palestine for the Jews," Blackstone advocates for the establishment of a Jewish homeland in Palestine, endorsed by 413 dignitaries. A portion of the memorial reads:

> We believe this is an appropriate time for all nations, and especially the Christian nations of Europe, to show kindness to Israel. Millions of exiles, by their terrible sufferings, are piteously appealing to our sympathy, justice, and humanity. Let us now restore to them the land of which they were so cruelly despoiled by our Roman ancestors.

The early history of Christian Zionism is long and complex but infrequently discussed. As Cox reminds us: "Maybe the authors [of most standard histories of Zionism] would prefer to forget about this peculiar part of the story."

Unholy Alliance: A Functional Symbiosis

> The Israeli-U.S. fundamentalist alliance is not a confluence of theological doctrine or spiritual beliefs. Rather it is a working partnership founded on factors that are more political and military than theological"
>
> *(Halsell, 197)*

Fast-forwarding nearly a century from the time of Blackstone, we find ourselves in what Ralph Reed, former Executive Director of the Christian Coalition, deemed the era of "Evangelical-Jewish alliance" (Solomon, 27) with the common purpose of preserving the State of Israel. "Both Israeli right and Christian right leaders are nationalistic, militaristic, each with a dogma that demands the highest priority in their lives—a dogma centered around Israel and a cult of land" (Halsell, 159).

However disparate the reasoning of these groups, the alliance has proved politically efficient for both sides thus far. The relationship was conceived during the 1970's and reached a peak in the 1980's under the Reagan presidency, only to ascend to a different peak in the 1990's after the election of Benjamin Netanyahu.

An example of this alliance in its early phase includes the contentious UN Resolution 3379 (1975), in which the UN declared Zionism to be a form of racism. After the 1967 war, Israel took the

West Bank, the Gaza Strip, the Golan Heights, the Sinai Peninsula, and Southern Lebanon by force. Although certain areas were bartered back to the originating Arab states, Israel continued to occupy Palestinian lands (and does so to this day). Most mainstream churches opposed Israel's occupation of the West Bank and Gaza Strip, and voted with the United Nations to equate Zionism with racism. Only the Evangelicals supported Israel's occupation. As mainstream Protestant support for Israel eroded after the 1967 war, "Israel played its fundamentalist card"(Weber, 9).

Largely due to the election of Jimmy Carter in 1976, the seventies were declared the "decade of the Evangelical." The Likud party was elected in Israel in 1977 after decades of Labor party rule; both the Israeli Right and American evangelicals anticipated the beginning of a new era of unconditional support for Israel (a new era of Zionism).

American evangelicals were horrified when Carter spoke up for Palestinians and took dramatic measures to mobilize their populations both for Israel and against Carter.[5] A Likud plan was published a year later outlining a strategy to encourage Christian fundamentalists to support the State of Israel.

When Netanyahu was the Israeli UN ambassador in 1985, he spoke at the National Prayer Breakfast for Israel: "There was an ancient yearning in our common tradition for the return of the Jews to the 'Land of Israel.' And this dream, smoldering throughout two millennia, finally burst forth in Christian Zionism"(Halsell, 138). In his speech, Netanyahu used the sentimental rhetoric of a common dream, a shared pseudo-spiritual vision of the "restoration" of the Jews to the "Land of Israel." Although Evangelicals and the Israeli right lack a common vision, they share a common end, and that end is the "Land of Israel".

The centerpiece of Christian Restorationist theology is its eschatological expectations, meaning that Jews must return to the "Land of Israel" in order to initiate the process of the Second Coming of Christ. As we will see in the latter section on the theology of Armageddon, the "restoration" of the Jews is a necessary prerequisite to the divine drama of the End Times. The evangelical groups that support Israel hence view the alliance as a sort of divine investment. Not only will they be able to participate in the messianic process, but they will also have ringside seats at the battle of Armageddon. Of course, it is imperative to note that, according to this theology, two-thirds of the world's Jewish population is prophesied to be killed in this great battle, including the same people with whom the Evangelicals are making this alliance.

The Israeli government clearly has a different use for the Evangelicals. The Israeli Right, in particular, benefits from this alliance in the tangible form of political, financial, and institutional support. The Israeli government simply turns a blind eye to the eschatology of the Evangelicals and their often anti-Semitic theologies, in order to gain the support necessary to maintain their unconditional approval status with the United States. As Boyer states, "Privately ridiculing premillennialist readings of prophecy... [Israelis] recognized an important political bloc and dealt with it accordingly"(quoted in Weber, 9).

Therefore, the Jews are ignoring the eschatological theology of the Evangelicals, and the Evangelicals are ignoring everything else about the Israelis, i.e, the Palestinian situation; the fact that most Israelis are Jews; and the political, economic, and social realities of Israel. It is as if both members of the alliance are living in two completely different worlds—the Evangelicals in the spiritual world of the End Times, and the Israeli Right in the physical reality of the nation-state of Israel.

However different they may be, the two sides have their points of convergence. One clear area of convergence for both the Israeli Right and the Evangelicals is their shared sense of militarism. Included in this hawkishness is the support of arms sales to Israel, a support of Israeli military maneuvers in neighboring Arab states and in the Occupied Territories, in addition to a mutual "fear of the peace process"(Goldberg, 41). Both groups also share an investment in the mythology of "The Land" and in the ideology of Zionism. As for theology, the differences between the two could not be more vast. Yet, the consistent trump card is Israel—the "Land of Israel"—which both sides believe to be vital to their survival.

The Mythology of the Land: Symbolism, Redemption, and Preparation

> In the Land of Israel the Jewish people came into being. In this land was shaped their spiritual, religious, and national character. Here they created a culture of national and universal import and gave the world the eternal Book of Books.
>
> —David Ben-Gurion,
> *May 14, 1948, upon the declaration of Israel*
> *as an independent nation-state*

This "restoration" of the Jews to the land is the starting point for many Christian Zionists, who believe Jews to have, for all intents and purposes, an "unconditional divine land grant"(Halsell, 72). In the words of Ben-Gurion himself, the basis of Zionism is "the self-evident right of the Jewish people to be a nation, as all other nations, in their own sovereign state." That land was the land of Palestine, of which Jews only constituted 6.4% of the population at the time. The other 93.6.% of the population was comprised of the indigenous Palestinians, now the largest refugee population in the world.

Therefore, the spiritualized concept of the "Land of Israel" plays a powerful role in the alliance of Evangelicals and the Israeli right. For both the Evangelicals and the Israeli right, the "Land of Israel" holds symbolic import (which often supercedes the reality of the state of Israel), redemptive import, and definitive religious and spiritual import as the future site of the Third Temple.

Gershom Gorenberg, expert on the Temple Mount in Jerusalem, aptly states: "In the Middle East, the symbolic is what is most real" (Goldberg, 40). Centuries of history of religious expansion, imperial conquest, epic legends, wars, and conflict inhabit the landscape of Israel/Palestine. Distinctions between past, present, and future are eternally blurred, with competing mythologies of origin, possession, and relationship to "The Land." For Evangelicals, the "Land of Israel" exists on a metaphysical plane, transmitted directly from the dusty Sunday School Bibles of their childhoods to the future site of Armageddon. In the meantime, the earthly Israel/Palestine exists in political turmoil, but it is not the Israel of the Christian Zionists. Fishman comments that the term "Land of Israel" "was applied symbolically, but not practically. It was a metaphysical and metaphorical term connoting a distant past or a vague theological future, not a viable present. It had little to do with the national strivings of the contemporary Jewish people"(18). Furthermore, and perhaps more importantly, the term has even less to do with the reality of the Palestinians, including years of human rights abuses, deportations, home demolitions, torture, murder, and humiliation.

With the belief that the modern nation-state of Israel is actually the biblical "Land of Israel," Zionism, particularly Christian Zionism becomes a "moral absolute" (Halsell, 155). Protection of the Israelites and the land "promised" to them becomes a moral imperative as Christian Zionists attempt to prepare for the Second Coming of Christ.

However, it is important to note that notions of the "Land of Israel" (or, indeed, any land) were not originally central to Christian understandings of theology. As opposed to the heavy emphasis on "Land" in the Old Testament, the New Testament scarcely mentions land as related to worship or the teachings of Jesus. Rather, Prior reminds us that much of the theological emphasis in the New Testament involves a "critique of a theology of land, and a universalization of the concept, so that the Good News of Jesus Christ can be brought to the ends of the earth"(54). A trademark of early Christianity involves the universalizing of the physical Temple and of the earthly Jerusalem to a worship unattached to specific lands and a spiritual Jerusalem accessible to all. Hence, worship was universalized for the early Christians. Therefore, why has Christian Zionism reintroduced the centrality of "The Land" into its theology? What role does it play?

Redeeming the Land

> See, I place the land at your disposal. Go, enter the land that the Lord swore to your fathers, Abraham, Isaac, and Jacob, to assign to them and to their offspring after them.
>
> *(Deuteronomy 1:8)*

According to both the Israeli right and Christian Zionists, the "Land of Israel," in its mythological and political reality, is a prerequisite for redemption. Indeed, the redemption of "The Land" is necessary for the redemption of the people. For both Evangelicals and certain religious Jews, we are living in the "Age of Redemption," the preface to the first or second coming of the Messiah, depending upon one's religious leanings.

The "promise" of restoration to the "Land of Israel" is cited by both Christian and Jewish Zionists as backed by numerous scriptures, among them: Amos 9:13–15, Hosea 3:4–5, Jer. 3: 8–25, 30:8–24, 23:5–8, Is. 49:14–26, 54:1–17, 62:1–7, 65:16–25, 66:7–24, Zech. 2: 10 12, Luke 21:23–24, and Acts 1:6.

However, three additional scriptures are worth mentioning in more detail, beginning with Lev. 25:23–24, in which it is stated: "The land must not be sold beyond reclaim, for the land is mine; with me you are but aliens and tenants. Throughout the land that you hold, you must provide for the redemption of the land." Therefore, the Jews are in stewardship of "The Land," charged with "providing redemption," ie, fulfilling the covenant. There is no ownership denoted other than the eternal and divine possession of the Almighty him/herself. Therefore, what does it mean to fulfill the covenant? Is the land a means to fulfilling the covenant or is the covenant a means to gaining access to the land?

The scripture of Deut. 4:25–26 may offer some answers:

> When you have had children and children's children, and become complacent in the land, if you act corruptly by making an idol in the form of anything, thus doing what is evil in the sight of the Lord your God, and provoking him to anger, I call heaven and earth to witness against you today that you will soon utterly perish from the land that you are crossing the Jordan to occupy; you will not live long on it, but will be utterly destroyed.

Halsell believes that the Christian and Jewish Zionists actually reverse this Deuteronomic order in their theology, by elevating the concept of the land over that of the covenantal relationship. "Thus does the land issue become one of idolatry. The fervor over attaining and expanding the land eclipses any relationship to Yahweh, the Torah, and humane treatment of the sojourner"(64). Assuming one literalizes the "promise" of "The Land" to the Jews, one must also literalize the Law; according to the same scriptures, Israel cannot inhabit the land and oppress the poor at the same time. "Oppressing the poor" is the least of the worries of the Palestinian populations suffering from innumerable forms of Israeli oppression, dispossession, and systemic discrimination.

The last scripture to be mentioned in relation to the mythology of "The Land" in Zionism is Ezek. 37:12–28:

> I will bring you back to the "Land of Israel." I will take the people of Israel from the nations among which they have gone, and will gather them from every quarter, and bring them to their own land. Then they shall be my people, and I will be their God. My servant David shall be king over them. I will make a covenant of peace with them. My dwelling place shall be with them. Then the nations shall know that I Yahweh sanctify Israel, when my sanctuary is among them forevermore.

Ezek. 37 is most often cited as the justification for the necessity of the "ingathering" of the Jews to Israel, as manifest in the modern day nation-state. This ingathering will precede the messianic age for both Jews and Christians, although the "End Times" may look rather different according to which side of the alliance one is on. The restoration of the Jews will bring redemption upon the land, which will, in turn, bring redemption upon the Jews, and ipso facto, the Christians. "For the Zionist, the land had no history of its own, no culture of its own, no people living in its domain other than the history, culture, and people inscribed in its theological myth—the land itself was considered to be in exile"(Raz, 14).

The Third Temple: Solidarity in Terrorism

If they build it, He will come.

(Goldberg, 41)

Finally, both Christian and Jewish Zionists share a belief in the religious/spiritual import of the "Land of Israel" with specific regard to the city of Jerusalem and the Temple Mount. Jewish sovereignty over Jerusalem[6] and the rebuilding of the Temple are two prime messianic prerequisites for the fulfillment of biblical prophecy, shared by both Jewish and Christian Zionists. The building of the Third Temple (Ezekiel's Temple) is a prime project of the Christian Zionists who are eager to accelerate the coming of the messianic age, and are either unaware or unaffected by the dramatic consequences such an attempt would incur.[7]

Therefore, we find Zionism to fit the category of shared mythology, "a story invented as a veiled explanation of truth," "existing only in the imagination," yet "ostensibly related to history," and "given uncritical acceptance." The danger enters when the mythology is perceived of and interpreted as theology; biblical understandings of the "Land of Israel" are superimposed on the reality of the modern nation-state of Israel and the Occupied Palestinian Territories. Hence, the myth becomes a reality, and that reality is the subject of the next section-colonialism.

Ideology of Colonialism

Zionism appeals to an historical link between the settler population and the land to be settled: all Jews have an historical right to the land, in virtue of unbroken habitation there by Israelites/Jews.

(Prior, 189)

The ideologies of colonialism and Zionism are inextricably linked with one another, as Zionism is inextricably tied to the "Land of

Israel." Prior writes that in various forms of colonization, we find the theme of the "mythology of conquest." He comments that "The stereotypical myth of colonialism postulates that the land was in a *virgin state*, or that habitation was irregular; the people (to be) conquered were of an *inferior status*; and that the enterprise was one of *civilizing* (or even *evangelizing*) the natives" (emphases mine)(189).

Manifest Whose Destiny?

The theme of conquest and the land figure prominently in the connection of Christian and Jewish Zionists with regards to the notion of manifest destiny, a vestige of 19th century imperialist expansionism. In fact, Fishman speaks of the relation of the Puritan settlement of colonial America to the ideology of Zionism. He describes the "New Jerusalem" established by the Puritans as "the territorial symbol of religious faith and exemplary virtue"(16). The participation of the Puritans in the creation of the national manifest destiny of America through the settling of the land is congruous to the perceived "manifest destiny" of Zionism, Israel, and the Jewish people in relation to:

- The redemptive quality of the land,
- The conquest of the "unreligious" natives
  (ie, wrongly religious, ie, not Christian or Jewish), and
- The transformation of the landscape from the barren wilderness to productive, fruitful lands "flowing with milk and honey."

A complex psychology of conquest, pioneering, and frontierism, undergirded by a divine order, has imbued colonialism with "divine permission" to carry out its activities, attempting to legitimate, and even glorify, the conquering, conversion, and consequent destruction of indigenous populations. Prior speaks of the different hermeneutics utilized by the colonizers and the colonized, in that the "victims of colonialist plunder" do not benefit from the ethnocentric God presented from Genesis to 2 Kings (not to mention the innumerable subsequent interpretations with varying political agendas). Therefore, he asks the basic epistemological questions:

> Do texts that we recognize to belong to the genre of folkloric epic or legend, rather than of history, legitimize the 'Israelite' possession of the land and subsequent colonialist enterprises, when their original legitimacy depended on the presumption

> that the biblical narrative was factual history? Does a judgment which was based on the premise that the genre of the justifying text was history not dissolve when it is realized that the text belongs to the genre of 'myths of origin,' which are deployed in virtually every society in the service of particular ideologies? (182).

Christian Zionists believe that the Bible gives them a proprietary interest, and indeed, investment in the colonized "Land of Israel." It is the "Holy Land" as much as it is the land of the Jews. Because "they think the Promised Land belongs to them as much as it does to Israelis"(Weber, 2), the establishment of Israel can be viewed as one of the largest "joint ventures" of the century.

Armageddon Approaching: Theology Meets Prophecy

> We have entered the final days of history. There is a terrible, bloody battle about to be waged, far worse than anything we witnessed in World War II. The Bible predicts this war will be fought at Armageddon and will involve the nation Israel against forces from the north, probably Russia. There has never been a war as terrible as the one we are about to witness. Nation will fight nation, and brother will battle brother.
>
> *anonymous Evangelical Revivalist,*
> *quoted by Wagner*

Thus far we have witnessed the convergence of Christian and Jewish Zionists on the issues of the mythology of "The Land" and the ideology of colonialism. However, theology is the fork in the road, which destabilizes the Evangelical-Israeli right alliance. Both Christians and Jews ascribe to a common basic belief in messianism and assert that the establishment of the modern nation-state of Israel is a vital part of the messianic process. However, that is also where the similarity ends between Christian and Jewish theologies of the "End Times."

Goldberg speaks of the "theologically improbable alliance [of Jewish Settlers] with evangelical Christians"[8](41); however, I would deem it a "theologically impossible alliance." The convergence factors that gel the Christian-Jewish Zionist alliance are political, social, historical (mytho-historical) and economic. Christian Zionists rely heavily on apocalyptic literature and apocalyptic interpretations of scripture, based on dispensationalist theology, which denotes that we are living in the last dispensation, in the last days.

The present era is believed to be the "time of the Gentiles," during which "dramatic events" will unfold and climax in the return of Jesus. According to the futurist premillennial scenario, the establishment of Israel in 1948 catalyzed this apocalyptic process. Christian Zionists claim that the numerous prophecies of the Old Testament are being fulfilled, attested to by the various Israeli military victories. "Israel would gradually attain international acclaim and become God's chosen instrument to fight the Antichrist"(Halsell, 24).

Again, the biblical "Land of Israel" is superimposed on the modern nation-state of Israel, not exactly an accurate fit. However, Christian Zionists use the lens of prophecy to interpret modern political events. For example, the "Antichrist" is no longer necessarily a fire-spitting fallen angel, but rather an enfleshed player on the political map, i.e. Hitler, the USSR, or perhaps even the Pope, all suggested by Christian Zionists as potential candidates. The "ten-member confederation" which is predicted to invade and destroy Israel is interpreted as the European Union in the Armageddon scenario, and the comprehensive destruction of the earth and all within it is interpreted as a nuclear holocaust.[9]

Before the battle of Armageddon, Zech. 13:8–9 prophesies that two-thirds of the Jews living in Israel will be killed. This prophecy is also known as "purging the Jews, to get them to see the light and recognize Christ as their savior"(Halsell, 26). Here is where the alliance gets messy.

Anti-Semitism: Apologetics and Proselytism

…Dispensationalists do not look at Jews as normal people.

Gershom Gorenberg

Indeed, the long history of anti-Semitism in strands of Christian theology is the fundamental barb between Christian and Jewish Zionists, rendering it impossible for a theological alliance to be sustained between them. Anti-Semitism has been a reality of various interpretations of Christian theologies throughout the centuries, as embodied in the image of Jews as Christ-killers, well-poisoners, and child-eaters during Passover. The results have been tragic: pogroms, massacres, forced conversions, and the Shoah.

However, here is the point at which we begin the rather ugly process of investigating the manipulation at the core of the Christian Zionist-Israeli right alliance. Certainly, the manipulation cuts both ways; everyone "wins" on some level. Everyone, that is, except the

Palestinians. As with all alliances, each side is expecting a benefit. What is the benefit of the Jews to the Christian Zionists? In more realistic terms, what purpose do the Jews serve for the Christian Zionists? Simply put, the "ingathering" of the Jews, as mentioned previously, is a necessary advent to the "Second Coming of Christ."

The question of conversion of the Jews, however, is more ambiguous. Their conversion is listed biblically as a necessary part of the preparation for the End Times, not to mention the fact that conversion put the "evangelize" into evangelical Christianity. Fishman states that the Jews are related to Christian millenarian expectations in only one way: "the conversion [of Jews] to Christianity would accelerate the messianic advent"(17). The Israeli government does not take kindly to proselytizers, as demonstrated in the 1977 Knesset law that declared it "illegal for anyone to proselytize or convert Jews from their Jewish beliefs"(Halsell, 103). Since that time, the Israeli government has pursued a strict policy of deportation of proselytizers and converts, as exemplified in the 1993 governmental vote to "expel certain Messianic Jews from Israel."[10] Through the process of proselytizing and conversion, Jewish nationalism, the destiny of the Jewish people, and the political future of all peoples in the Middle East become absorbed by the agenda of Christian eschatology.

The question has been asked as to how much of the Christian Zionist impetus of the Reformation Protestants was actually a guise for the greater motive of creating a Europe free of all Jews. In other words, the seemingly philo-Semitic act of working to help establish a Jewish state was, in fact, the ultimate act of ghettoizing the Jews. Bruzonsky corroborates this viewpoint of Christian Zionism as an advanced expression of anti-Semitism: "Zionism would never have been started without Christians wanting to put Jews in a ghetto called a Jewish state, exclusively for Jews. The tragedy is that after resisting the idea for about 200 years the Jews went along with it" (quoted in Halsell, 141).

Finally, anti-Semitism has also played a dominant role in Christian Zionism with respect to Christian apologetics. The extensive history of the persecution of the Jews is cited by Christian Zionists to historically justify their theological agenda of "restoring" the Jews to Israel. Additionally, despite the fact that numerous countries turned away large populations of Jews during the 1930's and 1940's, Christian Zionists cite the establishment of Israel as a necessity to "protect" the world Jewish population (protect them until two-thirds will be massacred at the battle of Armageddon?) from another Shoah:

Eighty-eight years later [after the First Zionist Congress], in Basle, facing a large portrait of Herzl, I listened to Christian and Israeli Jewish speakers repeat as a litany Herzl's credo: all the world hates Jews. All through history people have hated Jews. There's only one solution: the Jews have to live exclusively among Jews and be militarily strong."

(Halsell, 132)

What Does Israel Gain?

Your sympathy, solidarity, and belief in the future of Israel, this to us is tremendous. Your presence here will always remain a golden page in the book of heaven. May the Lord bless your hour of Zion.

Chief Rabbi Shlomo Goren, to the ICEJ

After the grim look into Armageddon theology, one may rightly ask what it is that the Israeli right gains from its alliance with Christian Zionists. No party persists in an alliance without some self-interest. The three prime benefits for the Israelis include: money, in the form of aid; more land; and unconditional institutional support from various Christian groups. The question remains as to whether these three elements will be enough to sustain the alliance.

Funding Redemption

Write out your check and do it now. Write it for 'Jerusalem, D.C.' If you think you can give only $25, make it $50. And if you think you can give only $50, make it $100. And If you can give only $100, make it $1000!

Mike Evans of Mike Evans Ministries

Christian Zionists figure prominently in assuring that Israel receives monetary aid, both officially and unofficially. Israel has long since been the recipient of the largest package of foreign aid available from the United States. The annual aid to Israel averages upwards of $6 billion, not including loan guarantees, annual compound interest, or tax-exempt donations. Malthaner estimates that in a given year, the total aid package to Israel is some $10 billion, meaning that the "U.S. government has given more federal aid to the average Israeli citizen in a given year than it has give to the average American citizen."

Christian Zionists play a role in assuring this unconditional aid package through PAC's such as CIPAC (Christian-Israeli Public

Affairs Committee), the sister organization of the influential AIPAC (American-Israeli Pubic Affairs Committee). CIPAC supported $10 billion in loan guarantees to Israel, among other forms of uncond-itional political support.

Christian Zionists also raise a tremendous amount of money unofficially through churches, Christian organizations, and tele-vangelism.[11] However, it is difficult to trace the comprehensive amount of unofficial funding. The National Unity Coalition for Israel also became the lobbying arm for the Christian Zionists.

According to Halsell, Zionism requires this two-pronged strategy of official and unofficial support in order to survive; both the United States government and the Christian Zionists are essential to the Israeli right. "The nature of Zionism has always been to seek a protector, a provider. Now the Zionists look to and depend entirely on the United States. And they have formed this alliance with the New Christian Right, which endorses any military or criminal action Israel takes"(162).

The Jerusalem Friendship Fund is an example of substantial "unofficial assistance" to Israel. Established by Rabbi Yehiel Eckstein of Chicago in 1983, the Jerusalem Friendship Fund distributes funds contributed by Christian Evangelicals to help Jews immigrate to Israel and support Jewish communities in Diaspora. The Fund has contributed a total of $65 million since its inception—so much that Jerusalem mayor Ehud Olmert appointed Eckstein the "special advisor for fundraising in the non-Jewish world"(Sheleg).

There is also collaboration on the financial and political levels of Jewish and Christian organizations that advocate the taking of the Temple Mount by any means necessary. Gershon Salomon, leader of the Temple Mount Faithful, regularly receives money from numerous Christian Zionist organizations. The goal of the Temple Mount Faithful is to reestablish Jewish prayer and presence on the Haram al-Sharif, followed by the eventual construction of the Third Temple (which, of course, presumes the destruction of the Dome of the Rock and the Al-Aqsa Mosque). The Temple Mount Faithful is responsible for provoking riots that left 17 Palestinians dead. Could it be that an alliance is also being formed between Jewish and Christian Zionists organizations for the purpose of terrorism? Could it be that Christian Zionists are being enlisted to do the dirty work of Jewish terrorists? "The mountain is within reach...God is waiting for us to move the mosques and rebuild. The Jews may not be ready, but the Christians are"(Goldberg, 43).

Adopt-a-Settlement

In addition to financial aid of various stripes, Israel also receives full Christian Zionist support in colonizing more Palestinian land.[12] As discussed previously, the concept of the "Land of Israel" is imperative to Christian Zionism, and hence, numerous modes of support are offered to assure that Israel can confiscate and maintain as much land as possible. Americans for a Safe Israel is an exemplar group with a neo-conservative agenda, which proclaims that "Israel has exclusive right to Palestine and Jerusalem." Certain Christian Zionist groups have taken a political stance on the subject of Israeli settlements,[13] illegal constructions on Palestinian lands in the Occupied Territories. One such group is the Christian Friends of Israeli Communities, which operates an "adopt-a-settlement program." This program has linked more than 40 churches in the United States to particular settlements in the West Bank, the goal being to garner enough Christian support to prevent the United States government from pressuring Israel to withdraw from the West Bank (Gradstein). "Churches, prayer groups and individuals commit themselves to an ongoing relationship with a community with the purpose of offering comfort and practical support" (www.virtualholyland.com).

"Comforting" the Victor?

> I saw all the oppressions that are practiced under the sun.
> Look, the tears of the oppressed—with no one to comfort
> them!
>
> *Ecclesiastes 4:1*

Christian Zionists profess that their role with regards to Israel is one of support and comfort. Beyond the semantic connotations, this "support" translates into unconditional, uncritical approval and advocacy for all actions taken by the Israeli government. One of the most prominent Christian Zionist organizations, the International Christian Embassy of Jerusalem believes that Christians have a "biblically mandated responsibility" to "comfort and support the modern Jewish state"(Halsell, 102). This "support" may take the form of monetary aid, political advocacy, and institutional support, but the motive is explicitly a "religious" one. The ICEJ proclaims "the role of the true Christian becomes one of perpetual support for the modern State of Israel, which the Christian Zionist sees as a criterion of faithfulness to God"(102).

The list of Christian organizations that support Israel is a long one. However, it is helpful to mention a few of these organizations by name:

International Christian Embassy of Jerusalem (ICEJ)
Christians' Israel Public Action Campaign (CIPAC)
Friends of Jerusalem
Bridges of Peace
American Messianic Fellowship
The Messianic Jewish Alliance of America
Jews for Jesus
Churches Mission Among the Jews
The Christian Friends of Israel
Evangelical Sisterhood of Mary

The ICEJ provides the best case study of the organizations for understanding the Christian Zionist support given to Israel. The ICEJ has been defined as "a Christian fundamentalist organization that supports Israel uncritically" and as a "parachurch agency"(Halsell, 50). ICEJ's budget of roughly $1 million annually allows for extensive economic, educational, and prayer programming in addition to political lobbying.

For example, the ICEJ raised several millions of dollars in 1990–1992 to fly more than 35 planeloads of Soviet Jews to Israel, and then assisted in their settlement. Another massive event staged by the ICEJ involves the Jewish holiday of *Sukkot*, the Feast of Tabernacles. Every *Sukkot*, the Jews of Jerusalem organize a parade and festival, "The March of Jerusalem." For the past twenty years, the Christians have marched with the Jews in the streets of Jerusalem, proclaiming Jewish sovereignty over the city, participating in one of the most nationalistic events of the year. The Christian Zionist attendance at the *Sukkot* "March of Jerusalem" of 1999 peaked at the astounding number of 5,000 Christians, constituting the "single largest foreign religious gathering in Jerusalem." Ehud Olmert, current Mayor of Jerusalem, called these Christian Zionists "the most wonderful guests that this city has"(Orme).

Lastly, the ICEJ has held four international Christian Zionist Congresses over the past twenty-five years: the first in Basle, Switzerland in 1985, the rest in Jerusalem, from 1998–2001. The first congress in September of 1985 was attended by 589 people from 27 countries, growing to 5,000 delegates from 40 countries by the third congress. In this first meeting, the congress passed a resolution calling on all Jews to leave the countries in which they are currently residing and move to Israel because of the "terrible suffering" the Jews have suffered, in addition to the "grave danger which they still face." In tandem with this resolution calling on Jews to immigrate, the ICEJ called on "all nations" to:

- "recognize Judea and Samaria as belonging to Israel" (Resolution 4);
- legitimate Begin's illegal annexation of East Jerusalem;
- move their embassies from Tel Aviv to Jerusalem ("Declaration of the First International Christian Congress");
- "desist from arming Israel's foes."

Finally, the congress called on Israel itself to annex the West Bank and East Jerusalem. Here is another point of divergence in the relationship between Christian Zionists and the Israeli right; the alliance, as we have seen, is not always a harmonious one. Despite the fact that the Christian Zionists and the Israeli right share the common agenda of Jewish sovereignty over the "Land of Israel," their methodologies of achieving this often diverge. Van der Hoeven, spokesperson of the ICEJ, proclaims, "We don't care what the Israelis vote! We care what God says! And God gave that land to the Jews!" (Halsell, 133). Regardless of the pro-Zionism implicit in this statement, the most important element is contained in the first part; Christian Zionist interpretation of "what God says" will always override the political reality of Israeli policy.

The Evangelical Gain: A Divine Role to Play

Harvey Cox outlines the "appeal" of Christian Restorationism to these Christians at the turn of the 21st century. His distinctions are useful for assessing the reasons underlying the modern version of this "improbable alliance."

- Christian Restorationism/Zionism assures Christians that God did, "after all, have a purpose for what appeared to be the meaningless onrush of history," acutely felt at the turn of the century. Similarly, the chaos of living in post-modern, post-industrial, "post-meaning" societies is assuaged by the prophecy of impending apocalypse in Christian Zionist theology of Armageddon.
- Christian Restorationism/Zionism gives gentiles "a real role in the fulfillment of the divine purpose for them." Despite the fact that they are not the "chosen ones," Christian Zionists are able to participate in the manifest destiny of the "End Times" through

their participation in the earthly affairs of the nation-state of Israel. They vicariously help to orchestrate their own destiny through shaping that of the Jews.

- Christian Restorationism/Zionism imbues individual and collective life with a unique sense of urgency, a rare commodity in a commodified society. Cox articulates this sense of urgency beautifully in his statement:

> Everyone likes to think he or she lives in a particularly critical and unique period, and this theology assured them that they did. Indeed, not for twenty-one centuries had anyone had an equal opportunity to help the hand of the Almighty to fulfill eternal promises. Furthermore, Christians in small town America who had never met a Jew and knew Jews only from the Bible, now had a chance to step into the pages of that big black-covered book and become a part of the greatest story ever told. It was an offer many found hard to refuse.

Not only do the Christian Zionists benefit "spiritually"[14] from their alliance with the Jews by assisting in ushering in the messianic age, they also benefit materially. Pro-Zionist Jewish lobbies use their money to endorse or destroy candidates, depending upon their stance towards Israel.

At this point it is important to point out that not only are the two members of the improbable alliance (Christian Zionists and the Israeli right) using one another for their own purposes, but there is a great deal of internal manipulation as well. The political motivations of certain leaders of the Christian Zionist/Evangelical movement, such as Falwell, feed off the religiosity of their followers—the 40 million-strong evangelical population in the United States. Large communities in the Christian Zionism camp spring from rural, poor communities, often from the southern and mid-western regions. Halsell explains that "Having no radio, television or public cultural events, we depended to a great extent on revivalists...to bring us knowledge and understanding"(1), including interpretation of the scriptures and locating oneself (and purpose) in the wider schema of divine history. Televangelists in particular feed off the money and hopes of these evangelical Christians who are seeking meaning in their often dire circumstances. The barter of money for hope is not a fair trade. However, just as alliances are not innately benevolent, neither are they innately just.

Palestine: Doubly Dispossessed

> Does God know the grief of these Palestinian people in their suffering? Does it matter whether they are Christians or Muslims? What do Christians have to offer in these situations?
>
> *Grace Halsell*

We have witnessed who the "winners" are in the Christian Zionist-Israeli right alliance and analyzed the reasons why they benefit from one another. We must also ask the question, who loses because of this alliance? The answer clearly is the indigenous Palestinian population, both Christians and Muslims. The Palestinians do not figure into the future of the "Land of Israel" for either the Christian Zionists or for the Israeli right; they simply do not exist at all, as far as the alliance is concerned. Beginning with the Restorationists at the turn of the 20th century, few "seemed aware of an indigenous population in Palestine to say nothing of an ancient Arab Christian community who already thought of it [Palestine] as their homeland"(Cox). Also mirrored in Lord Shaftesbury's slogan "a country without a nation for a nation without a country," the phrase and ideology that godfathered political Zionism, we find the Palestinian population nowhere in the "manifest destiny" of "The Land."

To be sure, the indigenous Arab Christian population has experienced great confusion and ambivalence with regards to the Christian Zionists, whom they find on the other side of the political fence, a barbed one at that. Palestinian Christians have consistently distanced themselves from groups such as the ICEJ, rejecting them as a "Western intrusion" as well as a sort of theological anomaly(104). There has traditionally been very little contact between Christian Zionists who tour the "Holy Land" as pilgrims and the native Palestinian population.[15] In fact, tours such as Falwell's "Holy Land Tours" deliberately prevent this contact.

Falwell maintains that Christian Zionist participation in supporting Israel is an apolitical act; therefore, one should not get embroiled in the politics of the conflict, but rather focus on "God's will," as revealed in the Bible. In this case, perhaps the 50,000 Palestinian Christians living in the Occupied Territories, in addition to the 106,000 in Israel proper should question the validity of "God's will." Not only are Palestinians absent from the Zionist mythology; they do not even figure into the Christian Zionist theology, leaving the Palestinians dispossessed both physically and spiritually.

The absence in biblical scholarship of concern for 'the natives' reflects the deeply ingrained Eurocentric, colonialist prejudice which characterizes virtually all historiography, as well as that discipline itself. An exegesis that is not sensitive to the dispossessed people is an accomplice by omission in the act of dispossession. Any authentic discussion of the Bible must include a moral critique which respects the discourse of human rights and international law(Prior, 173).

The "Arabs" (as a homogenous population) do, however, fit into Christian Zionist apocalyptic theology, as among the numerous "enemies of Israel" who will invade Israel before the battle of Armageddon.[16] The logic of this perception is that "if Arabs are enemies of Israel, it follows they are enemies of God." This theology results in another type of anti-Semitism, "a contempt for other Semites, the indigenous people of Palestine"(Halsell, 55). A typical expression of this anti-Arab sentiment was expressed in Christian Zionism's hostility to the peace process. The Proclamation of the Fourth International Christian Congress on Biblical Zionism reads:

> To Israel, we speak tenderly that we have borne witness to the tremendous pressures exerted on you to cede portions of your divine inheritance in exchange for unreliable assurances of peace. We attest that your nation has earnestly and sincerely pursued peace with your Arab neighbours, only to be met with terrorism and the sword of Islam…We firmly believe that your cause is just and that Lord God, King of the Universe, will preserve you and ultimately vindicated you before all nations.

Conclusion: The Hidden Prophet

> Could it be that one whom most Americans would dismiss as terrorist was a prophet?
>
> *Grace Halsell*

The improbable alliance of Christian Zionists and the Israeli right is an unstable and temporary one, subject to the whims of changing political administrations. The goal of maintaining Israel at all costs is shared, but is that truly the "end" that both parties are seeking? I believe not—Israel is an "end" in and of itself for the Israeli right, whereas it is a means to an end for the Christian Zionists. Symbiosis has its positive features, but the balance is always a precarious one. Indeed, the balance in the Middle East will continue to be precarious as long as the third party (and recipient of the effects of both sides of this alliance) of the Palestinians are left out of the game. As long as the Christian Zionists and the Israeli right assume that the Palestinians are not players in this divine/political drama, the higher the cost will be for all in the future. While the Christian Zionists and the Israeli right are busy learning new tactics to milk as much as possible out of their alliance, the Palestinians sink further into despair, misery, and invisibility. Instead of looking for prophetic signs in the breakdown of the peace process or in the new political alliances of the post-Cold War era, I would urge both parties to redirect their attention elsewhere for prophecy, beginning in the Palestinian refugee camps. Not only will the future of the Middle East emerge from these dusty alleys, but so will hope, assuming there is any to be found. Jerry Falwell has said that "God has blessed America because we have cooperated with God in protecting that which is precious to Him"(Halsell, 141). So I would ask what is "precious to Him?"

Sources

Cox, Harvey. "The Future Begins in Jerusalem: The Curious Career of Christian Zionism." Lecture of Colloquium on the Study of Religion: Harvard University, Feb. 28, 2000.

Goldberg, Jeffrey. "Jerusalem Endgames: Israel's Y2K Problem." *The New York Times Magazine.* Section 6. Oct. 3, 1999. 41–65.

Gorenberg, Gershom. *The End of Days: Fundamentalism and the Struggle for the Temple Mount.* New York: The Free Press, 2000.

Habib, Rafiq. *Masihiyah wa-al-harb: Qisat al-usuliyah al-sahiyuniya al-amrikiya wa-al-sira'a a'la al-sharq al-islami.* Cairo (Misr): Yafa lil'darasat wa-al-abhath, 1991.

Halsell, Grace. *Prophecy and Politics: Militant Evangelists on the Road to Nuclear War,* Westport: Lawrence Hill & Company, 1986.

Hedding, Malcolm. "Christian Zionism." *Fourth International Christian Congress on Biblical Zionism,* Jerusalem: International Christian Embassy of Jerusalem, February 2001.

Malthaner, Tom. "U.S. Aid to Israel: What Every U.S. Taxpayer Should Know." www.salam.org/palestine/usaidto.html, 1997.

The New Testament: Revised Standard Version, New York: Thomas Nelson & Sons, 1946.

Orme, Jr., William A. "Succoth in Israel, and Here Come the Evangelicals!" *The New York Times*. International Section. Sept. 29, 1999. A4.

Prior, Michael. *Zionism and the State of Israel: A Moral Inquiry*. London: Routledge, 1999.

Raz, Amnon. "Fearing the Religious: National Colonial Theology." *Tikkun*, Vol. 14, No. 3. 11–16.

Sheleg, Yair. "Christian Generosity Becomes a Rabbinical Nightmare." *Ha'aretz Daily*, Oct. 16, 2002.

Solomon, Alisa. "Beyond the Pale." *The Village Voice*, Vol. 40. New York: Dec. 12, 1995. 27.

Tanakh: A New Translation of The Holy Scriptures According to the Traditional Hebrew Text. Philadelphia: The Jewish Publication Society. 1985.

Wagner, Donald E. *Anxious for Armageddon: A Call to Partnership for Middle Eastern and Western Christians*. Scottsdale: Herald Press, 1995.

—. "Evangelicals and Israel: Theological Roots of a Political Alliance." The *Christian Century Vol. 115*, Chicago: Nov. 4, 1998, 1020–1026.

—. "Reagan, Begin, Bibi, and Jerry: The Theopolitical Alliance of the Likud Party with the American Christian 'Right.'" *Arab Studies Quarterly Vol. 20*, Belmont: Fall 1998. 33–51.

Weber, Timothy P. "How Evangelicals Became Israel's Best Friend." *Christianity Today Vol. 42*. Carol Stream: Oct. 5, 1998. 38–49.

Endnotes

1   John Hagee is an evangelical sensationalist preacher and modern "doomsday" prophet. Among his publications are: *Final Dawn Over Jerusalem, The Beginning of the End, From Daniel to Doomsday*. He is counted among the more fundamentalist and neo-conservative of the Evangelicals.

2   During the Reformation, Protestants also began to reassess and accept the concepts of messianism and millenarianism, both of which are pivotal to Christian Zionist theology and ideology.

3   Lord Shaftesbury coined the phrase of "a country without a nation for a nation without a country" in describing Palestine. This phrase was later picked up by the Jewish Zionists and used as "a land without a people for a people without a land."

4   Louis Brandeis (1865–1941), Chairperson of General Zionist Affairs, was the individual who named Blackstone as the "true founder of Zionism."

5   Indeed, one of the major reasons cited for Carter's defeat in the 1980 election to Ronald Reagan was his support for Palestinians.

6   The issue of the future of Jerusalem was one of the "Final Status Issues" to be negotiated between the Israeli government and the Palestinian Authority before talks broke down. Needless to say, this is a subject unto itself, but it is imperative to bear in mind the rhetoric that surrounds it, often in biblical language.

7 The Haram al-Sharif, now stands on the site of the first two Jewish Temples. The Haram is a platform on which the Dome of the Rock and Al-Aqsa mosque stand. Destruction of these holy sites of Islam would create what all sides of the conflict believe to be World War III, which is perhaps exactly what many of the Christian Zionists are looking for. For list of occurrences on the Haram since 1967, especially those involving Christian Zionist activity/terrorism, see www.ldolphin.org/chron.html).

8 Goldberg's phrase is the source of the title of this paper.

9 Hal Lindsey and his bestseller *The Late Great Planet Earth* (and subsequent series) popularized this strategy of political analysis via prophecy.

10 The deportations of Messianic Jews continues, with the most recent case occurring in February of 2000. Three Israeli women of Ethiopian origin were stripped of their citizenship, because they joined a Messianic group.

11 Public advocacy for Israel by evangelical leaders, particularly the prominent TV personalities, has been "endless," but the newer development in Christian "support" involves numerous small grassroots organizations offering institutional and financial aid. See Document 9 for an example of a Christian Zionist "ask letter" (source: Habib).

12 Indeed, Jerry Falwell told the Tyler, *Texas Courier–Times Telegram* in 1983 that he believed Israel should take all the land from the River Euphrates in the east to the Nile River in the west, which would include parts of modern day Iraq, Syria, Saudi Arabia, Egypt, the Sudan, and all of Lebanon, Kuwait, and Jordan.

13 The future of Israeli settlements was another issue to have been discussed in the "Final Status Talks" of now defunct Oslo II; however, settlement building in the Occupied Territories and East Jerusalem increased more than 80% after the beginning of the Oslo Agreement.

14 It is also important to note that the Christian Zionists also "benefit" psychologically from their alliance with the Israeli right, in that they often identify with the warriors of the Old Testament, especially the figure of Joshua. Therefore, they like being allied with "the victor."

15 Partnerships between Christian Zionists and the indigenous Arab Christian population do not exist, although it is possible to find Christian organizations (who are not Zionist in doctrine or practice) engaging in necessary human rights work and basic relief efforts. The Lutherans, the Brethren, the Anglicans, the Mennonites, and the Quakers are among the most active Christian denominations working in the Occupied Territories to assist the entire Palestinian population, Christian and Muslim.

16 It is also interesting to note that numerous characters predicted by Evangelicals to be the Antichrist over the past decades have included numerous Arab leaders: among them, the Ayatollah Khomeini of Iran, Momar Qadafi of Libya, and Saddam Hussein of Iraq. Yasser Arafat of the PLO and PNA has also been named as a possibility. Even more interesting is Falwell's 1999 statement that he believes that the Antichrist is a Jew currently living in the United States.

Part Two:

Voices from the Ground

CHAPTER SIX

A Most Ungenerous Offer

Jeff Halper

This essay originally appeared in The Link, *published by
Americans for Middle East Understanding, Inc.Volume 35, Issue 4
Link Archives: www.ameu.org September–October, 2002*

Consider a prison: If you look at a blueprint of a prison, it looks like the prisoners own the place. They have ninety-five percent of the territory. The prisoners have the living areas. They have the cafeteria, the visiting area, the exercise yard. All the prison authorities have is five percent: the surrounding walls, the cell bars, a few points of control, the keys to the door. The prison authorities do not need twenty or thirty percent of the territory to control the inmates. They only need to control the strategic points.

This analogy is useful for understanding why Barak's celebrated "generous offer" to the Palestinians was anything but generous. It also explains the callous impunity with which Israel relates to Palestinian national aspirations and rights. I would argue that Israel views the *intifada*, the Palestinian uprising, as a prison riot. Israel—and the Zionist movement before it—never recognized a Palestinian people possessing a distinct identity, culture or history with legitimate claims to a country. Although Israel required the P.L.O. to recognize it as a legitimate political construct and not merely a "fact of life," Israel in return did not recognize the Palestinian's right of self-determination. It never promised a Palestinian state at the end of the "peace process." In Oslo, Israel agreed only to negotiate "final status issues" with the P.L.O., without committing itself to any particular outcome. Indeed, given the fact that Israel doubled its settler population during the seven years of negotiations, constructed a massive highway system in the Occupied Territories that linked its settlements to Israel proper while creating barriers to Palestinian movement, and imposed an economic closure that impoverished the Palestinian population, no hint is evident "on the ground" that Israel ever contemplated the establishment of a viable Palestinian state.

Understanding this is crucial for comprehending Israel's fierce reaction to the second *intifada*, leading to its current efforts to dismantle the Palestinian Authority completely and create a permanent *bantustan*. It explains why Israel mistreats Palestinians and violates their human rights with impunity, why it thumbs its nose at international humanitarian law, why it is able to build a prison wall against the Palestinians "so high that even the birds cannot fly over it." For Israeli Jews, Palestinians are merely "Arabs" (Israeli Jews seldom use the word "Palestinians"), an undifferentiated part of an Arab mass that might just as well live in one of the "other" twenty-two Arab countries as in "ours." From their point of view there is only one legitimate "side" to this conflict, their own. Only Jews—wherever they live, Israeli or not—hold exclusive claims to the land. This is the source of Israeli human rights violations in both the Occupied Territories and within Israel itself. There is no symmetry, no "two sides," no more negotiation. Like prison guards, Israelis claim a "right" to put down the prison riot, the *intifada*. Inmates have no right to riot, and certainly no right to challenge the dictates of the authorities. Once we put them down, once they know their place, once they submit and accept their life in prison-*bantustan*, they will have a pleasant place to live; we will even liberate them from the rule of their own criminal leaders. But they must understand they are in our country, and we will brook no challenge to our exclusive rights.

House Demolitions

Now consider what it means to be a prisoner under Occupation.

Back in early 1997, when Bibi Netanyahu was prime minister and we were supposedly in the midst of a "peace process," his government would often demolish 20–30 Palestinian homes a week. Demolishing houses is one of the most cruel and oppressive aspects of the Occupation (even though Israel has been systematically demolishing homes and whole villages since 1948). Since the start of the Occupation in 1967, 9,000 Palestinian homes have been destroyed, some 2,000 since the outbreak of the second *intifada*, leaving more than 50,000 Palestinians homeless, destitute, and living in fear and trauma.

The motivation for demolishing these homes is purely political. Although Israel tries to lend its actions a legal façade through an elaborate system of planning regulations, laws and procedures—we are, after all, the "only democracy in the Middle East"—the practice of house demolitions violates international law and fundamental human rights. The purpose is to confine the three and a half million residents of the West Bank, East Jerusalem and Gaza to small, overcrowded, impoverished and disconnected enclaves, thereby foreclosing any viable Palestinian entity and ensuring Israeli control even if Palestinians achieve some nominal form of independence.

The renewal of massive house demolitions by Netanyahu in 1997 sparked the founding of the Israeli Committee Against House Demolitions (ICAHD), of which I am the coordinator.

ICAHD began as a non-violent, direct-action group composed of representatives of diverse Israeli peace and human rights organizations: Bat Shalom, Rabbis for Human Rights, Yesh Gvul, the Public Committee Against Torture, Palestinians and Israelis for Human Rights, Netivot Shalom, parts of Meretz and Peace Now. Having become somewhat dormant during the years of Rabin and Peres, when many of us believed that "peace" was painfully being achieved, we all felt that now something must be done to resist the increasingly oppressive Occupation. We chose to focus on house demolition because it lies at the juncture between a political policy crucial for perpetuating the Occupation and the human suffering it engendered. We had little appreciation, however, of how that decision would change our lives and the style of our work.

First, it required us to learn the "lay of the land." Israeli peace groups tend to set their own agendas, seldom consulting Palestinian organizations. We felt this only replicated the power relations inherent in the Occupation itself. Early on we decided that we would act only in the Occupied Territories in conjunction with a Palestinian organization. We therefore established close working relations with a number of grassroots Palestinian groups, in particular the Land Defense Committee, with branches throughout Palestinian towns, neighborhoods and villages, and LAW, a Palestinian human rights organization.

For the first few months of our work, as we got to know the workings of the Occupation and developed relations of trust with Palestinian organizations and families, we began to visit some of the thousands of families threatened with demolition orders. Here, too, our position as Israeli peace activists was challenged. The Israeli peace movement traditionally engaged in protest. It never promised to effect any concrete changes in Israeli government policy and was never called upon to "deliver"—which is why Palestinians had little faith in many of our activities. The Palestinian families we met would have nothing of protest or mere solidarity. They wanted to know if we could prevent the demolition, if we could help them get a permit, if we could arrange legal protection, if we could use our political influence. What would we do, they wanted to know, when the army and bulldozers arrived. Would we stand and resist together with them? And if the house was demolished, they wanted to know what would we offer: To rebuild? To help finance alternative quarters? To secure them a permit?

Suddenly, after decades in the peace movement and hundreds of demonstrations under our belts, we discovered how little we knew of the Occupation and of the people living under it. Who issues demolition orders? The army? The Civil Administration? The police? Another government body? [Answer: the Civil Administration in the West Bank and Gaza, though the army also has the authority if "security" is involved; both the Municipality and the Ministry of the Interior in East Jerusalem.] We had heard vaguely of the Civil Administration, but where was it located? [In Beit El settlement northeast of Ramallah.] And who exactly is responsible for issuing demolition orders? Could we obtain building permits, and how? What is the government's demolition policy and what numbers are we talking about? And we realized how little we actually knew about the workings of the Occupation we had protested for so many years. When a family contacted us from the town of Anata, part of which lies within the Jerusalem municipal boundary, none of us knew where it was or how to get there.

In fact, none of us had ever seen a demolition. Normally they are carried out at dawn, after the men have left for work and only the women and children remain at home. And they are randomized so as to diffuse the fear and uncertainty, to deter people from building at all. Once a demolition order is confirmed by the court, the bulldozers could arrive the next morning, or next week, or next year—or never. It is like a reverse lottery—you do not want to "win." In the end, the policy of house demolitions makes life so unbearable that those who have the means (especially educated middle classes so critical for Palestinian society) are driven from the country altogether.

A major change in our work occurred on July 9, 1998. At one o'clock in the afternoon, as members of ICAHD, the Land Defense

Committee, and LAW were preparing a demonstration opposite the Civil Administration in Beit El (30 houses had been demolished the previous week), we received word that the house of Salim Shawamreh was being demolished in the nearby village of Anata. It was the fifth house being demolished that day, and the Civil Administration had apparently gotten greedy, thinking that because of the lack of resistance, it would keep demolishing through the day.

Salim Shawamreh, his wife Arabia, and their six children were one of the families we had met earlier. Their village of Anata, with a population of some 12,000, is a microcosm of the Occupation. It is divided between Jerusalem and the West Bank. Almost all the village's lands have been expropriated to build Israeli settlements, leaving the residents crowded into a small "core." Twenty-three demolition orders had been served on Anata residents by the Jerusalem municipality, the Ministry of the Interior and the Civil Administration.

The Shawamreh house fell into Area C of the West Bank, which is under full Israeli control. After several unsuccessful attempts to obtain a permit, Salim, having nowhere else to live, built on his own private land. He promptly received a demolition order, but managed to live in his home undisturbed for four years. One fine day in July, as he was having lunch with his wife and six children, he heard a knock on the door. When he opened it, he found himself confronted by dozens of soldiers. Their leader, a field inspector of the Civil Administration named Micha, asked Salim: "Is this your house?" "Yes, this is my house," answered Salim. "No, it isn't," Micha replied. "This is now our house. You have fifteen minutes to remove your belongings before we destroy it."

When I arrived on the scene and managed to pass through the dozens of soldiers to reach the house, I found Salim lying beaten on the ground and his wife being carried unconscious to the hospital. Both had resisted the attempt to demolish their home, and both had been violently ejected from the house. The terrified children had scattered and were not to be found.

Together with Salim and his neighbors, I resisted the army's attempts to drive us away so that the bulldozer could begin its work. I sat in front of the bulldozer (something that would have gotten a Palestinian shot) and was pushed down the hill by the soldiers. Finally, lying with Salim and the others in the dirt, I witnessed a unique experience for an Israeli—watching through the eyes of a Palestinian as his house was systematically destroyed and all the fruit tress of his garden uprooted.

Demolition is a different experience for men, women and children. Men probably are the most humiliated, since the inability to provide a home for their families and to protect them destroys their very position as head of the family. The loss of one's home means loss of one's connection to the land, the family's patrimony. The message of demolition is clear: there is no place for you here; there is no place for a Palestinian on the face of the earth.

Men often cry at demolitions, but they also are angered and swear revenge, or plan to build again.

For women, the loss of the home is the loss of one's identity as a woman, wife and mother. For Palestinian women, most of whom do not work outside the home, the house is their entire world. In fact, they lose twice. They lose their own home in a traumatic act of violence—their most personal belongings thrown unceremoniously outside in the dirt—and they must go live in the home of another woman (a mother or sister-in-law), thereby losing their status as the head of the domestic household and even as a mother. Palestinian women tend to sink into mourning, their behavior—crying, wailing and then depression—is very much like those of people who have lost loved ones. The demolished home can never be replaced, and after demolitions women undergo personality changes. Some become more sullen or moody, often frightened by small sounds or unexpected events, prone to break into crying. Others step into the vacuum left by the emasculated husband and become the strong center of the family unit.

For children the act of demolition—and the months and years leading up to it—is a time of trauma. To witness the fear and powerlessness of your parents, to feel constantly afraid and insecure, to see loved ones beaten, to experience the harassment of Civil Administration field supervisors—and then to endure the noise and violence and displacement and destruction of your home, your world, your toys—these things mark children for life. The signs of trauma and stress among children are many: bed-wetting, nightmares, fear to leave home lest one "abandon" parents and children to the army, dramatic drops in grades and school attendance, exposure to domestic violence that occasionally follows impoverishment, displacement, and humiliation. One day recently, Israeli tanks appeared before the windows of the Shawamreh's rented apartment, and their 11-year-old daughter Wafa went blind for two hours. Her mind simply shut down under the weight of successive traumas.

A month after the demolition of the Shawamreh home, ICAHD brought hundreds of Israelis to join local Palestinians in rebuilding the house. It was promptly demolished a second time by Israeli bulldozers, but we all decided to rebuild it yet again as a political act of resistance. When we all had finished the home for the third time, Salim said: "Together with Israelis who seek a just peace, we have built here a House of Peace." In April 2001, the Shawamreh house was demolished yet again. We are now planning to rebuild it for the fourth time. We refuse to let the Occupation win.

Israel's Matrix of Control

As "the only democracy in the Middle East," Israel attempts to conceal its prison-like Occupation behind a legalistic façade Thus the Palestinians are cast as the "law-breakers." How else could Israel explain its demolition of thousands of Palestinian homes while at the same time constructing exclusive Jewish settlements on the occupied land—some 40,000 Jewish-only housing units in the West Bank since 1967, and 90,000 in East Jerusalem.

It also denies the very fact of Occupation. Israel claims it is merely "administrating" the West Bank and Gaza (having formally annexed East Jerusalem and the Golan Heights) until their final status is negotiated—a position unanimously rejected by the international community. But by embedding its Occupation in an elaborated bureaucratic and legal system, Israel hides the illegality of its Occupation policies under international law.

Since 1967, Israel has laid over the Occupied Territories what I call a Matrix of Control. It is a sophisticated, complex, and integrated system designed: a) to control every aspect of Palestinian life while giving the impression that "Occupation" is merely proper adminis-tration; b) to cast Israel's military repression as self-defense against an aggressive Palestinian people endeavoring to expel it; and c) to carve out just enough space to establish a dependent Palestinian mini-state—or worse, a number of feudal and disconnected cantons—that will relieve it of responsibility for the Palestinian population.

The Matrix operates on there interlocking levels:

Military Controls, Military Strikes and Close Surveillance
- Outright military actions, including attacks on civilian popu-lation centers and the Palestinian infrastructure, especially evident during the two *intifadas* (1987–1993; 2000–present), are

not Israel's preferred means of control. They are brutal, too visual, and generate both internal and foreign opposition. Citing "security" concerns, Israel uses military force effectively and with impunity to suppress resistance to the Occupation and as a deterrent ("teaching the Palestinians a lesson;" conveying a "message"). In the long-term, however, Israel prefers to control the Palestinians administratively—including the issuance of thousands of "military orders" and by "creating facts on the ground."

- Extensive use is also made of collaborators and undercover "*mustarabi*" army units. The dependency which Israel's stifling "administration" engenders turns thousands of Palestinians into unwilling (and occasionally willing) collaborators. Simple things such as obtaining a driver's or business license, a work permit, a permit to build a house, a travel document or permission to receive hospital care in Israel or abroad is often conditioned on supplying information to the security services. Extortion, the only word to describe forcing people into traitorous activities that undermine their own society, is an essential feature of the Matrix. So effective is this that Israel can pinpoint and assassinate Palestinian figures—"targeted prevention" is the euphemism—in their cars or even in telephone booths.

- Israel has at its disposal sophisticated means of surveillance. In May of this year it launched Amos 5, the fifth in a series of spy satellites, which can detect the tiniest movement even at night. Since the Occupied Territories are small and largely barren patches of land, surveillance is virtually complete.

- Mass arrests and administrative detention are also common features of the military side of the Matrix of Control. In the March–April 2002 raids on West Bank cities, towns, villages and refugee camps, about 3,000 people were detained, 280 of them held in administrative detention which can last for months or years, without being either charged or tried.

Creating Facts on the Ground

- Since 1967 Israel has expropriated for settlements, highways, by-pass roads, military installations, nature preserves and infrastructure some 24 percent of the West Bank, 89 percent of Arab East Jerusalem, and 25 percent of Gaza.

- More than 200 settlements have been constructed in the Occupied Territories; over 400,000 Israelis have moved across the 1967 boundaries: 200,000 in the West Bank, 200,000 in East Jerusalem, and 6,000 in Gaza. A key goal of the settlement enterprise is to foreclose the establishment of a viable Palestinian state (or, for some, any Palestinian state) by carving the Occupied Territories into dozens of enclaves surrounded, isolated, and controlled by Israeli settlements, infrastructure and military.

- While a number of Israeli highways were built in the Occupied Territories before the Oslo Accords, construction of a massive system of 29 highways and by-pass roads, funded entirely by the United States at a cost of $3 billion, was begun only at the start of the "peace process." Designed to link settlements, to create barriers to Palestinian movement, and, in the end, to incorporate the West Bank into Israel proper, this project, which takes up an additional 17 percent of the West Bank land, contributes materially to the creation of "facts on the ground" that prejudiced the negotiations.

  Another mechanism of control that came into being with the signing of Oslo II in 1995 was the further carving of the Occupied Territories into Areas A, B, C in the West Bank; H-1 and H-2 in Hebron; and Yellow, Green, Blue, and White Areas in Gaza. In addition, Israeli-controlled "nature reserves," closed military areas, security zones, and "open green spaces" restrict Palestinian construction in more than half of East Jerusalem. This system confines Palestinians to an archipelago of some 190 islands encircled by the Israeli Matrix. Israel formally controls 60 percent of the West Bank (Area C), 60 percent of Gaza, and all of East Jerusalem. Its frequent incursions into Palestinian territory and its virtual destruction of the Palestinian Authority between March and July 2002, have left it, however, in de facto control of the entire area.

- Hundreds of permanent, semi-permanent, and "spontaneous" checkpoints and border crossings severely limit and control Palestinian movement.

- Construction of seven of 12 planned industrial parks on the "seam" between the Occupied Territories and Israel gives new life to isolated settlements while robbing Palestinian cities of their own economic vitality. These parks exploit cheap Palestinian labor while denying it access to Israel. They also afford Israel's most polluting and least profitable industries an opportunity to continue dumping their industrial wastes into the West Bank and Gaza.

- Israel's Matrix of Control extends underground as well, using settlement sites to maintain control over the main aquifers of the Occupied Territories.
- Even seemingly innocuous holy places such as Rachel's Tomb in Bethlehem, the Cave of the Patriarchs in Hebron, sites in and around Jerusalem, and Joseph's Tomb in Nablus serve as pretexts for maintaining an Israeli "security presence."

Bureaucracy, Planning and Law—subtle control mechanisms

- "Orders" issued by the Military Commanders of the West Bank and Gaza—some 2,000 in number since 1967—supplement Civil Administration policies that replace local civil law with procedures designed to strengthen Israeli political control.
- Since the start of the "peace process," a permanent "closure" has been laid over the West Bank and Gaza, severely restricting the number of Palestinian workers allowed into Israel and impoverishing the Palestinian community whose own infrastructure has been kept underdeveloped.
- Discriminatory and often arbitrary systems of work, entrance and travel permits further restrict movement both within the country and abroad.
- Given Israel's goal of controlling the entire country and its "demographic problem"—Palestinians will soon outnumber Jews in the area between the Jordan River and the Mediterranean Sea—policies of displacement are actively pursued: exile and deportation; revocation of residency rights; economic impoverishment; land expropriation; and house demolitions, all are means of making life so unbearable that it will induce "voluntary" emigration. Schemes of "transfer" have become a common and acceptable part of Israeli political discourse, with two parties in Prime Minister Sharon's government, the National Union Party and Israel Is Our Home, now promoting transfer as their main political program.
- Zoning and planning policies are ideal vehicles for rendering the Occupation invisible, since they are couched in supposedly neutral terms and professional jargon but serve Israel's political ends by obstructing the natural development to Palestinian towns and villages. Central to this system is the restrictive use of building permits, reinforced by house demolitions, arrests and fines for "illegal" building, and daily harassment by Israeli building inspectors.

While the Palestinian population is being confined to small enclaves, planning for Israeli expansion employs "master plans" that encompass broad stretches of Palestinian land intended for future settlements. Within this framework Israel can cynically claim that its settlement building is "frozen" and that it is only "thickening" existing ones for purposes of "natural growth." In fact, small settlements often give rise to large settlement-cities which, of course, "do not count" because they share an existing master plan.

- Severe restrictions on the planting of crops and their sale hit an already destitute population hard, especially when combined with Israel's practice of uprooting hundreds of thousands of olive and fruit trees since 1967, either for settlements or for "security" purposes.
- Use of abusive licensing and inspection procedures limits the local economy and keeps it dependent on Israeli goods.

Barak's "Generous Offer"

If anything has turned public opinion in Israel and abroad against the Palestinians, it is the contention that Israel under Barak made far-reaching concessions to the Palestinians and that they rebuffed his "generous offer" with violence. In this popular view the Palestinians are to "blame" for the breakdown of the peace process and, in the light of terrorism, Israel's policies of repression are justified. Seen in the light of the prison analogy, however, Israel does not need more than 5–10% of the Occupied Territories to retain control and render a Palestinian state non-viable and non-sovereign. The fallacy lies in equating territory with sovereignty. Although gaining control of 95 or 88% of the territory is important—especially if the territory is contiguous—it does not necessarily equal a sovereign state. This is where the Matrix of Controls enters the picture, and where knowing the "lay of the land" is critical. If anything, Taba revealed how much Israel could relinquish and still retain effective control over the entire country. Looked at closely, this is what the "generous offer" in fact offered:

Consolidation of Strategic Settlement Blocs

Israel retains the three large blocs of Ariel and its surrounding "Western Samaria" bloc; the central Givat Ze'ev-Pisgat Ze'ev-Ma'alei

Adumin, and perhaps Beit El bloc; and the Efrat-Gush Etzion-Beitar Illit bloc.

The Creation of a "Greater [Israeli] Jerusalem"

The Givat Ze'ev-Adumin and Gush Etzion settlement bloc, with their 80,000 settlers, when annexed to Israeli-controlled "Greater Jerusalem," will dominate the entire central region of the West Bank. Because some 40 percent of the Palestinian economy revolves around Jerusalem in the form of tourism, commercial life and industry, removing Jerusalem from the Palestinian realm carries such serious economic consequences as to call the very viability of a Palestinian state into question.

Emergence of a "Metropolitan [Israeli] Jerusalem"

The ring roads and major highways being built through and around Jerusalem are turning the city into a metropolitan region, incorporating 10 percent of the West Bank. Within its limits are found 75 percent of the West Bank settlers and the major centers of Israeli construction.

An East Jerusalem Patchwork

Israel will not cede the entire area of East Jerusalem, where Israelis, now about 200,000, outnumber Palestinians. Palestinian presence in Jerusalem will be fragmented and barely viable as an urban and economic center. The Temple Mount/Haram al-Sharif issue remained unresolved at Taba, with Israel seemingly prepared to cede "functional sovereignty" (though not official) to the "upper" area of the mosques, while retaining sole sovereignty over the "lower" Western Wall.

Israeli Control over Highways and Movement

Over the past decades Israel has been building a system of major highways and by-pass roads designed to link its settlements, to create barriers between Palestinian areas, and to incorporate the West Bank into Israel proper. Even if physical control over the highways is relinquished, strategic parts will remain under Israeli control: the Eastern Ring Road, Jerusalem-Etzion Bloc highway, Road 45 from Tel Aviv to Ma'aleh Adumin, a section of Highway 60 from Jerusalem to Beit El and Ofra, and the western portion of the Trans-Samarian highway leading to the Ariel bloc. In terms of the movement of people and goods, this will divide the Palestinian entity into at least four cantons: the northern West Bank, the southern portion, East

Jerusalem, and Gaza. Plus, Israel insists on retaining rights of "emergency deployment" to both the highway system and the Jordan Valley.

Limited Palestinian Sovereignty

Such a Palestinian state would possess limited sovereignty only. It would be demilitarized and unable to form military alliances not approved by Israel. It would have jurisdiction over its borders, but would have certain restrictions as to who may enter, especially vis-à-vis the refugees. And the restrictions regarding military contingencies, as defined by Israel, would apply.

Defeating Palestinian Aspirations

Faced with the prospect of being locked forever into a tiny non-viable *bantustan*, Palestinians rose up in their second *intifada* in September 2000. It spelled the final rejection by the Palestinian people of the Oslo "peace process," which they considered a sophisticated form of *apartheid*. Since then, the *intifada* has turned into a full-scale war for independence. For Israel it has turned into a last-ditch battle in which Israel will emerge victorious and the Palestinians' aspirations for self-determination in a viable state will be dashed forever. The May 12th vote—by acclamation—of the Likud Central Committee against the establishment of any Palestinian state flowed logically and smoothly from "Operation Defensive Shield," the ferocious incursion into Palestinian areas in March–April 2002.

In the wake of this military action and the reoccupation of the Palestinian areas—all done with U.S. support for "reform" of the Palestinian Authority (read: implant a quisling leader)—the Sharon government believes it has defeated the Palestinians once and for all, and can thus drop the pretense of even a Palestinian mini-state. It has three good reasons for thinking so:

Jenin. Although the Israeli attacks of March–April 2002 extended far beyond the Jenin refugee camp, Jenin became the focal point and symbol of Israel's thrust to "destroy the infrastructure of terrorism." In fact, it represents for Sharon the final defeat of any Palestinian attempt to resist the Occupation. Palestinians, in his view, have nowhere to go. Their infrastructure is demolished, and given Israel's suffocating control of Areas A and B, they will never be able to reorganize. There may be isolated incidents, but the problem of terrorism/resistance has been reduced to manageable proportions.

Ramallah. Although the Israeli assault on Ramallah received far less press and was focused on events around Arafat's compound, it represents nothing less than the destruction of the Palestinian Authority's ability to govern. In Ramallah virtually the entire civil infrastructure was destroyed—all the data of the government ministries, hospitals and clinics, the land registry office, the courts and banking system, businesses, non-governmental organizations and research institutions, even the Palestinian Academy of Sciences. We already see Israel's Civil Administration stepping into the vacuum. Before the incursion, Israel recognized the documents/passports issued by the Palestinian Authority to Palestinians traveling to Jordan; now Palestinians will have to get travel documents from Israel. In addition, they will need special permits to leave their cities in order to travel to the bridge to exit, which they didn't need before. And we must not miss the "message" of the solders left behind: "Death to Arabs" scrawled on walls with excrement, excrement and urine spread throughout offices and homes, wanton destruction of furniture, equipment, artworks, and gardens.

The American Congress. On May 2nd, in the wake of the attacks and in anticipations of Sharon's visit to Washington, Congress overwhelmingly passed a resolution (94–2 in the Senate, 352–21 in the House), supporting Israel's campaign to destroy "the terrorist infrastructure and attacking the Palestinian Authority." The resolution showed clearly why the U.S. Congress is Israel's "trump card," allowing it to defy the international community while thumbing its nose at American administrations.

All this leads inexorably towards a three-fold permanent "solution" to the "Arab problem." First, Arafat will be transferred to Gaza, which will become one large prison for PLO members. At some point, probably when Arafat leaves the scene and a more compliant leader can be found, Gaza will become the Palestinian state as a sop to international demands for Palestinian independence.

The West Bank will then be divided into three separate cantons according to settlement blocs and Israeli highways already in place. A northern canton would be created around the city of Nablus, a central one around Ramallah and a southern one in the area of Hebron, with a possible separation at Qalkilya and Tulkarem from the rest. Each would be disconnected from the other and connected independently to Israel. A road or two might connect the different cantons, but checkpoints and cargo docks would ensure complete Israeli control. Each canton, whose residents would have a residency status similar to that of the Palestinians of East Jerusalem today, would be granted local autonomy to run its municipalities, schools and services, as envisioned by Begin.

Finally, Israel would ensure submission using a combination of controls. The administrative tools of the Matrix, together with the "facts on the ground," effectively foreclose any Palestinian organization beyond local autonomy. Fear of losing the economic opportunities promised by Peres's industrial parks and other enterprises would counteract moves towards renewed resistance. And then there is the "quiet transfer." By inducing the emigration of the educated Palestinian middle-classes, Israel renders Palestinian society weak, leaderless and easily controlled. Since the outbreak of the second *intifada* an estimated 150,000 Palestinians have left the Occupied Territories, the vast majority of them middle class, including many Christians from the Bethlehem and Ramallah areas.

What Must Be Done?

A just peace will not be achieved unless the following elements are present:

- An explicit declaration that the eventual goals of the negotiations are a viable and truly sovereign Palestinian state, together with an Israel enjoying security and regional integration (a position very close to the Saudi plan).
- A direct connection between the negotiations and the realities on the ground. Oslo was formulated in a way that put off the "hard issues," those most crucial to the Palestinians, for the final stages of the negotiations, which never happened. Jerusalem, borders, water, settlements, the fate of the refugees and the security arrangements—all these issues (except the last, important mainly for Israel) were put off during the seven years of negotiations. Although Article IV of the Declaration of Principles talks about preserving the "integrity" of the West Bank and Gaza during negotiations, it did not prevent Israel from "creating facts" on the ground which, as we have seen, completely prejudiced the discussions.
- Reference to international law and human rights. International humanitarian law provides a map for the equitable resolution of the Israeli-Palestinian "conflict." By guaranteeing the collective rights of both peoples to self-determination and prohibiting occupation and the perpetuation of refugee status, it leaves only

the details of an agreement to be worked out by negotiations. Boundaries, the just resolution of the refugee issue based on the Right of Return and individual choice and the other "final status issues" can be resolved only if they are addressed in the context of human rights and international humanitarian law—and not as mere by-products of power. Nothing is being asked of Israel that is not asked of any other country—accountability under the covenants of human rights formulated and adopted by the international community, which Israel pledged to respect as a condition for its creation by the United Nations.

- Dismantling the Matrix of Control. As we have seen, the strategic 5–15 % of the Occupied Territories Israel seeks to retain would frustrate Palestinian national aspirations. Viability, sovereignty and the end to Israeli control (along with addressing genuine Israeli security concerns) must be the markers of progress towards a just peace.

- Refugees. Some seventy percent of the Palestinian people are refugees. No resolution of the conflict is possible without addressing their rights, needs and grievances. Israel must acknowledge its active role in creating the refugee problem and recognize the refugee's right of return. Once that is done, the Palestinians, and the wider Arab world that endorses the Saudi plan, have indicated their willingness to negotiate a mutually agreed-upon actualization of that right.

- Involvement of the wider international community, civil society as well as governmental, in peace-making efforts. We must closely monitor whether peace proposals in fact further Palestinian independence in a viable state. Key to this is understanding the implications of the various discussions and proposals in terms of the reality "on the ground." This may involve initiatives on the part of civil society; investigating the events in the Jenin refugee camp, for example, since the U.N. has been prevented from doing so.

- Mobilizing public opinion. ICAHD's campaign to organize 1,000 house parties in order to raise funds for the rebuilding of demolished Palestinian houses is a meaningful act of resistance that involves Israelis, Palestinians and internationals in civil society peace-making. (For more information on this effort, see our campaign web site at www.rebuildinghomes.org.)

- Lobbying. Palestinian and Israeli delegations should be brought to parliaments and Congress.

The Occupation poses a bold challenge to the international community, whether to its elected representatives or to the civil society as represented by Non-Governmental and faith-based organizations. In an era of global transparency, of mass media, instantaneous news coverage and the internet, can a new Berlin Wall be built that locks millions of Palestinians behind massive fortifications, Israel's $100-million "security fence?" Decades after the end of colonialism and a decade after the end of South African *apartheid*, will the international community actually sit passively by while a new *apartheid* regime arises before our very eyes? In a world in which the ideal of human rights has gained wide acceptance, could an entire people be imprisoned in dozens of tiny, impoverished islands, denied its right of self-determination?

The cardinal mistake in the American approach is to believe that Israel will voluntarily relinquish its Occupation in return for full security or regional integration, or, as National Security Advisor Condoleeza Rice put it, that Israel has an interest in a strong, stable Palestinian state. The Israeli government does not consider its Occupation an "occupation," but merely an administration until such a time that its control can be formalized in negotiations. The recent July 2002 bombing in Gaza, in which 17 people were killed and some 150 wounded, most of them children, illustrates this clearly. The attack came just hours before the Fatah Tanzim were to declare a cease fire and when even Hamas was considering a similar change of policy. The attack was nothing less than an intentional escalation designed to scuttle any developments that might force Israel into real negotiations. Unless this fundamental point is grasped, all efforts to shake Israel's hold of the Occupied Territories will end in failure.

A Long Way From Hibbing…

Sometimes, while trying to explain the plight of the Palestinians to an Israeli public that doesn't want to listen or when facing arrest by soldiers while resisting the demolition of a Palestinian home or during testimony before a U.N. commission on Israeli human rights abuses, I think to myself: "This is a long way from Hibbing, Minnesota."

What brought me to Israel thirty years ago was a curious mixture of push and pull, and what has kept me here is an even more curious mixture of attachment and resistance. The "push" comes, I believe, from four sources. One was my home town of Hibbing (yes, where

Bob Dylan hails from), which possessed a strong socialist tradition deriving from its place at the center of the iron mining industry and from its working class Scandinavian and Central European immigrant roots. Hibbing is also the hometown of Gus Hall, the long-time head of the U.S. Communist Party, a fact which is also a source of pride. The mild radicalism that informed the ambience I grew up in pre-conditioned me for the second source of my activism: the Sixties. As a student at Macalester College in St. Paul, I was involved, as were so many others, in the activities of the New Left—the twin causes of civil rights and anti-war in particular. I called myself a "radical," as did so many others, but unlike New Left people who rejected "ideology," I remain part of what I call today the "critical left."

The third source of my activism—and the one that impelled me to move to Israel so many years ago—was the Jewish one. Since I was always extremely secular, my Judaism found expression in Jewish radical traditions—deriving from the "Prophetic tradition." Like many in the Sixties searching for "identity" and "roots," I was "pulled" towards Israel by my national Jewish—and incipient Israeli—identity.

Upon my arrival in Israel in 1973, I found myself drawn to the critical "leftist" community where I met my wife Shoshana, a refugee from an orthodox religious upbringing. Zionism seemed to me parochial, exclusivist and, in the end, oppressive. I did not share with the extreme Israeli left, and most Arabs, the view that Israel is a "colonial settler state." I did accept as legitimate Jewish national claims to the country; we were not merely "settlers," as were the British, say, in Kenya. But I had to admit that the Zionist movement had acted—and continues to act—as a colonial movement. It also seemed to me that trying to maintain an ethnically pure state in our globalizing reality is a recipe for discrimination, oppression and injustice. While I accepted my status as Israeli, I have tried hard over the years to reconcile my identity and national rights with those of the Palestinians and to work towards justice and co-existence.

I believe that my professional background as an anthropologist, the fourth source of my activism and worldview, has also helped me bridge those apparent contradictions. It certainly has given me the ability to see, get to know, and work with the "Other," the Palestinians.

As I look back over my life and my work in the cause of a just peace between Israelis and Palestinians, I hear the words of my hometown balladeer:

How many times must a man look up
Before he can see the sky?
Yes, 'n' how many ears must one man have
Before he can hear people cry?
Yes, 'n' how many deaths will it take till he knows
That too many people have died?
The answer, my friend, is blowin' in the wind,
The answer is blowin' in the wind.

CHAPTER SEVEN

Suicide Bombers

What is theologically and morally wrong with suicide bombings?

A Palestinian Christian Perspective

Naim Ateek

This essay originally appeared in Cornerstone, *the publication of* Sabeel Ecumenical Liberation Theology Center, *issue 25, summer 2002.*

Preamble

The issue of Palestinian suicide bombings has become a familiar topic to many people throughout the world. It is easy for people, whether inside Israel/Palestine or outside to either quickly and forthrightly condemn it as a primitive and barbaric form of terrorism against civilians or condone and support it as a legitimate method of resisting an oppressive Israeli Occupation that has trampled Palestinian dignity and brutalized their very existence.

As a Christian, I know that the way of Christ is the way of nonviolence and, therefore, I condemn all forms of violence and terrorism whether coming from the government of Israel or from militant Palestinian groups.[1] This does not mean, however, that all Christians believe in nonviolence. On the contrary, so-called Christian nations in the West have waged some of the bloodiest wars in history and have been responsible for the worst atrocities and violations of human rights.

Having said that clearly, it is still important to help the readers, whether Palestinians or expatriates, to understand the phenomenon of suicide bombings that tragically arises from the deep misery and torment of many Palestinians. For how else can one explain it? When healthy, beautiful, and intelligent young men and women set out to kill and be killed, something is basically wrong in a world that has not heard their anguished cry for justice. These young people deserve to live, along with all those whom they have caused to die. This article is, therefore, addressed to all people of conscience urging them to work for a speedy termination of the illegal occupation of the Palestinian territories. Such an act will, most certainly, bring this tragic phenomenon of suicide bombing to an end and ensure security for both Israel as well as Palestine.

Since this article is intended for a broad and diverse readership, it has not been easy to decide on the best format. It generally follows the principles of liberation theology, thus moving from context to theology. Be that as it may, the hope is that it will inspire the reader to become an "aggressive" advocate for the *right of both peoples* to live in freedom and security. So far, this right has been denied to the Palestinians, hence the resistance to the Occupation with all its multi-faceted forms including suicide bombings.

The Background

The Palestinian resistance to the Israeli Occupation of the West Bank and the Gaza Strip has taken a very important turn since the early 1990s. Young Palestinian men, and more lately women,[2] have begun srapping themselves with explosives, making their way to Israeli Jewish areas whether crowded with soldiers or civilians and blowing themselves up, killing and injuring dozens of people around them. Between the beginning of the second *intifada* in September 2000 and June 19, 2002, Palestinian militants carried out 56 suicide bombings in the Gaza Strip and the West Bank, including Jerusalem, as well as inside Israel, killing, according to Israeli statistics, 225 Israelis including soldiers, men, women, and children.[3] In the same period, the Israeli army killed 1645 Palestinians including police, men, women, and children.

To discover the root causes, one needs to consider the background. For the last thirty-five years, the Palestinians have been engaged in resisting the Occupation of their country. The whole of the Gaza Strip and the West Bank, including East Jerusalem, came under Israeli Occupation in the war of 1967. It has not been a benign occupation as Israeli propagandists claim. It has been an oppressive military domination. Today over three million Palestinians are longing for independence and freedom. Instead, most of them are under siege and are subjected to curfews and humiliation.

Israel has been consistently confiscating their land and building exclusively Jewish settlements on it, restricting their movements, demolishing their homes, devouring their water resources, and controlling every aspect of their life.

The Palestinians have tried through different methods to shake off the Occupation but to no avail. For many years they have worked through the international community to bring an end to the Israeli Occupation but they have been unsuccessful. Indeed, the United Nations has been powerless to implement its many resolutions on Palestine. In 1987, the Palestinians rose up in a largely nonviolent uprising to shake off the Occupation and achieve independence. Although this first *intifada* caused many people in the world to become aware of the Palestinian plight, it did not bring about the desired result.

After the Gulf War, the Palestinians went to the Madrid Conference in October 1991 with the hope that it would lead to the implementation of UN resolutions 242 and 338. Instead, the negotiations took a circuitous route and opened the way to the Oslo Peace Process in 1993. With enthusiasm on the part of many and skepticism on the part of others, most Palestinians entered the Peace Process with the hope that it would lead them into a negotiated settlement with their Israeli neighbors. People expected that the presence of the Palestinian Authority with its democratically elected leadership would certainly enhance that process. Instead, Oslo led to entrenching the Israeli domination system, the deterioration of Palestinian economic life, increase in the confiscation of their land, and the deepening of their oppression.

With the apparent failure of the Peace Process, the second *intifada* started in September 2000 using nonviolent as well as armed resistance against the Occupation. Israel heightened its intransigence and intensified its oppressive policies. With the benefit of hindsight, it seems that the second *intifada* was also indirectly pointed at the Palestinian Authority that failed to deliver a just peace. Or at least, it was a defiance of its authority. Most of its active perpetrators were extremist militant Palestinian groups who were critical of Arafat's policies. In other words, it is possible to say that the anger of the people was directed not only against Israel but also against the Palestinian Authority that seemed unable to curb the injustice. With the increase of Palestinian resistance, there has been an immeasurable increase in Israeli oppression. Every aspect of Palestinian life worsened as the Israeli army escalated its malevolent policies against them. It has become a slow but steady process of strangulation of hope, greater despair, and deepening hate. Without understanding this background, it is difficult to grasp the evolution of the phenomenon of suicide bombings.

The Underlying Causes: an attempt to understand but not to justify

Historically speaking, the Palestinians did not begin their resistance to the Occupation with suicide bombings. These came at least 25 years later when the political and security situation deteriorated considerably and when it became certain that the international community is powerless to implement its own resolutions. There were no suicide bombings before the Oslo Peace Process. They are the result of despair and hopelessness that started to set in when an increasing number of Palestinians became frustrated by the deepening Israeli oppression and humiliation. As an illustration, one can cite the story of Abdel Baset Odeh, who blew himself up in the Park Hotel, Netanyah, last March 2002 killing 28 Israelis and tourists and sparking the largest Israeli incursion in the West Bank since 1967—Operation Defensive Shield.

Six months before, Odeh was prevented by the Israeli authorities from crossing into Jordan to get married to his fiancee from Baghdad. The Israeli Shin Bet (security intelligence) kept sending for him. He refused to go because he suspected, as often happens, that they would blackmail and pressure him into becoming an informer. He was 25 years old, ready to get married, start a family, settle in Jordan, and enjoy life. When everything was shut in his face and his future plans were shattered by the Israeli army, he turned to suicide bombing. His father attributed his son's action to humiliation and a broken heart. His family first heard about the bombing from the TV.[4]

Such stories abound in the Palestinian community. They all include one or more basic elements resulting from humiliation by the army, and/or seeking revenge for the killing or injury of a relative or a friend, desperation and frustration from the oppressive Israeli Occupation, unemployment and confinement, imprisonment and torture, hopelessness, racism, discrimination, as well as other reasons.

In other words, these young people were not born "terrorists." No one is born a terrorist. They were born in the image and likeness of God. They were born human beings with love of life and freedom. All of them, with no exception, were born under the Israeli military Occupation. The only Jews they knew were Israeli soldiers carrying guns and dehumanizing them. It was in the crucible of the Occupation that they were shaped and formed. And if Israel labels them as terrorists, they are, after all the product of its own making.

Moreover, these young Palestinians did not blow themselves up because they simply wanted to commit suicide. Before 1993, they were resisting the Occupation of their country through the traditional methods available to them. All they wanted was the end of the Occupation and the establishment of their own state alongside the state of Israel. However, with increasing Israeli oppressive and punitive measures against them—the use of helicopter gun ships to assassinate Palestinian leaders, F-16 fighter planes to kill people and destroy homes, the mushrooming of military checkpoints to control and humiliate people, closures and siege of Palestinian cities and towns, army incursions into Palestinian areas, and much more—suicide bombings came to be perceived as a more potent tool of resistance that can reciprocate the pain and hurt they were experiencing. And as they were driven deeper into despair, their desire to hit back in any way possible grew in intensity. From a Palestinian perspective, therefore, the real sequence of the cycle of resistance has been this: Israeli occupation, Palestinian resistance, greater Israeli oppressive measures, and greater attempts on the Palestinian side to increase the resistance, and the vicious circle goes on.

Besides the basic political injustice and the oppressiveness of the Occupation, there are four major areas that constitute the breeding ground for suicide bombers. To begin with, many young men have become permanently unemployed. Even when other older men were able to find employment within the pre-1967 borders in Israel, most young men were barred from entering because Israel considered them a security risk. During the second intifada, the unemployment rate has soared to an alarming 75% in some quarters. This led to the fact that approximately 65% of the Palestinian population was living below the poverty line. It has been extremely difficult for many people to find any form of work. Unemployment creates frustration and despair, and can lead to extreme action.

Moreover, it is the young men more than others who are humiliated, harassed, and provoked by the Israeli soldiers. Some of the worst humiliation takes place at checkpoints. The occupied areas have become infested with them. Some reports have mentioned more than 180.[5] Many of them have become permanently fixed; others are arbitrarily mounted at whim. The Occupied Territories have been literally segmented into numerous small cantons where it is impossible to move from one area to another without running into military checkpoints. It takes hours to pass through areas that normally take a few minutes. Humiliation is perhaps one of the worst methods used by Israel to dehumanize the Palestinians. It is clearly a policy that strips people of their self worth and dignity. It is directed at all echelons and age groups of Palestinian society.

Furthermore, there is hardly any Palestinian family in the West Bank and the Gaza Strip that has not experienced some kind of pain or injury. Many families have lost their loved ones—a spouse, a sibling, a child, a relative, or a close friend. The level of bitterness and hatred keeps rising daily. Almost every aspect of Palestinian life is controlled by the Israeli army and many people have lost the ability to dream of a better future or envisage a better life. Therefore, the desire to avenge their wasted life, take revenge against the Occupation, and at the same time take away with them as many Israeli lives as possible becomes an objective.

There is another group of young Palestinian men and women that must be mentioned. Many of these have been arrested and tortured in Israeli prisons and "concentration" camps. In fact, Israeli prisons have become the "factories" for creating and "manufacturing" collaborators.[6] Young men are detained for indefinite periods of time and are pressured into becoming spies and collaborators. They are simply trapped and some of them do not know how to shake off the pressure. This phenomenon causes some of them to exist in constant self contempt and scorn for having betrayed their own people. Forced collaboration has stripped them of their self worth. They are ready to become suicide bombers in order to purify and redeem themselves and express their utmost loyalty and patriotism for their country and people.

To sum up, these young people's daily life has become an experience of death. It is vividly symbolized in the daily funerals of their colleagues that they have to attend. Indeed, many of them feel that Israel has practically pronounced a death sentence on them. It is only a matter of time. Death is surely coming to them whether through a slow economic strangulation, or harsh political negation, or daily personal dehumanization. Since they have been stripped of their human dignity, their only possibility for existence is to exist as slaves under an Israeli *apartheid* system of domination. They feel they have no options and very little to lose. Consequently, they are willing to give themselves up for the cause of God and the homeland (*watan*) believing that with God there is so much to gain.[7]

From the perspective of those who believe in and carry out these suicide operations, there is a simple and plain logic. As Israeli soldiers shell and kill Palestinians indiscriminately, Palestinian suicide bombers strap themselves with explosives and kill Israelis indiscriminately.[8] They perceive every Israeli as the enemy who has robbed them of their land and is responsible for their misery. If Israel can carry out its incursions with the most sophisticated American-made war machinery, the Palestinians carry out their resistance with even the most elementary crude homemade explosives. If Israel drives its tanks to destroy and devastate Palestinian areas, the suicide bombers use their own bodies as tanks and shells to destroy and devastate Israeli areas. If the oppressors have the heart (or should one say lose the heart) to kill women and children and to make the life of Palestinians miserable, the suicide bombers are not going to spare Israeli lives as well.

Moreover, Sharon has insisted repeatedly that Israel is involved in a war with the Palestinians. In war, soldiers give themselves up on behalf of their country whether their country is the aggressor or fending off aggression. Officially speaking, some countries argue that the Palestinian suicide bombers are not proper soldiers that belong to an internationally recognized state and their resistance, therefore, cannot be considered legitimate. Some Palestinians would, however, argue that if what is going on is a war as Israel claims it is, then in war the whole nation is mobilized and different militia groups become engaged in resisting the occupation of their country as happened in France during WW II. Furthermore, in war, most armies and militias do not always comply with codes of war ethics and many civilians as well as military are killed.[9] Some have argued that the suicide bombers are also fighting a war and killing as many of the enemy as they can so that the psychological warfare can create panic and fear as well as contribute to weakening and capitulation. In this same vein, how does one view the US atomic bombing of two major cities in Japan during the WW II and the killing of over 170,000, most of them civilians?

The militants go on to argue that what they are doing is precisely like a soldier in battle who carries out a heroic act by storming a club within a military camp and blowing himself up, killing soldiers as well as women and children who happen to be enjoying a party. If one looks at it in this context of warfare, then it happens all the time. No war has been free from such acts and its actors were labeled heroes and were awarded medals posthumously. They were not called terrorists. In the West such acts are deemed heroic, but in Islam, due to the close ties between God and country, they are given a religious character and the people involved are considered "*shuhada*" (martyrs); their act is martyrdom and its prize is paradise rather than a human military medal. When one considers it from the angle of being engaged in war and the defense of one's homeland, these militants would argue that the suicide bombings could be a legitimate way of resistance.

A Muslim Perspective

The suicide bombings become a more powerful phenomenon when their religious underpinnings are emphasized. According to Hamas leader, Khaled Mash'al, there are three main reasons, namely, the religious, the nationalist or patriotic, and the humanitarian. The latter means that the suicide bomber sacrifices himself in order for his people to live.[10]

It is difficult to determine whether the religious dimension followed and enhanced the political decision for its use or whether the religious significance preceded and prompted it. It is most likely that both went hand in hand since any Palestinian killed by Israel whether a militant or an innocent bystander, was regarded as a martyr. Consequently, groups like Hamas were referring to these acts not as suicide bombings but as "martyrdom operations" and "martyrdom weapons."[11] Nationalism and faith have been fused together and imbued with power. People regarded the suicide bombers as martyrs and believed that paradise awaited them. Their rewards include forgiveness, companionship with the prophets, becoming friends of God in heaven, and intercession on behalf of their families on the Day of Judgment.

In one of the sermons preached by Sheikh Isma'il al-Adwan and broadcast on Palestinian TV, the Sheikh said, "The *shahid*, if he meets

Allah (Arabic for God), is forgiven his first drop of blood; he's saved from the grave's confines; he sees his seat in heaven; he's saved from judgment day; he's given seventy two dark-eyed women; he's an advocate for seventy members of his family."[12] Be that as it may, these martyrs believe they are fighting for the cause of God and their place in heaven is, therefore, guaranteed. An important quotation from the *Qur'an* in this regard is "Count not those that were slain in God's path as dead, but rather living with their Lord, by Him provided."[13]

Other Muslims argued strongly that Islamic law forbids the killing of non-combatants and therefore, the killing of innocent Israelis is wrong. Imam Yahya Hendi is a *Qur'anic* scholar who is the Muslim chaplain at Georgetown University. In his website[14], he gives a *Qur'anic* view of *Jihad*, martyrdom, and terrorism and violence. On *Jihad*, he emphasizes the personal form of *jihad* which is the intimate struggle to purify one's soul and spirit from sin. This *jihad* takes precedence over the physical *jihad* in which Muslims wage wars against oppression and transgression. He quotes the verse "Fight in the cause of Allah those who fight you, but do not transgress limits; for Allah loves not transgressors."[15] This verse speaks of a defensive war that is waged to stop the aggression but not to go beyond it. "The idea is that justice prevails. You don't fight because you enjoy fighting, but because there is an oppression," the implication being that it does not involve the killing of civilians.

On martyrdom, Imam Hendi says clearly that those who die in the service of God are martyrs, "...though that service needs to be of a different sort than that provided by terrorists." He gives a number of illustrations. "Suppose I'm on the pulpit teaching and giving my sermon; if someone shoots me because of what I'm saying about God, the *Qur'an* says I'm not really dead because I'm with God. If I'm feeding the poor, and calling for justice, I can't be called dead. My soul is alive and God sustains me...So to claim martyr status, all terrorists have to do is convince themselves that they are fighting for 'justice,' which is, of course, highly subjective....[Terrorists] think if they hurt Americans, they serve the cause of justice. They use these [*Qura'nic*] verses". Imam Hendi says that the *Qur'an* has many verses about martyrdom that must not cause harm to others. He quotes prophet Muhammad as saying, "Do not attack a temple, a church, a synagogue. Do not bring a tree or a plant down. Do not harm a horse or a camel..."

Finally, Imam Hendi has a section on terrorism and violence. He clearly states that, "the *Qur'an* doesn't condone terrorism, though

Muhammad was the leader of a military force and therefore used violence....While there are passages in the *Qur'an*, like the Old Testament of the Bible, that celebrate military victory, the overall gestalt of the *Qur'an* promotes a more restrained view....'We ordained for the Children of Israel that if anyone slew a person—unless it be for murder or for spreading mischief in the land—it would be as if he slew the whole people: and if anyone saved a life, it would be as if he saved the life of the whole people.'[16] This passage places a great value on the sanctity of a single life. 'If you kill one person it's as if you kill all humanity'" says Imam Hendi. He ends this article with the words, "the *Qur'an* goes one step further in chapter 8, verse 61, 'But if the enemy incline towards peace, do thou (also) incline towards peace, and trust in Allah.'"[17]

Hamas Perspective

The suicide bombings have been carried out by four militant Palestinian organizations. These are: Hamas, Al-Jihad Al-Islami (Islamic Jihad), Kata'ib Al-Aqsa, the Popular Front for the Liberation of Palestine, and the Democratic Front for the Liberation of Palestine. The first two are religiously based while the third is mainstream and connected with Fatah. The latter two are left wing and secular. It is significant to point out that the Popular Front did not carry out any suicide bombing except after Israel assassinated its secretary general Abu Ali Mustafa on 27 August 2001.[18]

A variant Islamic view is expressed by Khaled Mash'al, one of the leaders of Hamas. In the same interview on Al Jazeera satellite TV station on June 29, 2002, Khaled said that had the international community done justice to the Palestinians, there would have been no reason for it to resort to martyrdom operations. He considered these operations as very effective. He mentioned several reasons. The cumulative number of casualties and losses which Israel cannot continue to sustain; their impact in causing the emigration of Jews out of Israel; the rise of the unemployment rate in Israel and the worsening of its economy; the low morale of the people; but most of all, the fact that the Israeli army does not have a weapon that can match these operations.

In other words, militant Islamic groups saw the suicide bombings as a powerful weapon that inflicted not only a heavy human toll but also a psychological trauma affecting a large segment of Israeli society and exposing Israel's vulnerability. Indeed, the suicide bombings shook the Israeli state and caused widespread panic and terror. Consequently, Israel heightened its media warfare against the Palestinians, locally and internationally, comparing its predicament to that of the United States in its fight against terrorism; and comparing Palestinian "terrorism" with that of Osama Ben Laden and his Al-Qa'ida network. Israel did not mention its illegal Occupation of the Palestinian territories and domination of a whole nation. Therefore, many people in the West, especially in the United States fell in the Israeli trap, not discerning the great difference between what has happened in the United States on September 11 and what is happening to a people who have been subjected to a harsh and brutal occupation.

In fact, it is important to point out that with the tremendous imbalance of military power between the Palestinians and Israel, some Palestinian militants have commented that due to the effectiveness of the suicide bombings there has been a relative balance of fear. The casualties on the Palestinian side were approximately four times higher than on the Israeli side but the suicide bombings brought an equalizing effect in the spread of fear and terror within Israel thus raising drastically the number of Israeli casualties. For those who believe in the armed struggle, such statements are considered significant. It reflects that the weak are not as weak as they seem to be, and the strong are not as strong as they think they are.

Mash'al mentioned that 120 persons have already given themselves up for the sake of God and the homeland. Half of them were university graduates and most of the rest are graduates of high school with only few who only finished primary school. Another Hamas leader reported on TV that 75% of all the Israelis killed by Palestinians were killed through suicide bombings: "And if Israel wanted to call it 'terrorism', so be it. Did not Yitsak Rabin, the late Prime Minister of Israel, himself call terrorism the weapon of the powerless?"[19]

Effects and Outcome

Although Israel was deeply hurt by suicide bombings, the consequences that the extremists were hoping would happen did not take place. One can ponder the following:

- Israel had many more options than the Palestinians thought they did. As it turned out, Israel had a good number of military options; and due to its successful media campaign, everything it did was justified as self-defense. In spite of its gross violations of international law including the perpetration of war crimes, it managed to escape the censure of the international community. Israel did not exhaust all its options, while the Palestinians had very few.

- The West Bank is not southern Lebanon. Hizballah was, indeed, successful in driving the Israeli army from southern Lebanon after 22 years of occupation. According to the 1919 Zionist map, southern Lebanon was clearly envisioned as part of the future Israeli state. So was most of the eastern side of the Jordan. Israel recognizes, however, that not everything envisaged is realizable. It made its calculations and withdrew from Lebanon. Undoubtedly, Hizballah's resistance played a crucial role, but there were other factors. The West Bank is different. Religious Jewish settlers and right wing Zionists find strong biblical and historical roots in the West Bank and it will not be easy to evict them from there. The presence of the illegal settlements is one of the most difficult issues in the struggle for peace.
- The United States is the only great world power today and has an unflinching commitment to the well-being and security of the state of Israel. It will come to its rescue politically, militarily, and economically whenever needed.
- Israel was successful in its media campaign internationally. Many countries in the world are against suicide bombings.
- The Israeli society did not crumble economically in spite of hardships.
- The vast majority of the Israeli people, perceiving the struggle as a fight for the very existence of the state of Israel, supported Sharon and his right wing policies.

Palestinian Condemnation

Although suicide bombings were condemned by some Palestinians including the Palestinian Authority, they were accepted popularly by many as a way of avenging the Israeli army's daily killings of resistance fighters and innocent Palestinians. And while the American government rushed to condemn suicide bombings and expected same from the Palestinian Authority, Israel's killing of Palestinian leaders and ordinary civilians did not abate and passed as self defense and was not condemned publicly by the United States.

Be that as it may, it is important to reiterate clearly that the Palestinian community is not totally in support of the suicide bombings. Although there are Palestinians who are sympathetic, many have denounced them. On Wednesday, June 16, 2002, 58 Palestinian men and women, Muslims and Christians, among whom are well known personalities, signed a public statement published by the most read Arabic daily, *Al-Quds* asking for a halt to all suicide bombings. They made it clear that such operations only widen and deepen the hate and resentment between Palestinians and Israelis. It also destroys the possibility for the two peoples to live in two states side by side. The statement mentioned that the suicide bombings are counterproductive and will not lead to the fulfillment of the Palestinian national aspirations. It only allows Israel to justify its increasingly vicious attacks on Palestinian towns and villages. The statement was published in the paper on five consecutive days before it was transferred to the website with hundreds more signatories. Over 500 people expressed their desire to see a termination of any suicide operations.

Israeli Reaction

There were voices inside Israel that were calling for more drastic and severe measures to curb the suicide bombings. One of those was Gideon Ezra, the deputy public security minister who openly on television on August 19, 2001, called on his government to execute the families of Palestinian suicide bombers. He argued that if potential suicide bombers know that their families will be wiped out, then they will refrain from committing the act. Apparently, Ezra was basing his suggestion on a Nazi practice that used to arrest and inflict suffering on the families of those who were suspected of undermining the state. Historian Moshe Zimmerman of the Hebrew University has stated that under the Nazis if someone shot a German soldier and was not caught, fifty people would hang. Shockingly, Ezra's words did not draw any protest or criticism from the Israeli government.[20] Certainly, not all the voices inside Israel are as extreme as that of Ezra.

By contrast, there are courageous voices that called on their Israeli government to examine its harsh policies against the Palestinians that breed suicide bombings. In one case, Rami and Nurit Elhanan lost their 14-year-old daughter, who was killed by a Palestinian suicide bomber in September 1997. In spite of the tragic loss, the parents became actively involved in peacemaking. They blamed the Israeli Occupation calling it "a cancer that is feeding terror. Israel is becoming a graveyard of children. The Holy Land is being turned into a wasteland. Our daughter was killed because of the terror of Israeli Occupation. Every innocent victim from both sides is a victim of the Occupation." In spite of the fact that Rami's grandparents, aunts, and uncles had perished in the Holocaust, he said, "The pain of losing our beautiful daughter is unbearable, but our house is not a house of hate...." Nurit said, "Hamas take power from the anger of people. If you restored people's dignity, honour and prosperity by ending Occupation, Hamas would lose power." The couple established the Bereaved Family Forum with Izzat Ghazzawi, a Palestinian whose 16-year-old son Ramy was killed by Israeli troops.[21]

Another example is that of Shamai Leibowitz who on June 27, 2002, wrote a letter entitled "An Israeli Officer's Response To President Bush." He introduced himself in the following way: "I am an Orthodox Jew and a criminal defense attorney in Tel Aviv. I am also a tank gunner in reserve duty, and part of a group of 1000 soldiers who have refused to serve in the Occupied Territories. Many of them were imprisoned in military jails in the past few months." Then he added the words, "Now that President Bush has enlightened us with his new 'Plan' for the Middle East, we can only wonder how long it will take him to realize that his plan is useless and meaningless....His [Bush's] failure to understand that no progress can be made while a whole nation [Palestinian] is being brutally occupied is the basic flaw in this policy. Bush fails to comprehend that the suicide bombings are a product of mass starvation and humiliation of the Palestinian people. Bush's aides are doing us so much harm by refusing to acknowledge that only an immediate end to the Israeli Occupation will bring an immediate end to the Palestinian uprising.

"We are now witnessing a situation in which 3.5 million people have no future, no hope, no vision, other than to become terrorists and avenge the continued harassment and shelling by the Israeli army's helicopters, tanks and artillery. While Bush has never set foot in this region, we have been living here, watching how the Palestinians were trampled and denied basic rights on a daily basis, besieged and occupied in every possible way. Our Jewish sources teach us that where there is no justice, there is no peace....Most Israelis know deep in their hearts that once we stop humiliating and oppressing this nation, we will return to become a safe and secure democratic Israel living next to a viable Palestinian State..."[22]

A Christian Response

One definition of a martyr is "one who chooses to suffer death rather than renounce a religious principle; one who makes great sacrifices for a cause or principle; one who endures great suffering." From their political and religious perspective, the suicide bombers have made the supreme sacrifice, the offering of themselves for their faith (in the way they understand God) and for their homeland.

In Arabic, the verb *shaheda* means to witness. *Shahid* is a martyr, that is, a person who has suffered death as a witness to his faith or the principles he/she stands for. In the Palestinian struggle, it has been used to refer to those Palestinians killed by the Israeli army as well as for those who voluntarily sacrificed their life for Palestine. The death of a *shahid* including those suicide bombers became a cause of pride for the family though that in itself does not lessen the pain and grief of their loved ones.[23]

In English the word for martyr is derived from the Greek *martus* and, like the Arabic, simply means a person who has given himself up as a witness. It was first used in the early Christian centuries to indicate the witness for Christ of the early apostles. When Christians were persecuted the word started to refer to those who underwent some form of suffering for their faith. Eventually, it was used exclusively for those who died for the faith.[24]

In discussing suicide bombings from a religious perspective, it is worthwhile to reflect, though briefly, on the story of Samson. His story occupies four chapters in the book of Judges (13–16). Many Christians have been held spellbound when they, as children or adults, heard its fascinating details. It is a story of a strong young man who rose up to save his people who were oppressed by the coastal powerful neighbor, the Philistines.[25] Obviously from the perspective of the Israelites, he was regarded as a hero and a freedom fighter while from the perspective of the people of power, namely, the Philistines, he was, in today's language, a terrorist.

According to the story, Samson was very successful in his brave adventures against his enemies. Eventually, he was captured by the Philistines and tortured. They pulled out his eyes and kept him in jail. In order to celebrate their victory over their archenemy, Samson, the Philistines brought him to a big event attended by three thousand men and women including their five kings. His final act of revenge took place when he pushed the two main columns of the building and pulled it down killing himself and all the attendees. Samson's final prayer seems very similar to the prayer of a suicide bomber before he blows himself up: "Lord God, remember me and strengthen me only this once, O God, so that with this one act of revenge I may pay back the Philistines for my two eyes."[26] Our purpose can well be served by a barrage of questions.

Read in the light of today's suicide bombers how do we evaluate the story of Samson? Was not Samson a suicide bomber? Was he acting on behalf of the God of justice who wills the liberation of the oppressed? Was God pleased with the death of thousands of men and women of the Philistines? Are we confronted with many similar stories today in the experience of suicide bombers? Is it legitimate to tell the story today by substituting the name Ahmad for Samson? Is it possible that the God of justice is as active today in working out the liberation of the oppressed Palestinians through the likes of Ahmad? Is the dynamic under which God operates that of Jew versus other people or is it that of oppressor versus oppressed? Do we see the divine involvement of God in one story and not the other? Is the story of Samson legitimate because it is written in the Bible while the story of Ahmad is rejected because it is not and therefore he is condemned as a terrorist? Do we have the courage to condone both as acts of bravery and liberation or condemn both as acts of violence and terror? Is not injustice considered injustice whether inflicted by the ancient Philistines against the Hebrews or by the modern state of Israel against today's Palestinians? Or do we hold a theology of a biased God who only stands with Israel whether right or wrong?[27]

Although some people in our Palestinian community admire the sacrifice of the suicide bombers and view it as the ultimate in the offering of oneself for the sake of the homeland and the liberation of the people, and although we understand its deeper motivation and background, we condemn it from both our position of faith as well as a legitimate method for resisting the Occupation. Our reasons are based on the following points:

- We condemn suicide bombings because they are a crime against God. Ultimately, it is only God our creator who gives us life and who can take it. Therefore, the sixth commandment, "you shall not murder" applies as much to murdering oneself as it does to murdering others. If it is a crime to shed another person's blood, it must be equally criminal, if not more seriously so, to shed one's own blood. If the second greatest commandment is to love our neighbor as we love our own selves, then to kill one's self is a greater sin since it eradicates the basis for loving the other.

Suicide is a sin against God who has blessed us with the gift of life.[28] Those who love God do not kill themselves. Moreover, those who love God do not kill themselves for the sake of God. Indeed, they should be ready to die and even be killed for God's sake, but they will not do it themselves.

Christian history is full of examples of people who suffered torture and death rather than renounce their faith and love of God. In the New Testament, we have only one case of suicide and that was Judas Iscariot.[29] Although we understand the reasons behind his suicide, we believe that he committed a sin. Instead he should have repented of his crime in betraying Jesus and would have certainly received forgiveness. It is true, we do not find anywhere in the Bible a condemnation of suicide but the implication is that it is God who gives and takes life. Later on, the church condemned it. Inference was made from passages such as I Corinthians 6:19–20 where Paul writes, "...do you not know that your body is a temple of the Holy Spirit within you, which you have from God, and that you are not your own? For you were bought with a price; therefore glorify God in your body." And Ephesians 5:29, "For no one ever hates his own body, but he nourishes and tenderly cares for it, just as Christ does for the church...."[30] The person who has committed suicide was considered the only true atheist who has no faith or hope in God and who has totally given up on life. Probably this is why traditionally the church did not allow those who committed suicide to have church burials. Taking one's own life was considered a sin against a loving, creator God.

One can look at it from another angle. According to the Gospels, Jesus Christ knew that he was going to die in Jerusalem. "...The Son of Man must undergo great suffering, and be rejected...and killed...."[31] Yet he did not try to escape from danger but set his face to go to Jerusalem where he was killed. We believe that he voluntarily offered himself for the sin of the world. We see his death as vicarious and redemptive. He said, "No one has greater love than this, to lay down one's life for one's friends."[32] This means that to give oneself on behalf of others is the greatest sacrifice of all. Christians believe that this is precisely what Christ has done. He died for us. Although one offers oneself to die, he does not pull the trigger and kill himself. He is open to sacrificing himself for the cause but he is not the one who does it.

- We condemn it because we believe that we must refrain from inflicting suffering or death on others. From a Christian point of view, the tragedy lies in the fact that these young men and women do not only kill themselves but also cause the death of others, many of whom are civilians and innocent. We must hasten to add that we equally condemn the state of Israel's killing of Palestinians. Indeed, it constitutes the underlying cause of the conflict. Be that as it may, from our position of faith we say that even when the cause for which a person kills himself/herself is noble, as it is in the case of Palestine, nothing justifies the killing of innocent people. Christ accepted suffering on himself and did not inflict it on others. When we intentionally inflict suffering and death on others and generate untold suffering on their relatives, we are sinning against God and neighbor.

In fact from a New Testament perspective, when Christians suffer, it should make them more compassionate for the suffering of others rather than bitter and vengeful. The greatest form of bravery is, therefore, to bear suffering rather than to inflict it. In the struggle for civil rights in the United States, Martin Luther King Jr. recognized the heavy price that needs to be paid for freedom but refused to accept any violent method to achieve it. He said, "Rivers of blood may have to flow before we gain our freedom, but it must be our blood." Indeed, "King insisted on the teaching of Jesus and Gandhi that unearned suffering is redemptive. The willingness to suffer is the utmost expression of human freedom."[33] If the choice is between inflicting suffering on others or bearing suffering, it is better to accept suffering on oneself rather than inflict it on others. This is tantamount to taking the high moral ground in the conflict, the very thing that we as Christians must take. Furthermore, for the Christian, suffering endured can serve as evidence of Christ's victory over suffering and death.[34] It can also be a way of exposing the evil and the injustice that must be resisted.

- We condemn it because we believe that when we are confronted by injustice and evil, we must resist it without using its evil methods. We must endure suffering when inflicted upon us by unjust governments. We bear it but do not accept, submit, or succumb to it. Nonviolent resistance is an important tool for use against the enemy. Violence only breeds violence. Some Christians have developed nonviolent direct action as a method of resisting unjust governments and systems. Martin Luther King Jr. expressed it well when he wrote: "The ultimate weakness of violence is that it is a descending spiral begetting the very thing it seeks to destroy. Instead of diminishing evil, it multiplies it. Through violence you may murder the liar, but you cannot murder the lie, nor establish the truth. Through violence you murder the hater, but you do not murder hate. In fact, violence merely increases hate. Returning violence for violence multiplies violence, adding deeper darkness to a night already devoid of stars. Darkness cannot drive out darkness; only light can do that. Hate cannot drive out hate; only love can do that."[35]

The Israeli Occupation of Palestinian land is evil and unjust. It must be resisted for the sake of both the oppressed as well as the oppressors. It is our faithfulness to God that drives us to work for justice and for the ending of the Occupation of Palestine. But it must be carried out through nonviolence no matter how long it takes. It is only nonviolence that can guarantee the restoration of the humanity of both when the conflict is over. Moreover, nonviolent resistance contributes to a speedier process of reconciliation and healing because it does not impinge on and violate the human dignity of people.

- For the Christian, the supreme example is Christ. "When he was abused, he did not return abuse; when he suffered, he did not threaten; but he entrusted himself to the one who judges justly."[36] This is not passive resignation. It is total surrender to the God of justice who established this world on justice and who is going to make sure that injustice does not have the last word. This does not mean, however, that we must not combat injustice and resist it, but it means total surrender and faith in the God who will ultimately vindicate us. Archbishop Desmond Tutu has often said that this is a moral world and God will not allow injustice to continue.[37]

We condemn suicide bombings because they are trapped in the same violent logic exercised and perpetrated by the Israeli government. They are based on the law of revenge expressed in "an eye for an eye and a tooth for a tooth". Although it is very difficult for us as humans, we are still encouraged as Christians to seek a higher law. "Beloved, never avenge yourselves, but leave room for the wrath of God; for it is written, 'Vengeance is mine, I will repay, says the Lord.' No, 'If your enemies are hungry, feed them; if they are thirsty, give them something to drink; for by doing this you will heap burning coals on their heads'. Do not be overcome by evil, but overcome evil with good."[38]

- It is probable that Prime Minister Sharon (along with the right wing religious extremist ministers and settlers around him including some Christian Zionists) believes that the war against the Palestinians can be justified biblically because he is doing exactly what Joshua did in the Old Testament. Therefore, as Joshua's actions pleased God so must Sharon's actions. Similarly, the suicide bombers believe that by blowing themselves up and killing those around them they are fighting in the cause of God by ridding their land of the injustice inflicted on it by "infidels," and so earning for themselves a place in paradise.

Our basic problem with both lies in their concept of God. We reject any understanding of God that reflects war, violence, or terrorism. The God that we have come to know in Jesus Christ is a God of peace, mercy, and love. Moreover, God is a God of justice, but God's justice is not expressed in violence or in terrorizing people. God's justice is expressed supremely in love, peace, and forgiveness.

- In the midst of the injustice, suffering, and death inflicted on us, we believe that God in Christ is there with us. Christ is not in the tanks and jet fighters, fighting on the side of the oppressors (although many Jewish and Christian Zionists believe that). God is in the city of Gaza, in the Jenin camp and in the old cities of Nablus, Ramallah, and Bethlehem suffering with the oppressed.[39] God has not abandoned us. We reject suicide bombings because, from a Christian perspective, they reflect feelings of total despair and hopelessness. We must never lose hope. Our hope must be anchored in God who is ultimately our savior and liberator. The words of the psalmist are very apt to our situation, "I say to God, my rock, 'Why have you forgotten me? Why must I walk about mournfully because the enemy oppresses me?' As with a deadly wound in my body, my adversaries taunt me, while they say to me continually, 'Where is your God? Why are you cast down, O my soul, and why are you disquieted within me? Hope in God; for I shall again praise him, my help and my God.'"[40]

- We condemn suicide bombings because they practice, in essence, collective punishment against people many of whom are civilians. They are guilty of the very things Palestinians detest in the Israeli government. When suicide bombers commit collective punishment, they become what they loathe. One of the most hated and resented acts of the Israeli army is its exercise of collective punishment against the Palestinians. It is possible that the protagonists of suicide bombings would say that collective punishment is not intentional or deliberate. It is an unfortunate collateral that comes with the resistance. This is basically the same rationale that Israel gives when it imposes curfews, siege, and closures on hundreds of thousands of Palestinians. Whatever justification the government of Israel or the perpetrators of suicide bombings may have, the end result is what counts. Innocent people are harmed and killed. When the Israeli army incarcerates whole towns for long periods of time or a suicide bomber blows himself up in a market place and indiscriminate killing ensues, both are collective punishment directed at largely innocent people. Consequently, the basic principle must be affirmed: it is unjust and immoral to punish people collectively.

Moreover, if the Israeli government carries out collective punishment frequently, that should not be an excuse for Palestinians to follow suit. The old question expressed by Abraham to God regarding the destruction of Sodom and Gomorrah continues to persist today, "Will you indeed sweep away the righteous with the wicked?"[41] When that is done, it is a crime. To punish people indiscriminately, including the elderly and the sick, women and children, is one of the most savage and brutal behaviors exercised by people of power in the past as well as in the present.

In its primitive religious form, one can find examples in the Old Testament where God warns the ancient Israelites that he will punish the "children for the iniquity of parents, to the third and the fourth generation."[42] In another story, Achan disobeys Joshua's order and out of greed takes some of the spoils of war that were forbidden. Although Achan confessed his sin, he was taken, at the command of God, "with his sons and daughters, with his oxen, donkeys, and sheep, and his tent and all that he had...and all Israel stoned him to death; they burned them with fire, cast stones on them...."[43] Tragically, acts of collective punishment have been wrongly attributed to God by humans in order to justify their own beastly behavior against their fellow human beings. Such acts, basically contradict our concept of the God of mercy and love. Even God's justice is not void of mercy.

At the time of the exile, several hundred years later, many people believed that God had not dealt with them justly; that they were suffering for the sin of others. They could only express it in the words of a popular proverb, "The parents have eaten sour grapes, and the children's teeth are set on edge."[44] Both Jeremiah and Ezekiel began to articulate a different theology that essentially said, only "the person who sins shall die."[45] It was a reversal of long held beliefs. Unfortunately, throughout history, people in power, whether religious or not, continued to exercise the indiscriminate punishment of people and justify it by giving it divine sanction.

In modern times, the United Nations' Fourth Geneva Convention clearly prohibits collective punishment. Article 33 of the Convention makes it clear that "No protected person may be punished for an offense he or she has not personally committed. Collective penalties and likewise all measures of intimidation or terrorism are prohibited." We know that the government of Israel practices collective punishment in order to control and bring the Palestinians into submissiveness—the extended curfews, the detention of large numbers of people for lengthy periods for alleged offenses, the destruction of homes, and many other techniques. Suicide bombings, whether deliberate or not, perpetrate collective punishment. They are punishing all Israelis for the evil policies of their government. Some Palestinians, as already indicated, might justify suicide bombing due to the heavy oppressive nature of Israel's Occupation or link it to human nature's propensity to retaliate by inflicting as much pain and damage against the enemy. In spite of all of that, it is important to lift up the moral and ethical principles of international law, namely, that collective punishment is wrong and must be stopped at all cost.

- Although people may be ready to die for their faith or even for their country, they need to do everything they can to stay alive and witness in life rather than kill themselves. So long as they are alive, they have the opportunity to witness to the truth. Indeed, they need to remain faithful until death[46] but they must not give up on life and kill themselves. Their life is a gift from God and they must not destroy it. We must live the life we have to its fullest. Christ has come so that we might have life and that we might have it abundantly.[47] To end one's life abruptly is to end the opportunities God presents us with, and the possibilities of contributing to the building of a better society. Standing before Pilate Jesus said, "For this I was born and for this I have come into the world to bear witness to the truth."[48] People in power tried to kill the truth by killing him, but he did not kill himself. When they killed him, the truth could not be silenced. It was revealed and exposed more widely.

We reject suicide bombings because we believe in life before death as well as life after death. In spite of the despairing situation, these young men and women deserve to live. Many times, even though life around us is difficult and frustrating, one can give and receive joy and love with family and friends. Even in the darkest of hours, it is possible to find some beauty and inner peace. Many times when things are very gloomy, it is possible to find some contentment in the service of others. Life can always offer new opportunities and it is worth living.

Conclusion

Our faith motivates and drives us to act justly, love mercy, and walk humbly with God.[49] We cannot condone suicide bombings in any way or, for that matter, any use of violence and terror whether perpetrated by the state or militant groups. By the grace of God, we must always try to take the high moral ground in any conflict. We must not allow ourselves to succumb to hate or walk the road of vengeance and malice. As we continue to struggle for justice, peace, and reconciliation in Israel/Palestine, we must keep lifting up the prophetic vision of a world without violence, a world where people (Israelis and Palestinians) will "beat their swords into plowshares, and their spears into pruning hooks; [where] nation shall not lift up sword against nation, neither shall they learn war any more."[50] This vision is realistic and achievable. Israelis and Palestinians can live together in peace if Israel will be willing to share the land with them and accept the establishment of a viable Palestinian state.

Unfortunately, the present policies of the government of Israel, and those internationals that support those policies, do not lend themselves to such a peace. In fact, Israel is creating *bantustans* (homelands, reservations) for the Palestinians and an Israeli form of *apartheid* that is much worse than what was practiced in South Africa. Today it is Israel that is creating and breeding extremism on the Palestinian side. Indeed, the Occupation of the West Bank, including East Jerusalem and the Gaza Strip continues to be the root cause of the violence and terror. This cycle of terror perpetuated today is simply shutting the door on the future for both people. It is killing not only the present but the future. We must guard against murdering the future. That will only shut the door to healing and reconciliation.

Ultimately, there cannot be room for hate if we want to live together. And live together we must. The sooner we put an end to the occupation the better our life will be. Ending the Occupation will certainly end the suicide bombings. All peace-loving people, whether people of faith or not, must exert greater concerted effort to work for the ending of the Occupation. Ultimately, justice will prevail, the occupation will be over, and the Palestinians, as well as the Israelis, will enjoy freedom and independence.

How do I know that this will take place? I know because I believe in God.

Notes

1 The American State Department defines terrorism as "Premeditated, politically motivated violence perpetrated against noncombatant targets by subnational groups or clandestine agents, usually intended to influence an audience". In the American definition, terrorism can never be inflicted by a state. This is a useful definition because, as Brian Whitaker writes, "it gets the US and its allies off the hook in a variety of situations. The disadvantage is that it might also get hostile states off the hook—which is why there has to be a list of states that are said to 'sponsor' terrorism while not actually committing it themselves." Under the State Department rules, if Palestinians attack a Jewish settlement with mortars it is considered terrorism. If, however, Israeli rockets attack a Palestinian community it is not because Israel is a state and states can never inflict terrorism (www.guardian.co.uk), May 7, 2001. To say that states cannot inflict terrorism betrays a lack of understanding of the depth of evil in our world and the direct involvement of many states in violence and terrorism. One wonders, is there really a clean and civilized "terrorism" committed by states and a dirty and barbaric "terrorism" perpetrated by militant groups? Palestinian daily experience has shown that it is the Israeli state injustice perpetuated through violence and terrorism against the Palestinians that has created and prompted its Palestinian counterpart. Ultimately, it boils down to whose definition it is. Brian Whitaker has written in the same article that a more honest definition of terrorism is this: "Terrorism is violence committed by those we disapprove of."

2 Out of 105 suicide bombers, three have been women.

3 Suzanne Goldenberg, "A Mission to Murder: Inside the Minds of the Suicide Bombers," *The Guardian* (UK), June 11, 2002. Since June 11th, the statistics have changed. As of August 1, 2002, 241 Israelis have been killed by suicide bombers; and total Israeli casualties are 593 (www.idf.il/daily). Number of suicide bombers who have died is 105 (www.phrmg.org). Total Palestinian casualties as of August 1,2002 are 1682 (www.miftah.org/report.cfm).

4 Khaled Abu Toameh, "Love and Hate," in *The Jerusalem Report*, May 20,2002, p. 27.

5 In an article entitled, "The Growing Hardships of Traveling in the West Bank," The Applied Research Institute, Jerusalem (July 2002) had given the following statistics on checkpoints: On the West Bank, 34 permanent check-points and 150 road blocks; in the Gaza Strip, 7 permanent and 7 road blocks. See www.arl.org

6 *The Phenomenon of Collaborators in Palestine*, PASSIA Publications, March 2001.

7 Apparently, some suicide bombers volunteer while others are recruited. The desperate political situation makes it relatively easy to have scores of can-didates. The preparatory stages are in effect accomplished by the Israeli army itself. It starts when these young people are traumatized, then brutalized, and eventually dehumanized by the impact of the Occupation. Once they reach that stage, they become easy recruits.

8 Some militant Palestinians would object to the use of the word "indiscrim-inate". They would say that they do not target children. A Hamas member stated, "There is nothing easier than putting a bomb in a school or sending a person with an explosives belt into a school, and the fact that Hamas has never done so, is evidence that they do take moral considerations into account...but in Israel, all of the civilians are soldiers, really. That's how we see" Amira Hass, "Driven by vengeance and a desire to defend the homeland," *Ha'aretz*, July 16, 2002, p. 4.

9 Scholars tell us that civilian deaths average 50% of all deaths in any given war. In the 1980's the percentage jumped to 74% and in the 1990's to 90%. It is estimated that in the 20th century 109 million people were killed in the dif-ferent wars, approximately half of those were civilians.Walter Wink, *The Powers That Be* (Doubleday, 1998), p. 137.

10 Al-Jazeera TV on 29 June 2002 in the "Open Debate" program with Khaled Mash'al.

11 See "Hamas Perspective" later.

12 Akiva Eldar, "'Ask Clinton what he thinks about Camp David," in *Ha'aretz*, August 21,2001. In an unpublished paper, Dr. Mustafa Abu Sway of Al Quds University maintains that the reference to the "seventy virgins" is neither mentioned in the Qur'an nor in the most authentic compendia of Hadith. It is, however, found in Mu'jam Al-Tabarani.

13 Qur'an 3:169

14 www.alhewar.org; e-mail: alhewar@alhewar.com

15 Qur'an 2:190

16 Qur'an 5:32

17 www.beliefnet.com

18 Amnesty Report in *Al-Quds* newspaper, 11 July 2002, p. 22.

19 Arno J. Mayer, Professor Emeritus of History at Princeton, has written in the wake of September 11, "...in modern times, acts of individual terror have been the weapon of the weak and the poor, while acts of state and economic terror have been the weapons of the strong." Quoted by Gore Vidal, *Perpetual War For Perpetual Peace: How We Got To Be So Hated* (Nation Books, 2002), p. xi.

20 Akiva Eldar, *ibid.*

21 Alexandra Williams, 'Our daughter was killed by a suicide bomber. But it is the terror of Israel's occupation that is to blame for her death," *The Mirror* (London), 25 June 2002.

22 Shamai Leibowitz, "An Israeli Officer's Response To President Bush," June 27, 2002, www.zmag.org. See also "The Ethics of Revenge", a moving speech of Yitzhak Frankenthal, chairman of the Families Forum given at a rally in Jerusalem on Saturday, July 27, 2002, outside Prime Minister Sharon's residence. magazine@tikkun.org. Frankenthal's son Arik was killed by Palestinians. He also blames the Israeli Occupation. He writes, "We lost sight of our ethics long before the suicide bombings. The breaking point was when we started to control another nation." He adds, "The Palestinians cannot drive us away—they have long acknowledged our existence. They have been ready to make peace with us; it is we who are unwilling to make peace with them. It is we who insist on maintaining our control over them; it is we who escalate the situation in the region and feed the cycle of bloodshed. I regret to say it, but the blame is entirely ours".

23 One of the criticisms voiced by Israel against the Palestinians and some Arab countries and especially Saudi Arabia has been regarding the payments given to the families of the martyrs.

Every family receives twenty five thousand dollars. Israel considers this payment an encouragement to young men to become suicide bombers and must be stopped. Most Palestinians, however, consider the money received not as an encouragement to suicide bombers but as a support to their families. One wonders whether Israel's condemnation of these payments implies that the families of the suicide bombers should be penalized. In fact, Israel has on numerous occasions demolished their homes mercilessly. Indeed, many times the family is not even aware of what their son is going to do. It is wrong, therefore, to inflict further pain and suffering on the family by starving them to death, or destroying their home, etc. as Israel would like to do. In the history of the church, a baby born out of wedlock was not penalized and thrown outdoor to die because he/she was born in sin. The baby was baptized and received as a child of God. It is right to support and comfort the family in spite of what its son/daughter has done. If Israel is so anxious to stop the suicide bombings it must consider stopping its oppressive Occupation and giving justice.

24 It is interesting to point out that some Christians have argued that the classic definition of a martyr should be expanded to include those who have been killed as a result of taking a prophetic stand against injustice and oppression; people like Dietrich Bonhoeffer, Martin Luther King, Jr., Oscar Romero, and others. These are people who have borne a witness and committed themselves to the struggle for justice and peace and consequently suffered for it. *Dictionary of the Ecumenical Movement*, eds. Nicholas Lossky, Jose Miguez Bonino, John S. Pobee, Tom F. Stransky, Geoffrey Wainwright, Pauline Webb, under "Martyrdom", by Rowan D. Crews, Jr. (WCC Publications, 1991), p. 660.

25 The Philistines are not racially or ethnically related to today's Palestinians. Some scholars believe that they were a sea people originating from the Aegean Islands and Crete. Others say that they came from the south and west coasts of Asia Minor between the 12–13th century B.C. and settled in the southern

coast of Palestine. Ultimately, during Roman rule, the whole area became known, by a slight variation of their name, as Palestine.

26 Judges 16:28

27 It is interesting that Samson's name is not mentioned among those who committed suicide in the *Interpreter's Bible Dictionary*. Although the word suicide does not appear in the Bible, there are people who committed the act. See for example, I Samuel 31 :4–5; II Samuel 17:23; I Kings 16:18.

28 The issue of suicide in today's world is not anymore black and white. It is a complicated phenomenon. There are people who due to terminal illness or deep psychological sickness and derangement attempt or indeed, take their life. Ultimately, it is only the merciful God who can judge. I am using it here in the context of our focus on suicide bombings.

29 Matthew 27:5

30 See also Romans 14:7–9

31 Mark 8:31; Matthew 16:21; Luke 9:22

32 John 15:13

33 *Dictionary of the Ecumenical Movement*, eds. Nicholas Lossky (& others) under "Suffering", by Dorothee Solie, p.963

34 2 Cor: 4: 14–18

35 From a sermon preached at Eutaw Alabama Church during the 1966 Alabama Tour. Poster produced by Community Printers and the Resource Center for Nonviolence in Santa Cruz, CA.

36 1 Peter 2:23

37 See highlights of Archbishop Tutu's address in a conference co-sponsored by Friends of Sabeel and the Episcopal Diocese of Massachusetts in Boston on April 13, 2002. *Cornerstone*, issue 24, Spring 2002, p. 3.

38 Romans 12:19–21

39 An eyewitness told me that in a meeting between Israeli officials and representatives of American Christian Zionist leaders, earlier this year, the request was made to the Christians to purchase arms for Israel. The Christian Zionists agreed to do that. When we hear such stories, we wonder whether we believe in the same God of love and peace.

40 Psalm 42:9–11

41 Genesis 18:23

42 Exodus 20:5

43 Joshua 7:24b–25

44 Ezekiel 18:2

45 EzekieI 18:20, Jeremiah 31 :29–30

46 Revelation 2:10

47 John 10: 1 0

48 John 18:37

49 Micah 8:6

50 Isaiah 2:4; Micah 4:3–4

CHAPTER EIGHT

Arab Christians— An Endangered Species

Riah Abu El-Assal

I n the second chapter of the Acts of the Apostles, we read of the presence of Arabs at the first Pentecost. Two millennia later, Arab Christians, largely unnoticed and in serious danger of extinction, still inhabit the land where the Christian Church and the Christian faith were born.

Although they are members of one the oldest communities of believers, present day Arab Christians are experiencing a new Diaspora. Not only is the psyche of every Palestinian Christian in Israel at peril; the very survival of the community is in gravest jeopardy. Some twenty-seven thousand Arab Christians inhabited Jerusalem in 1967; less than seven thousand remain. In Nazareth, the largest Arab city in Israel with a population of over fifty-five thousand, Christians formerly constituted a significant majority. Today; the figure is closer to thirty-four percent—and falling.

Arab Christians find these trends foreboding. Many in the Christian community in Israel today, especially the young, are voicing their fears of extinction. "So many people here are hoping we will simply disappear," they are saying. "All that would be left of our faith would be the holy shrines."

The causes of the new Diaspora are multiple. These include the manifold problems that Palestinian Christians in Israel share with their Muslim brothers and sisters: policies of economic, political and educational discrimination from a government which systematically violates the basic human rights of its Arab citizens.

Christians have always struggled to comprehend the mystery of the Trinity, three persons in One God. Palestinian Christians in Israel face a similar struggle of integrating the four persons within themselves: Arab, Palestinian, Christian, Israeli citizen. This struggle for identity is made all the more difficult when many of their Western brothers and sisters join with Zionist propagandists in distorting biblical teachings. The results of such distortions are political policies which drive Arab Christians, their children, and their children's children from the land of their birth—and the land of Jesus' birth.

The roots of Arab-Christian identity go deep into the soil of a region where, despite all difficulties, an indigenous Christian Church has survived for two thousand years. Such historic survival is nothing less than an awesome achievement. Arab Christianity has been buried beneath a superimposed Western veneer, the legacy of nearly one hundred years when the faith was closely aligned with European imperial power.

The history is complex, mingling alienation and hope. Not only were Arabs among the three thousand converts on that first Pentecost, but their numbers swelled when the Apostle Thomas reached Arabia on his way to India. In its first five centuries, the Church expanded broadly throughout the Middle East and North Africa. The Christian message profoundly influenced all the peoples of the region, including the founder of Islam, Muhammad. Arab literature records many individuals and tribes who altered the values of Arab society with their embrace of Christianity. (Also important was the social influence of those Arabs who converted to Judaism.) This historically-rooted indigenous character of Arab Christianity, however, has been concealed, not only from Western believers, but all too often from Arab Christians themselves,

Two highly significant events which took place in the sixth century had a deep and adverse effect on Christian life in Arabia, in the remainder of the Middle East, and in North Africa. In fact, their impact has been felt throughout the world.

The first event was theological. In an era when a multitude of heresies flourished throughout Christendom, one particular theology that spread through Arabia proclaimed a divine triad rather than a Trinity. The deity, according to this teaching, included God the Father, God the Mother, and God the Son. Muhammad refers to this teaching in the *Qur'an*: "God shall say, O Jesus, Son of Mary, hast thou said unto mankind, take me and my mother as two Gods, besides God?"(5:116). Therefore, when Muhammad appeared teaching the oneness of God, many Christians embraced Islam, initially unaware that it was a new and different religion. Likewise, in the West, much of European Christendom at first perceived Islam as simply another Christian, or possibly Jewish, heresy.

The second major event of this era was political. The spiritual imperialism of Byzantium, implemented in the Arabian Peninsula by its vassal Ethiopia, exerted a control so complete and so alien that, unsurprisingly, many Arab Christians welcomed Islam as a new indigenous power. They saw in it the promise of political liberation, and they saw in the Muslim army a force capable of restoring their freedom which had been lost for so many years.

These events conspired in the sixth century to cause those Arabs who clung to their Christian faith to do so at a cost to their Arab identity. Events of succeeding centuries did little to mitigate the growing perception of Christianity as an un-Arab religion. From the Crusades through the nineteenth and twentieth century, Western Christian missionaries have tended to view their Arab coreligionists as distant and somewhat backward cousins, rather than as full-fledged brothers and sisters in Christ. Moreover, they were almost invariably accompanied by mercantile entrepreneurs, military troops, and would-be political rulers. These forces all sought not only to bring the kingdom of God into "heathen territory," but also to promote the interests of Western economies and European princes and parliaments, inevitably at the expense of local business and Arab autonomy.

Muslim power structure, on the other hand, was indigenous to the region, rooted in its customs and mores, more tolerant of religious pluralism than their European counterparts. Until the time of the Ottoman Turks, Muslim ascendancy usually heralded periods of greater peace and tolerance than what ensued under Christian rule.

It should not surprise us, then, that the father of St. John of Damascus was the man to open the gates of his city to the incoming army of the Muslim Khaled ibn-al-Walid, or that the Jews of Spain welcomed the Muslim invaders as liberators. (In fact, for a short period, the Spanish Jews wrote Hebrew in Arabic script, as evidenced by the Geniza manuscripts.) Such events were symptomatic of a sort of religious/cultural schizophrenia already pervasive among Arab Christians that events of later periods would do little to alleviate.

The historical alienation of Arab Christians may have been made inevitable by certain philosophical underpinnings. Even in its earliest years, the development of the Christian faith was almost exclusively influenced by Western philosophy. For all its Eastern origins— Nazareth, Bethlehem, Jerusalem, Antioch, and Carthage in Tunis were, after all, the cradles—the shift of power to Rome and Constantinople in Christianity's formative years led to the notion that the faith was a Western invention.

Moreover, by the time of Muhammad, the true message of the Gospel lay buried under a heap of senseless superstition. Many believers were more enthusiastic about fighting over doctrinal controversies than spreading the word of God. In seventh century Arabia, distortion of the faith took such forms as worship of the wood of the cross and of images of holy men as well as extreme forms of Mariolatry. One sect, the Collydrian, allowed the Virgin to share the Godhead. Many Manichean ideas invaded Christian thinking, including the notion that Simon of Cyrene had been crucified rather than Christ. External rites and bodily exercises were emphasized at the expense of the inner spiritual life.

Furthermore, the whole structure of Church and empire was founded on a foreign hierarchy and an alien Greek philosophy. Christianity as Muhammad encountered it, was both error-filled and without indigenous identity. It was no longer the religion of the people with God personified one of their own; it had become the imposed faith of conquerors whose adherents were, all too often, rightly perceived as conspirators in the subjugation of their own people.

This perception was scarcely lessened in later centuries by the Crusaders. They came into Arabia more zealous than any Muslim force to slaughter the infidels, to destroy homes as well as mosques, and to assume temporal as well as spiritual power, The chivalry of that most unlikely of conquerors, Salah Al-Din, is not yet forgotten in the Holy Land, nor is the treachery and brutality of the Frankish Christians who opposed him.

Even in the past two centuries, Arab Christians in the Holy Land have rarely been encouraged to affirm the roots of their faith in native soil. Until very recently, most Church institutions resembled small colonies administered and controlled by Europeans, with only the most menial roles assigned to an underclass of Palestinian Christians.

European languages were taught in the schools and used in the homes and churches, a fact which, while adding to the 'sophistication' of the students, further fragmented the indigenous Christian community. The various colonizing and missionary groups sought to impose their own imported customs and traditions on the local Christian population without regard to their suitability to Middle Eastern life.

Much of the cultural legacy of the French, Dutch, British, Italians, and Americans has its comic side, like convincing Arab Anglicans to observe high tea at four o'clock, Greenwich time! But it has harmed Palestinian Christians, already adherents to a faith considered alien and aberrant by their neighbors, leaving them without control of their own Church or power to implement the tenets of their faith.

A very telling example of cultural imperialism is the Greek Orthodox Church. Though its present population in the Middle East is over 99% Arab in origin, it continues to be known as "Greek." Its patriarchs, archbishops and bishops are all natives of Greece, and only recently has any of its liturgy been read or chanted in Arabic. The same pattern is generally true of the indigenous Roman Catholic and Anglican Churches, where only recently have some Arab bishops and patriarchs been named.

It is no wonder, then, that many Arab countries continue to view the Arab Christian community as foreign to the land and collaborators with Western dominated governmental and economic forces. Even smaller wonder that Arab Christians, who have endured such domination for centuries, sometimes wonder if their neighbors may not be correct. For young Palestinian Christians, the struggle for self-determination and justice is exacerbated by the tendency of some Christian Arabs, along with many Jews and Muslims, to view Christians as not Arab at all. Many young Lebanese Christians, to be 'true' to their faith, deny their very nationality, styling themselves Phoenicians rather than Lebanese.

This centuries-long effort by the West, reinforced by policies of the State of Israel, is reminiscent of efforts to create indigenous "European communities" in India and Africa. As the Lebanese example illustrates, the efforts have met with some success, convincing many Christians, not only in the Holy Land but also throughout the region that their roots are not in the soil of their countries but in Europe and America. They have come to believe that Christian belief is indivisible from Western social structures, forgetting the earthly roots of Jesus. The long years of oppression have done their work.

Modern Arab Christians, particularly if they are also Palestinians who are Israeli citizens, not only look west but also go west—often to stay. Encouraged by Western political powers, the exodus has reached such proportions that in Sweden some forty thousand Syrian and Iraqi Christians are now living in special villages. In every major city in the U.S., Canada, and Western Europe, there are now Arab quarters of significant population, most of them growing ever larger and nearly all of them predominantly Christian.

These migrations have a profound impact on global geopolitics. They tend to foster single religion states throughout the Middle East: Judaic in Israel, Muslim in the remaining countries. They also place at great risk the very survival of Christianity over an area extending from the Bosporus to the Indian subcontinent and from the Suez to the African Atlantic shore.

Many believe that, if current policies within Israel and among the Western democracies persist, the extinction of Arab Christians in the region is not only possible, but probable. It seems increasingly credible that, in the very foreseeable future, the Holy Land will have become only a place of pilgrimage, holy shrines without an indigenous Christian community. The new Diaspora may threaten not only Christians but their Muslim brothers and sisters as well.

Such is the stated goal of the growing political movement of the Israeli right, especially followers of politicians Kach and Moledet, who are calling for "transfer" of Arabs. Public opinion polls confirm an increasing support of this proposal, particularly among young Israeli Jews. The expulsion of Arabs from their homeland may be promoted by Israel as justified for security and may be implemented at a time when the international community is either busy with some crisis away from the Middle East, or as a result of ignorance of the facts on the ground and the indifference that comes as a result of such ignorance. This apparent indifference by the international community, including the worldwide Christian community, reinforces the perception of Palestinians that, in addition to currently being forced to live under a near *apartheid*-style regime, their potential "transfer" will evoke no outcry in the West.

Palestinian Christians face a particular dilemma. The universal animosity of Jews toward Christians as a result of centuries of anti-Semitism is readily understood. Yet, that same animosity directed against Christian Palestinian Arabs who originally welcomed the new Jewish settlers to their country is less easily comprehended.

The psychological problem is enormous for Palestinian Christians. Younger Palestinians are generally more conscious of their Arab and Palestinian identity than their parents. They analyze their situation and their options, wary of their historical heritage and the current fragility of democratic institutions in Israel, and they increasingly voice their concerns openly, as do many of their Jewish compatriots disturbed by current trends in Israel.

The choices open to Palestinian Christians are few. By accepting the status quo, they doom themselves and their children to second- or even third-class citizenship. By remaining in their homeland, they accept economic deprivation, substandard education, inadequate housing and social services, cultural rejection, and, in the best of circumstances, the muzzling of effective political participation. In the worst of circumstances, they would face overt repression and violation of the most basic of their human rights.

Yet any peaceful change in their situation requires the moral commitment of the West. Palestinians know the effectiveness of such a commitment—they have witnessed its value for the Zionist cause. That same commitment, often sought by Palestinians, has been withheld.

Still, Palestinian Christians seek that moral partnership, crying out to the Western democracies, and especially to their brothers and sisters in Christ. "Know that we exist," they say. "Make yourselves aware of our situation. Join your cry with ours for justice in our native land. Tell all around you that we must have justice if there is to be peace in the land of our Lord." That cry has come for nearly forty years from a people wracked by psychological trauma and deep historical alienation. The cry of the Palestinians and of all Arab Christians is induced not by madness but by the fact that they are entirely sane. Their cry continues because they know the results when it is not heard.

The alternative is ever more violence in a land where violence is already a fact of everyday life. The violence of the oppressor is answered by violence from the oppressed until the violence of the past will be understood only as prologue to a saga of bloody struggle. That violence is a part of a story of Holocaust and Diaspora for a people who have lived since before the days of Joshua on land made sacred by the footprints of the Prince of Peace.

CHAPTER NINE

A Peace Movement of Her Own

Gila Svirsky

People often ask why Israeli women need "a peace movement of their own," to paraphrase Virginia Woolf, who envisioned the need for an independent woman to have "a room of her own." To begin to answer that question, let me tell a story about a peace action in Israel that happened in January 1999. Although by then Israeli women had had a decade of thriving peace actions of our own, this story helps explain why we need to have our own movement:

A group of about 100 of us from Jerusalem and Tel-Aviv—men and women—traveled to Kifl Hares, a village where two Palestinian homes had been demolished by the army. When our buses arrived, we disembarked and began to walk along the road leading into the village. Soldiers immediately blocked our way and demanded that we leave. Instead, we decided to try to access the village from another road, even though we knew the soldiers would block our entry from there as well. As we were walking along the perimeter of the village, one of the women suddenly broke rank and began to cross the field in the direction of the village. It seemed so simple, and a group of us followed her, spreading out to make it harder for the soldiers to stop us.

The soldiers came at us quickly, grabbing us to prevent our progress. I made a quick head count of them and climbed on a mound to call out, "There are many more of us than soldiers. Just walk through peacefully, no violence." A few more of us broke ranks, but soon the soldiers were running back and forth to stop more of us from walking through the field. Against some, the soldiers were more violent than others. Gail was forcefully thrown to the ground. My arm was well twisted. Although the soldiers were blocking us only with their bodies—twisting arms, pushing, grabbing—I guess it was the M16's slung across their backs that prevented more of the larger group from following us. In the melee, seven of us made it past the soldiers and into the village. The rest fell back and returned to the buses.

Inside the village, we went to the site of the demolished homes and met the families. We expressed our horror at the events and pledged to return to help the families rebuild their homes. While we were talking, I had a call on my cell phone from someone in the group outside who told us that, following negotiations with the army, an official delegation of the peace activists who remained behind would be allowed through. Within an hour, we saw a group walking toward us along the main road.

It was at this moment that we looked around at ourselves and something struck us: Those of us who had taken the risk, broken through the soldiers, and reached the village were all women—while those in the self-appointed "official delegation"...were all men.

So what else is new? Women do the work and men are in charge. In Israel, women have consistently been a large part, and usually the majority, of the rank and file peace activists, and often led the pack in out-of-the-box thinking, as epitomized by Gail's breaking of rank in the above story. In fact, I think even more can be said: Ever since Women in Black began its first vigil in January 1988, women's peace activism in Israel has consistently been more varied and more progressive than the peace activism of the mixed-gender peace groups. It was more varied, because we didn't just hold the occasional rally but engaged in a wide variety of activities—conferences, lectures, marches, street theater, dialogue groups, along with bringing food and medicine to refugee camps and a seemingly endless series of vigils. It was more progressive because we took daring positions well before the mixed-gender groups did, from asserting "The PLO is the legitimate representative of the Palestinian people" to declaring "Jerusalem must be a shared capital."

The First Women in Black

The first women's peace movement in Israel was Women in Black, founded in January 1988, one month after the first Palestinian *intifada* (uprising) broke out. It began by a small group of Israeli women carrying out a simple form of protest: Once a week at the same hour and in the same location—a major traffic intersection—they donned black clothing and raised a black sign in the shape of a hand with white lettering that read "Stop the Occupation." Within months, by word of mouth, women throughout Israel had heard of this protest and launched dozens of vigils.

This began the 15-year history of the Women in Black movement, as it spread spontaneously from country to country, wherever women sought to speak out against violence and injustice in their own part of the world. In Italy, Women in Black protest a range of issues, from the Israeli Occupation to the violence of organized crime in Italy. In Germany, Women in Black protest neo-Nazism, racism against guest workers, and nuclear arms. In Bangalore, India, Women in Black hold vigils that call for an end to the ill treatment of women by religious fundamentalists. And during the war in the Balkans, Women in Black in Belgrade set a profound example of inter-ethnic cooperation that was an inspiration to their countrywomen and men.

Women in Black are often the target of attack by those who promote narrow nationalist views over reconciliation and peace. Verbal abuse on sexual themes is common. In both Israel and Serbia, where Women in Black have spoken out against the policies of their own political leadership, women in these vigils are frequently threatened and sometimes violently assaulted, accused of being traitors to their own country. Yet Women in Black have refused to step down from their courageous stand, preferring to serve as a continuous, public reminder that the oppression of others is an unacceptable option.

Outside Israel, the movement has received international recognition. In fact, the international movement of Women in Black was nominated for the Nobel Prize for Peace and won the Millennium Peace Prize awarded by the UN Development Fund for Women (UNIFEM), both in 2001.

Inside Israel, however, there has been a deafening silence. In fact, when we sent press releases to the Israeli newspapers about our nomination for the Nobel Peace Prize, and then called to ensure they were noticed, we were told that the story would not get in the paper. Why not, we asked? "Because this is not the right time for that sort of story," said the reporter for *Ha'aretz*, referring to the intense levels of violence raging. Not a single newspaper published it: in times of violence, one apparently should not be talking about peace!

The Coalition of Women for Peace

But talk about peace we do, especially during periods of violence. It took the women's movement only one month to get together and gear up after the start of the *Al Aqsa Intifada*, currently being waged. We called an emergency meeting and representatives of nine women's peace organizations showed up. We named ourselves the Coalition of Women for Peace and agreed to work together: to support each other's peace work, to avoid scheduling activities that would conflict with each other, and to plan major actions that would include everybody. These are the names and basic aims of each member of the Coalition:

Bat Shalom: the Israeli side of The Jerusalem Link, an Israeli-Palestinian partnership of women for peace;

The Fifth Mother: the re-grouped Four Mothers Movement, which played a major role in bringing an end to the Israeli occupation of Lebanon;

Machsom-Watch: a human-rights group that monitors checkpoints and seeks to prevent abuse by Israeli soldiers of Palestinians who cross these checkpoints;

NELED: an organization of "Women for Coexistence;"

New Profile Movement for the Civilization of Israeli Society: addresses issues of militarism and gives support to conscientious objectors to military service in Israel;

Noga Feminist Journal: news and analysis of feminist issues in Israel and broad;

TANDI: Movement of Democratic Women for Israel, an organization of mostly Palestinian citizens of Israel that seeks equality for an empowerment of women;

WILPF: the Israeli chapter of the Women's International League for Peace and Freedom;

Women in Black: a weekly, one-hour vigil throughout Israel, in which women dressed in black call for an end to the Israeli occupation.

At the second meeting of the Coalition, although we were a broad coalition—from Zionist to anti-Zionist and all points in between—we nevertheless managed to hammer out a set of principles that was acceptable to all 9 organizations. These are the principles we approved:

- An end to the Occupation.
- The full involvement of women in negotiations for peace.

- Establishment of the state of Palestine side by side with the state of Israel based on the 1967 borders.
- Recognition of Jerusalem as the shared capital of two states.
- Recognition by Israel of its share of responsibility for the results of the 1948 war, and for finding a just solution for the Palestinian refugees.
- Opposition to the militarism that permeates Israeli society.
- Equality, inclusion and justice for Palestinian citizens of Israel.
- Equal rights for women and all residents of Israel.
- Social and economic justice for Israel's citizens and integration in the region.

For us it was important to have a broad view of peace, one that couples peace with justice. We could not imagine doing it otherwise. And we were surprised by how quickly we came to agreement about the principles. This cooperative spirit was a direct product of the sense of urgency we each felt about doing things and not just talking. We were determined to use our combined strength to make a powerful statement and to model cooperation among ourselves while doing it.

The first activity of the Coalition was a mass vigil and march in Jerusalem, with 2,000 Israeli and Palestinian women calling for an end to the Occupation and negotiation of a just peace. Subsequently, we held a series of demonstrations demanding an end to the military "closure," in which Palestinian towns and villages are kept under siege—entry and exit prohibited. In the first of these actions, women lay down on the street and blocked access to the Ministry of Defense in Tel-Aviv in order to "illustrate" the problems of closure. The police were not amused, and seventeen of us were arrested.

Subsequent actions, often in cooperation with mixed-gender peace organizations, involved other nonviolent acts of resistance to closure. These included the removal of blockades and filling in of trenches, both of which are intended to be physical barriers to prevent Palestinians from entering or leaving their villages. In other actions, individual women—young women, in particular—pushed resistance one step further by lying down in front of army bulldozers or chaining themselves to olive trees in an effort to prevent further destruction of Palestinian homes and property. Many of these actions ended in arrests. In the autumn of 2002, we have been helping Palestinians with their olive harvest, despite shooting and physical attacks by settlers on those working in the groves.

We have also held a series of very dramatic mass actions, seeking to involve both local and international audiences. In June 2001, the Coalition organized an international "Women in Black" day, mobilizing 150 vigils around the world to protest the Israeli Occupation, and held a vigil of 3,000 Women in Black in Jerusalem. It was the largest Women in Black event that had ever been held across the globe. In December 2001, we also held a 5,000-person March of Mourning in Jerusalem under the banner "The Occupation is Killing Us All," followed by a Concert of Peace and Hope, with Israeli and Palestinian performers and over 100 solidarity events held simultaneously around the world. Another major rally was held in June 2002 to mark 35 tragic years of Occupation.

And yet, despite all this activism—and much more, not reported here—we have had virtually no publicity in the local media. Some of this "ignoring of us" has to do with the unwillingness of Israeli media to portray activity that falls outside the consensus—the "wrong" time for this kind of story. And some of it—especially when an action does get coverage, but someone else gets credit for it—has to do with how women continue to be silenced or regarded as marginal to the main business of society. Even when we engage in some highly dramatic events, such as reaching across "enemy lines" to our Palestinian sisters, our efforts are ignored.

Israeli and Palestinian Women Crossing Bridges

Our Palestinian women partners have been no less determined to get to peace. In fact, secret meetings began between Palestinian and Israeli women about 15 years ago (even before the first *intifada* began). These meetings were secret because it was illegal for Israelis and forbidden for Palestinians to meet in those years. A number of groups were then getting together, but only one group persisted over time— resolutely grappling with the most difficult issues—and crafted an agreement that was signed and publicized several years before the Oslo Accords. Above all this agreement declared establishment of a free, independent and secure state of Palestine side-by-side with a free, independent and secure state of Israel as the core of a political settlement.

As profound as this moment could have been in the history of the Middle East, very few people heard about it. Why? Because the agreement was written by women. You may wonder whether the agreement was rejected for other reasons, perhaps because it was a radical statement dreamed up by utopians or marginal people. But each delegation included prominent political leaders—members of parliament, government ministers, an ambassador, and a party head. These women were neither marginal nor radical at all.

As for the content of the agreement, it too was neither marginal nor radical. Most of its principles have now become matters of consensus among both Israelis and Palestinians. Despite the current magnitude of brutality—or perhaps because of it—surveys consistently show that a decisive two-thirds of Israeli Jews would support a peace agreement that includes Israeli withdrawal from the Palestinian territories, evacuation of most Israeli settlements, and creation of a Palestinian state. Most Palestinians hold the very same views. Indeed, only extremist political leaders on both sides fail to understand that these principles will ultimately set the terms of peace between our nations.

It is hard not to reach the tragic conclusion that had the women who wrote this agreement been internationally recognized negotiators, the two *intifadas* that followed might have been prevented.

Israeli and Palestinian women continue to meet, often in the framework of actions organized by The Jerusalem Link. "A women's joint venture for peace" is the tag line. We have marched together under the banner "We refuse to be enemies." Indeed, the Israeli and Palestinian women's peace movements have already made peace: on paper, in our hearts, in the lessons we teach our children, and in the behavior we model. We are allies for peace, united in our struggle against extremists and warmongers on all sides.

Is it not preposterous that not a single Israeli woman and only one Palestinian woman has held leadership roles at a Middle East peace summit? Instead, the negotiators have been men with portfolios of brutal crimes against each other—military men who have honed the art of war and who measure their success by the unconditional surrender of the other. Is it any wonder that we are still locked in combat?

The Tender Core

As I look back over what I have written, I don't want to understate the role of some wonderful mixed-gender movements in keeping alive the peace movement in Israel. I am referring in particular to activists from Rabbis for Human Rights, Courage to Refuse (soldiers who refuse to serve in the army of occupation), the Israel Committee

Against House Demolitions, Gush Shalom, and Ta'ayush: Arab-Jewish Partnership. We share most of the views of these organizations, and we work harmoniously and well together with them.

But there is something different about the women's peace movement, and it is not just our steadfastness and vitality, not just our commitment to peace with justice. Before writing this article, I looked back at some of the reports I wrote about our work and tried to distill the essence of women's peace-building. I think I found a good example of it in a recent letter written by the Coalition of Women for Peace to the survivors of the Sabra and Shatilla refugee camps in Lebanon. We ended our letter to them with the following sentence: "We hope that you will accept the sincerity of our words and allow us to stand in solidarity with you as we strive to build peace with justice between Israel and Palestine." What I read in these lines is not just outreach, but humility and compassion, as we understand the sometimes terrible role Israel has played in causing the suffering of others, while also suffering at their hands. Perhaps this empathy, this tentative and self-effacing outreach to our partners across the borders, is the tender core inside the tenacious activism of the women's peace movement in Israel.

I believe it is.

For more information, write to intl@CoalitionOfWomen4Peace.org or see our web site http://www.CoalitionofWomen4Peace.org

CHAPTER TEN

The Intifada Journals

Henry R. Carse

Both Sides Now
Jerusalem, July 24, 2001

Through July the spiral of violence spins on. Two young Israeli soldiers are killed at a bus stop by a suicide bomber in Binyamina. Four Palestinians are assassinated by Israeli helicopter fire in Bethlehem. A Palestinian family is murdered by settler gunfire as they drove down the road near Hebron. The names blur, the incidents interface, the air is full of radio cover-ups and the advertisements of normalcy. "Cease fire," "Cooling Off Period," "International Observer Force"—all slogans, no substance. The killing in the Holy Land goes on at a hellish pace.

On July 18, early in the morning, my daughter Moriah was inducted into the Israeli Army. For months, the date loomed, the event slowly took on the quality of something real. Resisted, argued, discussed, cried over, yelled about, denied, rejected, embraced, planned and unplanned for—now real. My daughter, my only daughter, my little girl, is in the uniform of the IDF. Her heart, her body, her conscience, clothed in a moving target. Her days, her actions, her knowledge, her dreams, her weaknesses and her strengths, enclosed in the hugely powerful military machine of a police state under a dubious leadership and committed to an increasingly brutal policy of occupation and *apartheid*. Moriah is an Israeli soldier.

In my many conversations with Mori, during the long struggle to move her from the path in front of her, I described the indescribable. I did the research on conscientious objection (such as it is in Israel—

which isn't much). I brought her piles of printed information from the human rights organizations. I told her about Sharon and Sabra and Shatilla, about Barak and the Oslo illusions, and about war crimes and the evils we are all part of. I told her of my hours with the tiny Palestinian and Israeli nonviolent resistance movement, the visits to the bombarded homes, the brutal destruction wreaked by the armed settler gangs, the glowering presence of the military posts overlooking the homes of Beit Sahour and Ramallah, the desperate demonstrations at the barricades, the confrontations with the border patrols and the settler militias, the repeated scenarios of force and weakness, the tear gas grenades tossed, the guns pointed, the jeeps growling...and all in my direction, there where I stand, on both sides now.

I sketched in my words the impossible but possible: the image of Moriah in uniform on one side of the Occupation checkpoint, and me in a resistance demonstration on the other. We tried to give a name to the nameless. "What if...? What if...?" "Dad, it won't happen." "Mori, nothing is impossible. Just think about it...What if!"

We talked and cried and laughed, we drank numberless cups of coffee and we told our stories again and again. Moriah told me of the sense of belonging she feels, the bond with her Israeli friends and classmates, her unwillingness to leave them behind, to turn away from them, to deny her Israeliness and take the first flight out of here. She spoke of the frustration she feels at her country's wrong policies, the Occupation, the destruction of a whole generation's hope for peace and justice and a normal life. She spoke of her anger, but of her courage too. She, too, described the indescribable: the opportunity to work from within, to counsel and direct and be a voice of reason and conscience. She described the role she would play in uniform, the course she would take, the non-commissioned officer status she would reach, the connectedness she felt, the hope to be a force for good...

I looked into her eyes, and they were clear. She grew, and every moment a new facet of her was clearly outlined in the strong Jerusalem light. Her beauty and her honesty shone through the tears. She graduated from high school, she danced on the stage of her childhood one last time. She bought a knapsack and said she was going to Greece with her buddies but then they backed out and she stayed at home. She got a haircut and we read together the last chapters of "The Princess and the Goblin." I gave her my old guitar and she asked me to teach her to play "Bo Jangles." Still we talked and argued and talked. Then, inexorably, it was July.

On July 18, at the IDF mustering point in West Jerusalem, Moriah was inducted. She asked for us to be there; she couldn't have kept us away. On that day, I was not a teacher or a theologian or a guide or an advocate or activist. I was just a Dad, an Abba like every other Abba there. We were family. Mori's mother and I stood together, closer than I can remember we have stood since the divorce. Jonathan played the role of teenage brother perfectly, with just the right balance of cool and warmth. Jesse, upset, decided to stay at home, then wished he hadn't...We were simply there, to say goodbye to Moriah, to tell her the words of the song: "Take wing...and take good care."

Three of Moriah's classmates showed up too to see her off, and we all clustered around her in the parking lot where the big buses stood. There were a hundred young women—it was women's induction day—all dressed up, all gorgeous, all with designer shades and mobile phones and smart new knapsacks. Big hugs, some tears, some laughter. I slipped into Mori's bag a little box of my homemade "*intifada* chip cookies" and pinned an Irish shamrock talisman to her hem. Then we all hugged her, and Mori left us. She stood briefly in line, picked up her army unit file, shouldered her pack, and joined the other girls on the bus, and suddenly they were not girls any more. They were women, and soldiers, or would be soon. The bus pulled out of the lot, and Mori's face behind the glass disappeared, but her hand was still visible, waving, waving.

The next time I see Moriah, she will be in the uniform of an occupying army.

My heart and mind are reeling. How is it possible for two worlds to meet like this without an explosion? How can I find my way in the impossible maze of emotions this event evokes? Who will keep us together, who will prevent the realities of the Occupation, of the confrontations all around us, of the fears and passions of this poor land, from separating parents from their children, brother from sister, a daughter from her father? Even if no one can prevent any of this, God help us, can we not at least admit that it hurts us deeply, and try at least to recognize that we are not the only ones, and to tell the story of the two sides of every pain?

"To reconcile conflicting parties," writes the Buddhist teacher Thich Nhat Hanh, "we must have the ability to understand the suffering of both sides. If we take sides, it is impossible to do the work of reconciliation. And humans want to take sides...Are there people who are still available to both sides? They need not do much. They need only do one thing: go to one side and tell all about the suffering endured by the other side, and go to the other side and tell all about the suffering endured by this side. That is our chance for peace... But how many of us are able to do that?"

How many? I open my hand, here where I stand on the threshold between warring worlds, and as I watch you flyaway, my eyes follow until they can no longer see you through the window flashing in the sun, and then my heart goes further still. Moriah, my daughter, this threshold place that I thought to hide from you, to protect you from its wounds, is now your place, yours too. East and West, Israel and Palestine, meet in your story—both sides now.

Tell it well.

Mistaken
Jerusalem, September 15, 2001

At 8.48 a.m. on Tuesday morning, September 11, the first of the hijacked planes crashed into the northernmost of the Twin Trade Towers, and the horrible carnage began. That day, like countless others, I foolishly tried, from Jerusalem, to call some friends in the NYC and Washington areas. When I finally got an open telephone line, it was to Vermont, where I spoke with my father. He immediately told me about his memory of the exact moment in 1941 when he heard of the attack on Pearl Harbor. This, too, it seems, has become one of those moments marked by the question: "Where were you when...?"

The images of the smoking Pentagon, and of New York's collapsing skyline, of human beings in despair throwing themselves out of windows in the smoke are all seared into our minds. All around us, blindingly, are the white ash and thick darkness of too much death, the extinguishing of too many precious lives...And inside us, if we are honest, we find the shadows of unwelcome emotions, of hidden agendas, little glimpses of those parts of our hearts we would rather not own. The little jump of suppressed elation (Thank God, it wasn't me!). The lump of sheer undifferentiated shock in the stomach, suddenly turning into hatred, disgust, rage...Something terrible is suddenly making the world a playground for evil, and we can do nothing. We are overwhelmed, and our good intentions seem silly. All we can do is desire vengeance. So it seems.

For all of us, near and far from the ruins, this is the time to grieve, not to analyze. But, after grief will come...what? Confusion? Anger? Retaliation? Something better than these? Is anything else possible? Is it too soon to break the grip of shock, to speak about the impossible, before our fury blinds us?

I am in Jerusalem. Here, for my family, for my colleagues, for my neighbors, for myself, all this comes home. It is here that we will need to absorb into our lives the full realization of this horrible cruelty, and it is here that we will need to live through it, into something more human than hatred...But...is that possible? Or was all this "peace and justice" stuff blown into millions of meaningless grotesque fragments at 8:48 on Tuesday morning?

Where was I at that moment? No place dramatic, but I remember every detail. It was a hot dusty afternoon in Beit Hanina, a Palestinian neighborhood north of Jerusalem. I had arrived with two human rights activists (a Palestinian American and a Jewish American, as a matter of fact) to work on the construction of a Palestinian home that needs to be built quickly, before it is destroyed. It was a day of not-very-hopeful effort in the shadow of the Occupation's systemic heartlessness. It was a mundane and very ordinary day, I thought.

Here is how it works if you are a Palestinian living near Jerusalem. You can't get a building permit from the Israeli municipality, so you either have to leave the country (of course, that is difficult even if you wanted to, without a passport or travel papers) or build illegally. Or...live without a house. Abu Ali Shamri and his wife Uzziya chose to build, in the hopes that the army would leave them alone. They got the walls up and a roof on, and it began to look like they would make it. They moved in, although the floor was just rough chunks of rock. They and their kids, Ali, Ahla, Muhanned, Muayyad, gorgeous blonde Linda and little Muhammad, slept on tattered mattresses on the rocks. Uzziya cooked on a gas burner, as Abu Ali tried to find the money they needed to finish the house.

Then, on Monday morning, September 10, the Israeli police arrived, with a demolition order. Abu Ali and Uzziya were told that their house, built without a permit, would be destroyed the next day. They were not alone. Right down the dirt path, several more homes were served demolition orders that day. The owners got in touch with a lawyer in Jerusalem, and after a night of incredible efforts and appeals, supported by Israeli peace activists, Palestinian human rights and international groups, a judge was reached and convinced on humanitarian grounds to sign staying orders preventing the demolition of two of the doomed homes. Abu Ali's house was one of the two. They were given a reprieve of two weeks, within which time they had to complete the structures to the satisfaction of the court. Exhausted, Abu Ali and his family slept.

The next morning, Tuesday, September 11, the Israeli army arrived with bulldozers and demolition equipment. They were ready to knock down a half-dozen houses, and the officers in charge were not in a talking mood. The bulldozers started at the bottom of the dirt track, where a widow lived with one of her daughters. The Aisha house was soon a pile of rubble, and the demolition team turned next door to the home of Ramadan Ahmad Bader. His nine kids were all at school, so they did not see their home being attacked by massive equipment, or the trauma of their father being pushed away as he tried to show the soldiers the judge's staying order he had received the night before. Ramadan's home had been legally granted a reprieve, but the army bulldozers continued to crush it, until eventually someone got the message through. Too late.

Oops. A mistake had occurred. The judge's staying order was belatedly recognized. The bulldozers backed off, leaving the Bader house looking like it had been hit by several bombs, utterly savaged and irreparably damaged. A mistake. No one apologized; no one expected it.

Moving up the track, the army now approached the cinder-block home of Issa and Miryam Jabarin, who were at home with their four small children. The Jabarin family was stunned to see the bulldozer coming near. They had received no demolition order, but it made no difference. They were able to toss some bedding and furniture out of the windows, and then the big blade quickly leveled the house, leaving a tiny almond tree scarred and lonely on the plot.

When Abu Ali's turn came, it was past 11:00 a.m. The sun was getting hot and there was so much dust in the air that it was hard to see what was going on. To the great relief of the family, the IDF officers accepted the staying order (this time they actually looked at it!) and the house was spared—for the time being. Abu Ali Shamri would have to complete his home very, very soon, or lose it next time around.

I got a phone call around noon, heard the story, and joined the volunteer team to work on the Shamri home in Beit Hanina that very day. So, that is where I was at 3:48 p.m. on Tuesday, September 11. Relevant or not, that is just where I happened to be.

At the moment the first hijacked plane ripped into the first Trade Tower, and the dying began, I was mixing cement with Abu Ali and his brother the Haj, and Adam and Huweida, and a couple of other volunteers. We were all sweating and covered with the gray grime of splashed concrete, as we wrestled the old mixer over to pour the sloppy cement into buckets, to make a smooth floor for Abu Ali's family to sleep on. It was heavy work, and we moved fast, aware that it was going to be very difficult to get the house completed to the court's specifications with so few workers and in such a short time. In our minds were images of the houses down the track: the Aisha house, nothing but broken cement blocks and twisted reinforcement bars, the Jabarin family sitting next to the pile of stuff where their home had stood, and the Bader home, with the huge gashes in its roof and sides, Ramadan standing in the road talking to the human rights observers in their Land Rover, the women of the house sitting dejectedly on the crushed veranda, and the kids playing on the piles of debris that used to be their bedroom, before the army made that mistake.

There was nothing (yet) remarkable about the day, but it felt good to be working; it felt good to see the Shamri kids smiling, and it felt good to be building, not destroying. And somehow, that was enough. Then, someone's mobile rang, and the news of the unthinkably brutal attacks on the Trade Towers and the Pentagon found us, and changed us, and our world, totally.

Now, the televisions blare. Sky News and BBC show—over and over—those ugly little clips of Palestinians rejoicing in the streets of East Jerusalem and elsewhere, laughing and whooping it up as someone (back to the camera) hands out celebratory sweets to the raucous kids. The Trade Towers flame and crumble. Beit Hanina, East Jerusalem, all the Occupied Territories, are just a speck of worthless Middle Eastern grime. No one dares whisper a word about human rights from this mistaken corner of the human village. In a moment, the systematic destruction of the Bader home, the Aisha home, the Jabarin home, and the impending blow awaiting the Shamris—are all irrelevant. Worse—they are "understandable," even "justifiable." Or are they?

Is all this justice-for-Palestinians stuff now just an ugly joke? The voiceless lives of Ramadan and Abu Ali and their kids, of Miryam and Issa and the widow and her daughter, are swallowed up in a great roar of eloquent outrage. Terrified by the recycled images of terrorist mass destruction in Manhattan and Washington, wounded by the recycled shots of Palestinians rejoicing as Americans die, America cries out for vengeance. And vengeance will be found. And whatever commentaries remain to be written on this dark day, we can be sure of one thing. No one will give justice in Beit Hanina a second thought.

Because Palestinians, you know, all support terrorism. Or do they? Arabs deserve their suffering. Or do they? The Pentagon is our business, Manhattan is our business, and the ruined homes of the Baders and the Aishas and the Jabarins—well, too bad, but they're just none of our business. Or are they?

As the cry is raised against global terrorism that threatens civilization, a word of wisdom is reiterated again and again from a most unlikely oracle. President Bush, not wanting to promise the impossible, can only say: "Make no mistake. We will strike back. Make no mistake—the free and democratic world will fight this war and win. Make no mistake." And as he speaks, how many Americans and Europeans are ready to burn a mosque, or brand an Arab—any Arab—as a public enemy, or declare a crusade against jihad, and that means anything Islamic?

Make no mistake. But we will. Already, reports from the States tell of anti-Arab and anti-Muslim acts of hatred. And it is not irrelevant, that right here where I live the Israeli army has encircled and entered Palestinian towns, taking advantage of the confusion in America to imprison without trial the guilty with the guiltless—Arabs for whom today not a single advocate can be found.

Is it too soon to speak? It is true—I did not feel the fireballs explode. I cannot claim to see the entire picture or know the global score. I can only speak from the tiny spot of dusty rock on which I stand—but this I can do. Is it too soon to listen?

You may not hear the voices of hundreds of Palestinians gathered at a candle light vigil in East Jerusalem to mourn with America. You may sneer at the photo of Arafat giving blood for the victims, or at Palestinian leaders' measured statements of contempt for the terrorists who struck America. You may not know that Arab children stood in silent mourning in Muslim schools and gathered at the American consulate with signs that said, "Terrorism is our common enemy," or that Arabs crowded Jerusalem's Anglican Church to pray and grieve for the American victims and their families. You may not care, and I can't say I blame you, about any of this right now. But... someone has to say the unsayable. Terror is not forged by invisible devils but by wounded humans. "Why?" is a valid question. Vengeance will not bring us peace. Justice still matters and cannot be silenced as war drums roll.

Very soon, we will be swept into action, and told in no uncertain terms: Here is your enemy; strike! We will hear about collateral damage, and we will believe there was no choice. And we will be mistaken. The same wounded hearts that demand the death penalty for a single murderer, will now demand the death of many, and for the same reasons. And it will be as wrong.

What About the Kids?
Jerusalem, September 30, 2001

On Thursday, September 20, a young mother named Sarit Amrani was mortally wounded by Palestinian gunmen on the road to the settlement in the West Bank where she and her family lived. As the attackers raked the car with bullets, Sarit's husband was badly hurt, but, according to the newspaper report, "Their three young children, two toddlers and a 3-month-old infant, escaped the attack with no injuries."

I don't think so.

When Nidal Abu-Salamah takes his old truck of furniture through the IDF checkpoints in the Jordan Valley, the army will not let him through if he is alone, so he takes his children with him. Fathi, aged 6, and Nur, aged 5, miss school for days on end, because their father is often turned back at gunpoint at the checkpoint and has to try again and again to get his furniture to market. The kids get to see the abuse and insensitivity of the soldiers, the humiliation and the fear in their father's eyes, day after day, from their perch in the hot and dusty truck cab. And they are the lucky ones. At least their house is still standing when they finally get home.

God only knows what kind of trauma and long-term damage is done to children in this war zone. We seem all too ready to give our attention to the eloquent expressions of rage and grief voiced by the parents, but the silent scream of the very young goes unheard. And yet, if there is any hope for anyone at all in this long-running trauma battle between Jews and Arabs, it is the young children who might, just might, have a chance to see that hope become real.

So...What about the kids?

Here are a few statistics. During the past year [September 2000–October 2001], since the beginning of the present *intifada*, over 547 Palestinians have been killed, including Palestinian Israelis killed within Israel. This includes 432 civilians killed by Israeli security forces, 13 killed by the police (in Nazareth), and 11 civilians killed by Israeli civilians (settlers). The remaining 91 were Palestinian security forces killed in combat with the IDF. In other words, in this war, only 20% of the Palestinians killed were actually combatants in the accepted sense of the word. "Collateral damage" of 80% is not a good figure, no matter what any army says. From September 28, 2000 to January 9, 2003, 2,046 Palestinians were killed, including 439 children under the age of 17. The number of Palestinians disabled in the West Bank/Gaza is 5,500 (for current figures, see www.miftah.org).

Israelis have also been killed—171 as of September 14, 2001. Their names appear with short tributes in that day's *Jerusalem Post*. Of these, over half were civilians. "Collateral damage" of over 50% is not a good figure either. One thing for sure—if this is a war, it is a very dirty one.

Now what about the kids? On the Israeli side, the dead include four 17-year-olds, two boys and six girls of 16, three girls and a boy of 15, two boys and a girl of 14, a boy of 13, a girl of 10, a girl of 8, a boy of 4, a boy of 2, a ten-month-old baby girl and a five-month-old baby boy. That is 26 young people aged 17 and younger—some killed by Palestinian terrorist attacks within Israel, some killed in attacks on settlement targets in the Occupied Territories of the West Bank and Gaza.

Twenty-six young lives cut short is a heavy toll to start counting. But the real accounting cannot begin until we look at the Palestinian kids as well. Here I turn to the B'tselem Human Rights Organization figures for September 12, 2001, and find that 127 Palestinian children aged 17 and younger have been killed. Twenty-eight 17-year-olds, twenty-four 16-year-olds, twenty-five 15-year-olds, twenty-three 14 year-olds, ten 13 year-olds, seven 12-year-olds, three 11-year-olds, two 10-year-olds, two 9-year-olds, two 8-year-olds, and a 4-month-old baby girl. All of these kids, the "older" ones armed (sometimes) with stones and slingshots, were shot dead during confrontations with Israeli soldiers, or were shot dead at a distance by Israeli army snipers. In addition, a 2-month-old baby Palestinian girl was killed by Israeli settlers, and a 12-year-old Palestinian boy was killed by Palestinian gunmen when Palestinian civilians tried to stop the gunmen from shooting at an IDF post.

My mind cannot grasp all this. Conflict aside, how is it humanly possible for adults to kill so many children? Isn't there some kind of built-in safety catch, an evolutionary taboo that would tear the finger from the trigger? I don't get it. I can only come up with the middle-class middle-of-the-road complaint: "What were those poor kids doing there in the first place?" I cannot fathom how grown-ups can allow their children to become victims. Then, I come up with the even less impressive rhetorical question: "What on earth can I do about it?"

Good question.

Here is a little glimpse of real life. An email arrived yesterday from an Israeli peace activist in a Palestinian village in the West Bank. I just had to file it and move on. What else could I do? Now, I share it with you, and I ask you this: what else can you do?

> Dear Friends,
> Another example of life under Occupation that doesn't make headlines. Billal Muhamed Akel is fourteen years old. This evening he was found guilty of living near the by-pass settler road in his native village of Hares. For this he was beaten as his parents watched helplessly and taken away by Israeli soldiers. His whereabouts are still unknown. The soldiers said they knew the boy had not been throwing stones but they beat him and kidnapped him so that he would tell them who was throwing stones. The villagers claim that there was no stone throwing before the boy was attacked.
> Regards, Neta

Even if a miracle happens, and the army returns Billal to his home tonight, he is already injured, deeply. The wound is there, unseen, in every child I can see around me, Jew or Christian or Muslim, Israeli or Palestinian or both. Some have it better hidden, some are tough and glib, but all are torn and bruised. "Jew or Arab," "Occupied or Occupiers," "victors and victims"—these are the roles the grown-ups play. For the kids, there is only the wounding.

So, what about the kids?

As If
October 14, 2001

An ad in a local Israeli paper caught my eye just before *Rosh HaShana*: "Celebrate in Israel, and feel as if you're abroad!" This is interesting. Why would Israelis want to celebrate the New Year in Israel while feeling as if they were in—say—New York? Considering recent events "abroad," one might think most Israelis would prefer observing the Jewish Holidays at home. Isn't the very best place to celebrate the Jewish New Year in Israel, the Jewish homeland? So what is all this "as if..."?

The atmosphere of dissemblance has become thick enough to choke us, and still we go on with our celebrations. When the Jerusalem municipality set off fireworks to usher in the holidays near the walls of the Old City, it was natural that some of us flinched, wondering if the IDF was launching rockets at Abu Tor. Just a few days ago, under heavy security guard, thousands of citizens in Jerusalem marched into a green municipal park, waving blue-and-white flags and playing patriotic music. Meanwhile, during the Jewish High Holy Days, Palestinians in the refugee camp of Shuafat, just a few miles away, and still inside the Jerusalem municipal lines, watched as 14 of their homes were destroyed by army bulldozers. In days of awe, in times of shame like these, what kind of pride or comfort in their nation can even the most patriotic of Israelis feel? Is this why so many Israelis are choosing, discreetly, to go abroad?

This is not just a local story anymore. We are all "as if" abroad, all the time, even if we play house in the "security" of our backyard. To understand the extent to which we are deceiving ourselves, listen closely to the gossip in the global village. Just a few weeks ago (it seems a century ago now!), terrorist attacks in West Jerusalem might have seemed to the American on the street like disturbing but distant distractions from normal life. Suddenly, responding to terrorism is the buzz word for relevance. Just a few weeks ago, Israel's elimination of Palestinian leaders (with American weapons, and in broad daylight) might have struck the average New Yorker as a rather exotic example of foreign policy. Now the whole world seems divided between those trying to "take out" bin Laden and those trying to keep him in. "Retaliation" is well on its way into the lexicon of universal virtues.

As soon as he heard of the terrorist attacks on the Twin Towers, a construction worker in Burlington, Vermont, summed it up: "Somebody pays for this. Someone's got to pay." But who? Even as the combined technological might of America and Britain is bombing Afghanistan around the clock, transforming mud huts into rough little molehills in the desert and killing civilians, too many of us are still swallowing new versions of the "might makes right" philosophy that has seduced us for so long. For all our talk of "war on evil," we just want someone to pay. As if that would make us feel safe.

We have had some weeks now to think this through. How are we doing? Are we getting beyond vengeance to a glimmer of wisdom? A week before the awful realities of September 11, Fouad Ajami wrote a (partially) courageous article in *US News & World Report*, warning that the "path of the martyrs," the glorification of religiously motivated suicidal terrorism, is leading Palestinians further and further from freedom. As correct as this is, and as important as it is to decry the folly of viewing "suicide martyrs" as heroes, Ajami's warning still cannot answer the essential question: "Why do they do it?"

"Why do they hate us?" This is not a question anyone willingly asks. It is a question that has to be dragged out of us only by the shock of a brutal run-in with the truth. Are we ready? On September 3, Ajami attributed Palestinian suicide terrorism to blind anti-modernism, to "furious envy" at Israeli prosperity, as if hundreds of youths from Jenin and Nablus and Gaza are willing to kill themselves and others simply because they are jealous of people with swimming pools in Tel Aviv. With all its insights, Ajami's article never mentions the one word that truth requires: "Occupation," or even its synonym: "humiliation." In the midst of an important and prophetic message, Ajami simply stops short, unwilling to really ask: "Why do they hate?"

And now, a full month after the September 11 attacks, are we any closer to being ready? Yes and no. At least, we now see that Israel's moral dilemma is not unique; terrorists don't just hate Jews. Israelis, however, can hardly celebrate this revelation. Rather than passing the buck, they should be among the first to seek the reasons for hatred, and to address those reasons with social change. Jewish history is filled with the cries of hatred's victims, and the plea not to forget. If six million Jews and millions of other ethnic minorities could be wiped out, deemed "subhuman," by a Nazi regime sure of its moral superiority, and if the founding of the State of Israel is some kind of redemption for the remnant that remain, the question is relevant to Israeli society. Israelis (and Americans, too) would do well to be more concerned about finding the reasons for hatred, rather than acting as if it is an alien phenomenon, a murderous but mindless scourge.

Not to ask Why? is to cling to innocence. Too many Israelis (and Americans, among others) are choosing innocence over truth—as if it ended there.

Unbounded hatred is not something any individual should have to bear alone. When Hila Hershkovitz lost her husband Assaf in a Palestinian terrorist shooting in the Jordan Valley, she and her two children took a break from their life in an Israeli settlement and visited her family in London. "It was nice to get away to a place where no one shoots at you and no one tries to blow you up as you stand at a bus stop," she said. On the flight back to Israel, reality kicked in. "When I saw the lights of Tel Aviv from the plane window I began to cry and thought, 'What are we coming back to?'"

Hila's question is a heart-rending one, if only because she seems so alone in asking it. Her society, which for decades has been preaching an Israeli manifest destiny of forcibly colonizing the Jordan Valley (as well as the rest of the West Bank), can offer Hila false innocence, condolences and loans, but not answers. And so, not once does she allow herself the real question: "Why was my husband killed?"

Or does this question have only one answer? "They hate us, not for any wrong we have done them, not for any suffering that may have broken them, not for any reason we can ever understand, but simply because we are who we are. We are Jewish, they are not. We are free, they are not; we are modern, they are not; we are prosperous, they are not. We are good and normal people, and they are evil hateful mutants. This is why they hate us."

As if this line is anything like good enough. Innocent or not, citizens need wisdom from their leaders; society needs truth; it cannot build futures on yesterday's prejudice. Generation after generation of Israelis has been taught that Arabs hate them; are Americans now going to follow suit? Golda Meir's famous dictum, "We can never forgive the Arabs for forcing us to kill their children" has all the pathos, and all the obtuseness, of a full-fledged falsehood. This works for so long, as a self-fulfilling scenario, that it finally is hailed as truth. Now, generals who bomb Afghanistan will quote Golda. And still, no one asks.

I wish I could say that Israeli public wisdom is ready for the big question...but I don't see much evidence. Even as American and British planes drop punitive ordinance on—let's face it—more victims of an "as if" new world order, Israeli voices publicly play on the deepest fears of local "innocents." A chilling essay in *Ha-aretz* on October 12 is as belligerent as anything from Washington or Kabul. "The enemies of the West," writes Avi Shavit, are "the new evil." They are "the new Saladins," and the "tenacity of their faith in their god (sic)...[has] transformed them into...the enemies of life itself." Once upon a time, we are told, we learned to our astonishment from the poet/singer Sting, that our old demons, the Russian Soviets "love their children too." Not so "the new people," the purveyors of this "new evil." They do not love their children. Their "god" is spelled with a small "g." They are outside the pale.

This is the nightmare of "Independence Day"—a Hollywood blockbuster that some sensitive soul may now be regretting the making of. When all of humanity is threatened by sophisticated aliens who show nothing but cruel loathing for their human prey, America's cities crumble like card houses. The only catharsis this nightmarish scenario can offer is the farcical scene of Israeli and Arab fighter pilots joining cause with mighty America against the alien menace, and the final annihilation of the alien spaceship by a courageous suicide mission. It all rings absurdly false, and suddenly we are living it.

It is still so fresh that the shock still makes us tremble. 285 million Americans mourn the death of nearly 3,000 innocent victims of the terror attacks on the World Trade Towers and the Pentagon. Such a loss in one day is inconceivable. It surpasses all measure, all comparison. It is as if such suffering could only have been inflicted by a mutant strain, not by ordinary mortals. It is a *sui generis* suffering. Or is it?

In less than one year, from September 1940 to June 1941, the German Luftwaffe dropped 18,000 tons of high explosives on English cities, killing 40,000 civilians: men, women and children. I know a man who was a child in London then, and he reminds me that when the United States finally entered the war, revenge was quick. "We made the German raids on England look like small potatoes. We turned Dresden into an inferno of fire...Did it make us feel any better? Did it bring meaning out of the insanity? Actually, it did not...Nor did it bring back one of [the dead], not even one child."

Some years after the war, German and English teenagers embraced and wept in the ruins left by their parents' hatred. Not then, and not since, have the victims of all that slaughter been taught to think that their enemies lacked love for their children, or hated life itself.

There is no "new evil." The world has not changed after September 11, but our vision has. If our perception is that those who hate us can be nothing but godless and heartless mutants, then we need to search the mirror of our souls. For this, Israeli society does not need to look far. There are around 3 million Palestinians living under Israeli Occupation in the West Bank and Gaza, and they have lost 600 precious lives in the last year, many of them children...Percentages mean nothing to the heart. So, just stop a minute, if you are one of the 285,000,000 Americans who might read this, and imagine, if you can, that 57,000 Americans have been shot dead over the last year. That's the equivalent. How would that kind of mourning feel?

Can we imagine a human being enduring loss and humiliation, being filled with rage, becoming a terrorist, committing mass murder—and remaining human? Or is that a privilege we reserve only for history's victors who drop mass death on Dresden, atomic holocaust on Japan, liquid fire on Asia, or "smart" bombs on the Middle East? We, too, have sinned. Little yellow bags of American food rations in the Afghan desert, small groups of Israelis rebuilding Palestinian homes... these are tiny potential symbols of the campaign we really need—not of righteous wrath but of repentance and decisive change.

It is time to ask where terrorism comes from, not just where it is going. Only then will we know what to do about it.

"The means may be likened to a seed, the end to a tree: and there is just the same inviolable connection between the means and the end as there is between the seed and the tree." Gandhi had it right. If our means to fight evil is to terrorize others, then terror will be our end.

As if we didn't know.

Jacob at the Checkpoint
Jerusalem, January 6, 2002

On the afternoon of Christmas Day I found myself with several hundred internationals and Palestinians at the IDF military checkpoint north of Bethlehem, nose to nose with a line of Israeli soldiers armed with M-16s equipped with grenade launchers, backed up by an APC and several army jeeps with mounted machine guns. Demonstrators wearing *keffiyehs* sang "We Shall Overcome," soldiers in flak jackets glowered and shoved their rifle butts into our stomachs, and the Book of Genesis suddenly made sense...But I am getting ahead of my story.

The Christmas Day march of internationals and Palestinians on the Bethlehem checkpoint was just one of a series of actions in the context of the International Solidarity Movement (ISM) nonviolent campaign against the Israeli Occupation. The preceding two weeks had been a whirlwind of professional training, group formation and some fairly experimental initiatives like staging a "die-in" at an Israeli military position in Ramallah, marching under the gun-barrels of tanks in Nablus, challenging the military curfews in Hebron, and dismantling road barricades which isolate besieged Palestinian communities like Bir Zeit University, Kifl Haris and Deir Istya.

In general, the core group of international delegates, and their Palestinian hosts, acted with discipline, common sense and courage. More importantly, the campaign attracted the attention of the Palestinian public and was covered daily in the local papers (although unfortunately not so often in the foreign press). The actions were coordinated with Palestinian organizations and (when appropriate) with Israeli organizations, and some were joined by considerable numbers of Palestinian (and some Israeli) activists, who gained valuable field experience for the future. It is not impossible that the

2001 ISM campaign may bear fruit in a grassroots nonviolent movement for justice and peace in Palestine.

The campaign had a coherent message ("The Occupation Kills," and "The Occupation Must End") and remained true to the principles of nonviolent direct action, civil disobedience and legitimate protest. If I had to sum it up in terms of my experience since the outbreak of the present *intifada*, I would call it successful. It showed that international presence (i.e. the cooperation of committed and trained foreign activists) can encourage a dramatic change in the Palestinian perception of the value of nonviolence in the struggle for freedom. Although most Palestinians (and Israelis) still regard some form of armed confrontation as inevitable, we now have a core group of local nonviolent activists who can plan and realize complicated and sometimes risky actions without losing ground to provocateurs and reactionaries on both sides.

In addition, Palestinian nonviolent spokespersons are emerging who can clearly present their goals: a peaceful end to the Israeli Occupation of the West Bank and Gaza, and the realization of a democratic Palestinian State alongside Israel. This is remarkable at a time when among rejectionists there has been dramatic emphasis on terror—especially suicide terror against Israeli civilians—as a desperate (and doomed) reaction to increased levels of oppression. One of the most powerful assets of the Palestinian nonviolent movement today is its readiness to condemn terror unequivocally, even as it defends the right of an oppressed people to defend itself legitimately, and demands an end to the systemic "state-sanctioned" terror suffered daily by civilians.

The International Solidarity Movement numbered (eventually) over two hundred committed individuals (in delegations from France, Italy, the U.K, the U.S. and others) who gathered to galvanize the Palestinian and Israeli peace movements into cooperation and action at a critical moment. I heard one participant comment: "It feels like the 60's when the white students from the North went to the southern states to support the civil rights movement." The analogy is, of course, only partly correct. The Israeli-Palestinian conflict is about two nations, not one. "Internationals" visiting Palestine and Israel are not usually fellow-citizens with those engaged in the struggle; their solidarity is a broader one based on universal human rights. Because they come from "outside," international peace activists here open themselves to the charge of "meddling" in affairs they don't understand. However, in an area of the world that has been brutally manipulated, colonized and subjugated by the West for over a hundred years, we could use a few more "meddlers" with their priorities straight.

Day after day, night after night, the "intees" have for some time now managed their own well-orchestrated version of the long-requested and always-denied international observer force for human rights in the Occupied Territories. At checkpoints, they take snapshots of IDF soldiers harassing Palestinian civilians. In bombarded towns, they sleep with families under fire by Israeli tank-shells and rockets. At demonstrations, they place their bodies and their voices between irate Israeli settlers and irate Palestinians.

I am no expert in political theory, and my experience of nonviolent direct action is limited. While some of my contemporaries were storming East coast nuclear installations I was studying Biblical Aramaic and New Testament Greek, and while others were joining Greenpeace I was showing adventurous pilgrims the way up Mount Sinai. I missed most of the proverbial "action," but all in all I am happy to have taken the road of practical theology rather than politics, if only because now I begin to see where the two may meet and enhance each other.

A day after the closing of the ISM campaign, I started getting crowing emails from participants celebrating their victory over Israeli aggression and bragging about their courageous exploits. These emotions are understandable, and it is indeed satisfying to stand for something worthwhile, but we would be wise, I think, to await the verdict of history. Israel's Occupation of the Palestinian homeland has a complex past, in which neither side can claim the moral high ground. We are a long way from the compassion needed to resolve this thing. It is a big step from resistance to reconciliation, but that step must be made. And for this, will-power is not enough. Some sort of spiritual guideline will be needed.

After living here for three decades, I doubt that I have learned anything new in political or social terms in the past two weeks. Politically speaking, Israel's territorial gains in 1948 and 1967 are still exacting their heavy toll, crippling Israel's ability to integrate into the region and placing an impossible burden on Israel's democracy, as well as sparking violent political upheavals on the Palestinian street. From the point of view of sociology, the fact still remains that many (if not most) Israelis are too traumatized by the role of victim imposed on them by Western history to admit their complicity in an ethnic cleansing of their neighbors. Palestinians (most if not all) still feel too beaten and humiliated by their misfortunes in 1948 and 1967 to welcome a permanent and dynamic Jewish presence in the Middle East. Both peoples, socially speaking, are still living in societies more ruled by adolescent urges and tribal instincts than by the perspectives of the Enlightenment. This will all take time to change, and a few hundred peace marchers carrying torches and singing "We Shall Overcome" are not going to do it.

As a theologian, however, I may just have something to say. This is because, for better and for worse, the political conflict here is shot through with ancient religious themes. Land-grabbing "heroism," suicide "martyrdoms" and all kinds of other travesties of the human condition are here celebrated daily as divinely inspired and rooted in spiritual conviction. My scriptural and theological training has taught me the power of the word, especially the "sacred" word, as a raw material for the forging of past identities and future motivations. I can hear the thrum of Hebrew and Arabic poetry under the conflict's ugly screech of metal and stone. This worries me, but gives me hope as well. People who care enough about their texts to kill and die for them are at least not apathetic and should theoretically be able to transcend their fear and hatred of each other and follow the higher messages those same texts teach.

When Gandhi formulated his practice of *satyagraha* in South Africa, he was inspired by the Sermon on the Mount. When Martin Luther King and Rabbi Abraham Heschel marched together against racism, they looked to the Old Testament prophets and the Book of Exodus. When Palestinians and Israelis march together—and march together they will—what will be the sacred narrative, the guiding story, that will give them the new name they will need to re-write their common history of hatred?

One aspect of that creative narrative of compassion—and a good one for the nonviolent struggle in these specific circumstances—is in Genesis. It is a story of family feuds, of petty vengeance and illicit passions and shadowy love affairs. One of my favorite scenes in that story is the tragic-comic struggle between Jacob and Esau. Two brothers, torn apart by a common inheritance and by treachery, they live estranged until they meet at the ford of the Jabbok river. There Jacob wrestles with a mysterious divinity and is wounded even as he struggles free. It is not an angel that grips him, but a man—or more accurately, a person (*'ish* in Hebrew). Someone he knows and yet cannot admit he knows, someone who can claim intimacy and give Jacob a new name, and not stay for long nameless.

It is a dark story, without a moral high ground and without "satisfaction." Like so many good "sacred texts", the tale in Genesis does not lay claim to clarity. When Jacob and Esau meet and embrace in the light of day, it is a limping sort of rapprochement, without victory and without moral gain. The brothers will part, and both will return to lives of struggle. But when brothers wrestle at the river in the dark of night, a love—a kinship—is remembered.

This I saw, these two long weeks in the December mud at the impassable ford of the Occupation. Eyes turned down for years have been lifted, to look with shame but with pride into the eyes of the enemy. Voices have been raised, in Arabic and Hebrew, and there is the edge of intimacy here. This may be the only really original contribution and intention of nonviolence: it brings enemies face to face. I am now convinced that political science alone cannot move us forward. We need to build on sacred insights of intimacy, bringing to bear on each other the steady gaze of compassion, until we simply cannot bear to hate each other anymore. This year, when Israel and Palestine meet at the checkpoint, they will not meet to destroy each other. Not if one side remembers to speak the other's name.

Banalities and Blessings
Jerusalem, May 9, 2002

From Western Easter to Eastern Easter, for five long weeks in the warming springtime of the Promised Land, as the anemones and poppies have been blooming, sordid and brutal events have been unfolding all around us. Anyone can see that news and views are all over the map; no one can guess what cruel absurdities and griefs lie ahead. Still, can we dare to count our blessings?

On Western Easter Sunday, the last day of March, I visited friends in Beit Sahour, on the outskirts of Bethlehem. I arrived at the Orthodox Church and found the place overflowing with worshippers. For Orthodox Christians this was just another Sunday during Lent, but the church was so packed that I could barely squeeze into the gate. Kids were all over the place, dressed to the nines. A bunch of official-looking fellows showed up outside the church, hanging big Palestinian flags and photos of Arafat on the church fence, then adding a long banner supporting the Palestinian President. Children played peek-a-boo behind the banners and the flags, and one kid rushed around handing out photos of dead Palestinian heroes, all bearing the title *shaheed* ("martyr").

As the last blessings were intoned from the sanctuary, crowds were already gathering in the street. It was a support rally for Arafat, confined as he was to his offices in Ramallah and surrounded by Israeli tanks. It was also a general demonstration of resistance to the Israeli incursions into Palestinian areas. There was no doubt that people were expecting an imminent Israeli army invasion into the streets of Bethlehem, Beit Sahour and Beit Jala, towns already familiar with Occupation, resistance, firefights, assassinations, retaliations, and dread. One of my hosts, a municipal employee, with her 7-year-old daughter Luna, joined me at the church door, and we walked through the thronged streets toward the equivalent of a town square. A few internationals, mostly youngish participants in the International Solidarity Movement, gathered with the townsfolk. Under a banner supporting the imprisoned "Rais," town notables were giving short speeches. The bearded and handsome parish priest, in the impressive black robe of the Orthodox clergy, addressed the crowd under an incongruous array of local icons: Arafat in his *kaffiyeh*, the Virgin Mary in a blue dress, and Saddam Hussein in a pressed uniform, gazing benignly on the crowd.

My host gave me a running commentary while keeping an eye on her daughter scampering among the groups of townsfolk. Just when I thought it could not get more chaotic, a youth who looked thirteen, with his head completely wrapped in a checked *kaffiyeh*, leapt to the top of the nearest building and let off into the air an ear-splitting live round from his Kalashnikov. Jolted and shaken by the shooting, my hostess immediately rushed off to make sure little Luna was okay. Some of the kids around me were cowering against their parents, and not a few adults were shaking their heads and saying, "Why?—Why?"

Why indeed? Shows of juvenile aggression translate well into patriotism in most Middle Eastern languages. But no amount of nationalist lingo can make firing guns over the heads of toddlers anything but banal.

Luna's mother returned through the crowd not only with Luna, but with a Tanzim fighter she wanted me to meet. Atta (let's call him)— young, handsome, somewhat tense, obviously admired, and gracious. It was thought that I might like to talk with Atta about human rights, since he had announced the formation of a human rights committee for the local Tanzim militia under his command. Realizing that I had left my notes on the Tanzim militias at home, I managed to come up with a few questions about "purity of arms." After bit of translation footwork, the question reached him: As a commander of armed men, what were his directives concerning use of weapons or explosives against Israeli civilians? "Absolutely forbidden!" Atta was adamant. "I train my men to fight the Israeli army. They are forbidden to attack civilians, anywhere. Not even in the illegal Israeli settlements."

Atta and his men had their day. Five weeks later, when I returned to Beit Sahour, the city had been invaded and my hosts were under house arrest. Little Luna had put her head out the window to find tanks in the street and an Israeli soldier with his gun pointed at her face. Some neighbors were harassed and their houses trashed, others disappeared into military prisons, and over a hundred were besieged in the Church of the Nativity. Orthodox Easter came, and I had promised to visit my friends to mark the feast, so I made my way over incongruous roads to their home, where I found the entire family gathered. I brought them festive chocolates, cheese and cookies, and we ate and talked.

One of Luna's uncles engaged me in a conversation about the Israeli Occupation and Palestinian resistance. After a while, I asked him about the word "martyr." What does this mean to Palestinians? Oh, he said, anyone who dies fighting the enemy is a martyr. What about people who blow themselves up, killing Israeli civilians...Are they fighting the enemy? He leaned closer and told me a little secret: There are no Israeli civilians, he said. Everyone knows that they all serve in the army, from the age of eighteen to the age of fifty-six. Oh, I said. What about babies, and old people? Look, he said, do you think any of us condone these things?

Language can stretch just so far, and then it snaps.

I am slowly learning the meaning of banality. I thought that the banal was simply uninteresting. But "banal" comes from an old French word meaning "compulsory feudal service." Exactly. Israelis and Palestinians are trapped in the compulsory service of a benighted lord. "Nationalism is an infantile disease," wrote Albert Einstein. If so, this house we share with furious neighbors is a vast and curfewed hospital for miserable and angry infants.

Nationalism does things to communication. A correspondent for the Israeli newspaper *Ha'aretz* did a revealing study of Israel Radio's guidelines on vocabulary in its Arabic broadcasts. Statements by Israeli government spokespersons, for example, cannot be called "versions," because this seems to cast some doubt on their veracity. A member of Parliament cannot "refute" or "contradict" the Prime Minister. No, the right phrase is "expressed his objections." And, most importantly, "victim" must never be used to refer to a Palestinian civilian...he or she is simply "dead."

I love words, and I hate to see them brutalized. But even wordless images are pressed into the service of mindless politics. Here a bizarre and very banal example comes from the dusty margins of the Jenin fiasco. About Jenin what we know for sure is very little. Our ignorance will not bring back the dead, or turn back the clock, but maybe it will give us pause. In the words of an Israeli journalist: "Okay, so there wasn't a massacre. Israel only shot some children, brought a house crashing down on an old man, rained cement blocks on an invalid...used locals as human shields against bombs, and prevented aid from getting to the sick and wounded. That's really not a massacre."

One day, as the experts argued semantics, an Israeli Army spokesperson announced evidence of Palestinians in Jenin staging fake burials. An Israeli intelligence plane filmed Palestinians carrying a stretcher, and another Palestinian with a camera filming the stretcher-bearers as they made their way toward the cemetery. The man on the stretcher, however, fell off twice, and nimbly climbed back on, as the little procession proceeded. Conclusion: the Palestinians are staging funerals as "evidence" of deaths that did not occur. The banality of this episode can only really be appreciated when one reads the Palestinian response. Oh, yes, there were people filming in that place. Yes, indeed. It was, in fact, a Palestinian film crew making a film about a Palestinian funeral, a piece of local cinema with a relevant theme. In other words, this was not Palestinians faking a funeral for anti-Israel purposes...No, this was art!

Can anyone tell me what blessings might emerge to be counted out of such a sea of dissemblance? I can only offer a glimpse of goodness, but it has been enough to keep me going for these long weeks as the dust settles over Jenin and the sordid truth emerges from the shadows of Bethlehem, like the poet's "rough beast, its time come round at last." Even a single blessing deserves counting.

Imagine a small group of Palestinian and Israeli parents, meeting for the first time around a table, to discuss a shared future for their kids. Actually, the idea is very simple. What if twelve children aged 11 and 12 could get out of the conflict zone for a week or so, fly to a neutral place, and enjoy each others' company at a summer camp? The question became a dream, the dream a plan, and before we knew it, here were twelve pairs of hopeful and cautious parents, willing to talk it over, and courageous enough to entrust their kids to the making of an experiment in education for peace.

I listened and watched, as if a celestial apparition had suddenly shone into our cell of cynical despair. These Israelis and Palestinians, who simply do not accept the "state of war" between them, who care about the hearts and souls of their kids and about a sane future for them, cannot be stopped or silenced by the banality of hate. Get the kids together, let them learn to trust each other, even as the adults have failed. The project is new, but the idea is as old as time. Even Isaac and Ishmael, life-long rivals, were reconciled as brothers when the day came to bury Abraham their father.

In another time there was another Abraham, a simple and profound man, who had to see, as we now see, the price paid by brothers for injustices endured through generations of mutual bondage. In 1862, Abraham Lincoln wrote that "in the present civil war it is quite possible that God's purpose is something different from the purpose of either party." Although he led one side, he could transcend his agenda and think beyond nationalism. Three years later, as the slaughter neared its end, Lincoln wrote words that could perhaps be spoken today from the devastated rubble in Jenin or the smoldering ruins in Rishon LeTsion: "Both parties deprecated war; but one of them would make war rather than let the nation survive; the other would accept war rather than let it perish."

We may not be ready to examine the wisdom of his words, but Abraham Lincoln had the audacity to see a hidden blessing in a banal conflict. It was not the victory of one side or the other that gave him hope, but the reconciliation he desired. He had a vision that is lacking today on the ideological battlegrounds of Jerusalem, Ramallah, Bethlehem and Tel Aviv, but which, if we act wisely, may yet be encouraged in our children. Education for peace, a summer camp, a few days of shared time for our war-shocked kids: these may be all we can manage while the tanks and bombs seem to drown out reason. But when the shooting stops, as it will one day, what then? If these same children are nourished with the blessings of each other, not the banality of hatred and suspicion, then Israelis and Palestinians may yet find the heart and the strength to build an entirely different kind of future together, "with malice toward none, with charity for all...to do all which may achieve and cherish a just and a lasting peace."

Some Peacemakers
July 28, 2002

An unbearable pall of killing and maiming has spread like the dust of summer over the landscape of the once holy land. Towns and villages are either armed camps or helpless piles of devastation and rubble, in which people robbed of life still try to live. The countryside that was once a medley of farms and inviting hillsides has shrunk to wartime proportions. Once again, the "situation" has robbed us of time: of the simplicity of days and the normal flow of summer. Children, out of school, are either confined to their homes by curfew or by fear of terror. Only the foolhardy or the brazen go hiking or vacationing, even if they are free to do so. For many, the idea of a day at the beach or an afternoon at the mall is as fantastic as a stroll in the Garden of Eden. The conflict between Israelis and Palestinians is swallowing up life and sanity for all. Voices once raised in protest are now dulled and silenced by terror and rage.

Albert Einstein once said that only two things are infinite: the universe and human stupidity—"and I am not so sure about the former." The lethal combination of human stupidity and human desperation is so rich in the air we breathe that the Israeli Air Force bombing of a residential neighborhood in Gaza at around midnight on July 24 had to come as a shock but not a surprise. It should have been obvious that the Israeli assassination of Salah Shehadeh, a veteran Palestinian terrorist, would necessarily become an act of terror in itself. Nothing, in a way, could be more inevitable than the brutal slaughter of almost twenty innocent bystanders and the maiming of over one hundred more, when a policy of extra-judicial killing is ordered by one man and okayed by a telephone call from another who is thousands of miles away. What other results could we expect when ferocious ideologies of revenge are allowed to parade unchallenged through our minds and hearts in place of the simple human knowledge that "the end can never justify the means."

I confess that with that bombing in Gaza, I lost my voice and my vision—I felt paralyzed into silence, into an almost beastlike dumbness. The lexicon of shock, already thumbed thin, simply ran out of words. "Ghastly" and "imbecilic" were once good descriptions of the use of sophisticated weapons against unarmed civilians...now they seem bland. What do we do now that our ability to kill has outstripped our ability to talk?

A handful of Israelis and Palestinians, apparently simply unable to abandon the cause of justice, compassion and peace, continue to resist the rape of language and common sense, the brutalities of the Occupation and the equally brutal reactions to it. In a remarkable twist of human logic, their efforts seem more powerful even as their effectiveness seems ever more unlikely.

Less than a week before the Gaza bombing, I returned from a "Kids4Peace" summer camp near Houston, Texas, where I had accompanied a group of twelve Palestinian and Israeli kids aged 11 and 12. We had savored the peace and security of the American countryside, the sweet normalcy of sports and swimming and good fun, with hundreds of other kids and their counselors. Fun it certainly was, but a challenge too, as the kids from Israel and Palestine struggled to find a way to communicate their real feelings to each other in the very act of forging miraculous friendships. It was an "education for peace" experiment that left me thoughtful and inspired and wondering what other windows might open for these kids through the walls of fear they are now destined to return to. In all this, I was most struck by the courage and honesty, not only of the kids, but of their parents. Mothers and fathers who entrust their treasured children to a process of reconciliation are always heroes, but more so when the prevailing attitudes around them are unsupportive to the extreme. Several of the parents told us that their neighbors and friends had warned them that "this was not the right time" for sharing anything with "the enemy." It is a tribute to the wisdom of these parents that they knew that of all times this is exactly the right time to reach through the walls.

A few days after I returned to Jerusalem, I received a call from the Rabbis for Human Rights, concerning an initiative in Jerusalem hospitals. Two visits were being planned, one to a Palestinian hospital on the Mount of Olives and the other to the Mount Scopus Hadassah Hospital. In both of these places there are patients being treated for injuries sustained during *intifada*-related violence. A small group of Jewish, Christian and Muslim clergy had organized the visits to visit the injured, to speak with them, as well as to bring the message that we are all made in the image of God and that a common thread of compassion in our different faiths must motivate us to reject and resist inhuman acts of violence.

Although invited to join, as an non-ordained person I was a bit hesitant; in the end it was an experience I am glad I did not miss. As we gathered outside the Makkased Hospital, with three Jewish rabbis, a Catholic priest, an Anglican priest and a Sufi sheikh, I found myself alternating between grins and tears. It was a surreal journey into the impossible as we trooped into the intensive care ward, engaged in a lively exchange of traditional attitudes toward visiting the sick. The Sufi said that in Muslim tradition if you go to visit the sick or injured, you are accompanied by an angel along the way who at every step asks God to bless you. One of the rabbis cited the Talmudic teaching that to visit the sick is an act for which reward is unlimited, and one of the priests pointed out that, for Christians, it is enough to read in the Gospel that to visit the sick was to visit Christ himself.

In room after room, we saw the broken bodies, shattered limbs, damaged spirits of the Palestinians injured by Israeli bullets and tank shells. One 14-year-old boy sat up in bed with his father at his side. His left leg was huge and misshapen, pierced with metal supports and trussed to the metal bed frame. The rabbis and priests took the boy's hand, said the traditional blessings and prayers for the sick, and the Sufi stood near and smiled, with a silent gentleness that was better than words.

For the second visit, to the Israeli hospital, we gathered again a few days later, this time with a larger contingent of Muslim clerics, all dressed in distinctive robes. The public relations representative who greeted us at the entrance to the Hadassah Mount Scopus Hospital told us that she could not help thinking that the days of the Messiah might have come, seeing rabbis and imams and priests in a motley band swooping together from bed to bed, taking hold of hands, putting their hands in blessing on the heads of the Israeli victims of terror attacks, who lay here wounded and crippled, reciting prayers in Arabic and Hebrew, chatting with family members, and bit by bit getting smiles from the at first impassive faces of onlookers and nurses...

Finally we came to Sharon's bedside and met his mother Gila, and the power of the powerless peacemakers suddenly became clear. Sharon is a young Israeli man of 22 who sustained serious head injuries in the terrorist bombing in downtown Jerusalem on December 1 of last year. He is still in the hospital, barely able to move one arm, barely able to smile. It was his mother, Gila, who spoke for him and for all of us. Gila received us with a broad smile, blessing all of these strange messengers of Islam and Judaism and Christianity in their various garbs, as if they were long lost cousins coming home to the perfect welcome of an ancient family. Gila's face radiated gentleness, her voice rose and fell as if she were singing, and her gestures embraced us and held us. She spoke directly to the Muslim clerics especially, switching from Hebrew to Moroccan Arabic, speaking of the days that once were, but are not forgotten.

"We have lived in peace for hundreds of years before all this," said Gila, and she held her wounded son's hand in both of hers. "We know how to live in peace. We have gone to each other's weddings; we have shared our times of mourning. God knows, we are made for each other, and we will live together. Nothing can come between us. We have one God, and he will bless us, *Insha'allah*, with peace. Look at my son, look at his face! He is smiling, my dear son...He is happy that you are here. 'I'm Yirtseh HaShem. If God wills it, we will live together in peace.'"

I could never reduce the pure presence of Gila, the mother of the wounded Sharon, to words that would do her justice. But here in Jerusalem, in the dark days of summer's harsh light, in the aftermath of yet another cruel act of human imbecility, while we all seek the lost words to communicate the most basic and obvious insights of common sense, Gila is not groping or confused. She stands over the shattered body and the wounded mind of her son, blessing those whom some would see as her enemies. I wish an impossible wish, and because I have met Gila, I no longer think it is impossible. I want the injured and grieving in Gaza to meet her and to be held by her, even as their hearts gasp in the bloody place between shock and hate. Something in me will not give up, will not be silenced, as long as Gila can still speak. And it is not her face alone that is beautiful now; somehow, because she simply gives the gift, not counting its worth, she has communicated her beauty to us. It seems to me that she has achieved, naturally and without pretension, what all of us would, in our better moments, like to transcend our selfishness in order to reach.

In Gila I know that I have met a peacemaker, and her name means joy.

Part Three:

Visions for the Future

CHAPTER ELEVEN

On Christian Advocacy

M. Thomas Shaw SSJE

Stepping into Public Advocacy

In October of 2001, the three bishops of the Episcopal Diocese of Massachusetts joined in a witness on behalf of Palestinians in front of the office of the Consulate of Israel in Boston. Bishops Bud Cederholm, Barbara Harris, and I wore our episcopal vestments, making it clear that we were there not as ordinary citizens but as officials of the church. Our pictures on the front page of the *Boston Globe* the next day elicited a barrage of telephone calls, letters, and emails. The story was front-page news for three days as other Christian leaders and members of the Jewish community spoke out in support of or objection to our action.

For many, there were three questions. Why would bishops of the church in Boston demonstrate on behalf of Palestinians in the Middle East? Why would Christians voice their public support for a people widely identified in the United States as terrorists? Why don't the bishops demonstrate on behalf of the Israeli victims of suicide bombings?

We were accused of being unfair and one-sided. We were accused of being anti-Semitic. We were accused of being naïve. We were also told that our actions were long overdue and that the Palestinians were indeed victims of oppression.

Some suggested that we had acted precipitously, but in fact the conflict in the Middle East had been on my mind and in my prayers for fifteen years. Our action that evening in October was part of a long journey of prayer and witness. By standing in front of the Consulate, we wanted to stimulate a dialogue about peace in the Middle East among Christians, Muslims, and Jews in Boston. We hoped that our concern for the people of Palestine, many of whom are Christians, would be understood as part of our church's historic presence in the region, which dates back to the 1841 establishment of the Anglican Bishopric in Jerusalem. Nor was our interest in the present conflict between Palestinians and Israelis new. The Episcopal Church had been concerned about Palestinians since the first *intifada* in the late 1980s, issuing several statements through its General Convention and Executive Council in support of United Nations resolutions calling for Israel to withdraw to the pre-1967 borders and to respect the right of Palestinians to have their own state alongside that of Israel.* We felt that the concerns of the national church, which we as leaders of the Episcopal Diocese of Massachusetts shared and had publicly endorsed—and our concerns as Christians for the fate of fellow Christians—had not been clearly heard by our Jewish brothers and sisters in Boston.

Events in the Middle East also demanded immediate attention. We feared for the future of the region and for the fates of Palestinians and Israelis in the face of escalating conflict and a second *intifada*. It was obvious that the peace process had come to a dead end.

A few days before our witness, on October 19, the Israeli Defense Force (IDF) had shelled Bethlehem. Tanks were in Manger Square. The second *intifada* had begun when Prime Minister Ariel Sharon had visited the Temple Mount in September 2000, setting off a firestorm of protest and anger. The incursion into Bethlehem was part of the Israeli military response to the uprising—and in retaliation for the killing of Tourism Minister Rehavam Zeevi by the radical Popular Front for the Liberation of Palestine. The incursion was brutal. This violation of one of Christianity's most sacred places shocked me. It reminded me of the vulnerability of the many institutions supported by Christians in Israel and Palestine—including Episcopal hospitals, schools, and relief programs—without which the Palestinians could not survive. When one of our priests, the Rev. Robert Tobin, asked me to join the witness in front of the Israeli Consulate, I agreed.

I was ready to make this step into public advocacy.

My personal concern for the people of Palestine and Israel goes back many years, to the first *intifada* in 1987. At that time, I was in residence at one of our Anglican institutions in East Jerusalem, St. George's College, a continuing education center created just after World War II. One day, I was on the roof doing my laundry when I heard the nearby sound of gunfire. I went down to the street, where I saw a young Palestinian man who had been shot and killed by an

Israeli soldier. He was unarmed. He had not been throwing stones. I had been in combat situations before, during the revolution in Nicaragua, but I had never before been confronted by an innocent victim, dead, like this, in the street. It shook me. A few weeks later, I came upon the scene of an Israeli bus destroyed, along with the five Israeli men in it, by a Palestinian terrorist. In those two events, in the murders of those six young men, I understood the intractable horror at the heart of this conflict. And I did not know what I could do about it. As a monk, my first response to uncertainty is prayer, and that day I went to the Western Wall to pray.

Located in the midst of the Old City in Jerusalem, it is the section of the supporting wall of the Temple Mount remaining from the Roman destruction of the Second Jerusalem Temple in 70 C.E. The most sacred spot in Jewish religious and national consciousness, it has become a center of religious communion with the hope for restoration of Israel's former glory. For me, however, it was a place to be with God at the heart of the land where God has known us most intimately.

At the Western Wall, I vowed that I would pray for peace in the Middle East every day as part of my spiritual practice. And I have done that. My witness before the Israeli Consulate that cold evening in late October was an extension of my prayer for peace, in which I was not only speaking to God but listening to God. My prayer was also, perhaps mainly, for others. I understand this form of inter-cessory prayer to be one that leads us to be with those who suffer. In such prayer we tell God not about the suffering of others but of our willingness to be with them and God in that place of suffering. Such prayer is not passive. If we pray in earnest, prayer eventually leads us to take action.

Our prayer includes witness and advocacy in various forms. Indeed, our Christian faith in the Risen One cannot be merely about the survival of the soul (about my personal salvation); it is about, as Elizabeth Schussler Fiorenza puts it, "the transformation of the world as we know it....The Easter message is a proclamation that requires action..."(Fiorenza 121, 123).

Standing in the street in Episcopal vestments can be helpful as a call to attend to suffering or to point to injustice. But it is seldom enough. Following our witness at the consulate, we engaged in a series of conversations with Jewish community leaders, working with them to find new ground on which to continue work that we were already doing together around issues of homelessness and hunger in Boston. They were shocked by our actions, which many of them felt were precipitous. More than a few told me that we had not helped but had damaged Christian-Jewish dialogue. I felt that if we could not talk together about this issue that affected both of our communities in the Middle East, we could not talk honestly in Boston about our lives together as communities of faith sharing a common faith heritage.

Several years ago, I was invited to a synagogue service by the Jewish husband of one of our diocesan staff members. I did not have to speak or be an "official" presence. I remember discovering, as I listened to and recited the Psalms, a deep kinship with the Jewish faith. As a monk, I had been saying these same Psalms every day for twenty years. They were also my prayer, as they were theirs. I felt at home and, for the first time, understood that this was my parent faith. I took that recognition into my prayer for peace in Jerusalem. Even as I stood on the street in front of the Israeli Consulate, asking my Jewish brothers and sisters to attend to the pain of their Palestinian neighbors, I knew that their suffering was also great and could not be ignored. The existence of Israel itself is, as one Jewish friend has said, equivalent to the Christian resurrection. The Jews had experienced unimaginable terror in Hitler's Germany, while the so-called Christian world looked away. Their fears are not exaggerated; anti-Semitism is alive in the twenty-first century. Israel is a sign that the Shoah did not destroy the Jews. I understood that, and yet I had to say in any way I could to the government of Israel and to my Jewish brothers and sisters in faith that the Occupation of Palestinian villages and cities and the military action against the men, women, and children of Palestine was wrong. Violence, I wanted to say, will never bring about the peace that you and we desire.

Prayer calls us to be with the suffering of others. In the Spring of 2002, I led a pilgrimage of other Episcopalians from our diocese to Palestine. Once again, there was intense fighting in the West Bank. The IDF had reduced the town of Jenin to rubble. The Israeli military forces had repeatedly shelled Ramallah and destroyed the infrastructure of the Palestinian Authority and therefore its ability to control the factions contending for power in Palestine. Bethlehem had once again been invaded. The situation was dangerous to everyone in Israel and Palestine, and yet we felt that we had to be with our Palestinian friends in their agony. We visited the communities that had been most seriously damaged. We talked to the religious leaders and the peace-movement leaders. We met with representatives of Jewish government and mediating organizations. We took our intercessory prayer into the streets where people were suffering, where children were terrified, where the dead lay buried in the rubble of bulldozed houses.

That is what it means to pray for peace. This is prayer as truth-telling, as advocacy, and it is hard for many Western Christians, accustomed to a Christianity that avoids conflict, to understand what that means. This truth-telling is necessary for the transformation of the world promised in the life, death, and resurrection of Jesus Christ. Its goal is the restoration of right relations; it can lead, when we enter into the suffering of others, to wholeness and healing for all people.

What is Christian advocacy, and how can it be an instrument for peace?

Discerning the Spirits: Prayer and Prophecy

The summer after I returned from our pilgrimage to Palestine and Israel, I was invited by a close friend to meet with a rabbi and Jewish community leader for whom I have great respect. We sat on my friend's porch for the better part of a pleasant afternoon talking about the situation in the Middle East, about how hard it is to know what to do. Mostly, I listened and learned. We did discuss ways in which we might work together for peace in the Middle East, but I knew that there remained a gap between my concerns for Palestinians and Jewish concerns in this country for the survival of Israel.

As we parted, the rabbi said to me, "Tom, what I want you to hear is that your demonstration in front of the Israeli consulate shamed Jews. That was the impact your action had on us. And such public activity, such shaming, will not have the effect you want. What you have to do is work behind the scenes if you really want to accomplish anything. Quiet work and humanitarian efforts—getting to know each other as you and I have—will be more effective in the long run. Most importantly, one-sided advocacy just shuts down the conversation. I think what you want to be is a mediator. Advocates cannot be mediators."

He mentioned an exhibition of photographs we had shown in our Cathedral space during a series of evenings of education and prayer for peace. They were photographs documenting the devastating effects of the founding of the State of Israel on the indigenous Palestinian population.

"Those photographs," he went on, "told only one part of the story. The net effect did not make me more sympathetic to Palestinians. And it did not make me want to be in dialogue with the Episcopal Church."

I had heard similar comments before, but this conversation haunted me, perhaps in part because of my respect for this rabbi. The question he raised was also important. Does the kind of advocacy that we had engaged in over the past year separate people when our goal has been to bring people together, when our goal has been to bring peace? As Christians, are we called to be mediators? And if so, can we not be advocates for justice? As I reflected on the situation in which Palestinians find themselves in Occupied Territories, I wondered how their story could be told if we were not advocates for their cause. If the work that God calls us to do in our baptismal covenant, to "strive for justice and peace among all people, and respect the dignity of every human being," (*The Book of Common Prayer*, p. 305) is not advocacy, what is it? And how is the work of advocacy part of our vocation of prayer? And, finally, I wondered what it means for Christians, who are taught that nonviolence is God's response to violence, to support Palestinians, some of whom engage in terrorism.

As much as I admire and respect my rabbi friend, I came to the conclusion that advocacy on behalf of justice is deeply rooted in the Jewish and Christian tradition. Injustice has to be made visible if there is to be any reconciliation. Seeking justice and peace is not about avoiding conflict or protecting our brothers and sisters from themselves or unjust actions. It is about taking risks on behalf of the victims of injustice. That is what the prophets did in Israel, what Jesus did in the Roman Empire, what Ghandi did in India, what Desmond Tutu did in South Africa. The church is to be like that.

The Mosaic tradition is centered on the practice of justice, which Walter Brueggemann defines as "provision for neighborly mutuality and respect"(Brueggemann 644). This is the alternative to the practice of Pharoah, the opposite of imperial rule and economic exploitation that the Israelites experienced in Egypt. In his other writings, Brueggemann shows that the state of imperial rule is always the target of prophetic wrath because the system it imposes, by its nature, oppresses people by breaking neighborly mutuality and respect. (Walter Wink describes this rule as the "system of domination.") The ultimate model of such imperial rule is the concentration camp. The Exodus is the outcry of the people of Israel and Yahweh against injustice, an escape from domination, and it depends on mutuality and respect, under the reign of Yahweh. In the

Exodus story, Moses is Yahweh's advocate before Pharoah—and perhaps the most one-sided action in the Bible is the slaughter of the first-born of Egypt.

Yahweh is a God of Justice. To know God is to seek justice and remove oppression. The Anglican theologian Kenneth Leech writes in his book, *Experiencing God*, that the Law and the Prophets are focused on the question of justice in society. Insisting on the union of the spiritual and the social, the prophets invariably denounce worship without concern for justice as evil and unacceptable. They do not separate the secular and sacred as we tend to do (Leech 379). Separating the spiritual and the social (or political) is safe. Turning inward *and staying there* is escape from the covenant in which as Christians we live our lives of faith.

Almost any of the prophets will do as an example of the work of advocacy on behalf of Yahweh's reign of justice. During the time I was reflecting on this question, I was reading the prophet Micah. Here is Micah 3:1-4:

> Then I said,
> "Kindly listen, you leaders of the House of Jacob,
> you princes of the House of Israel.
> Surely you are the ones who ought to know what is right,
> And yet you hate what is good and love what is evil,
> Skinning people alive, pulling the flesh off their bones,
> Eating my people's flesh, stripping off their skin,
> Breaking up their bones, chopping them up small
> Like flesh for the pot, like meat in the stew-pan?"
> Then they will call to Yahweh,
> But he will not answer them.
> When the time comes he will hide his face from them
> Because of the crimes they have committed.
> (The Jerusalem Bible)

The target of this brutal attack is not some other power, another nation, but Israel itself. Micah's language is stark and vivid. And he is clear in identifying as cannibalistic policies that deprive people of their very lives. You are eating the poor, Micah says to the rulers of the nation. You are no better than cannibals, and so long as you continue to behave contrary to the word of God, Yahweh will cut you off.

There is only one side to this accusation, no weighing of evidence or opportunity for the accused to rebut Micah's charge. Indeed, how might the accused reply to an accusation of cannibalism? It is an absurdity. We can imagine the response: "Who can listen to such irresponsible accusations? How can you possibly deal with people who say such things?" The prophet does not even pretend to speak for Yahweh. What is his authority?

The prophet simply denounces oppression and the oppressors because that is who the God of Israel is—one who denounces oppression. There is no defense except to change one's way of living. Such accusations are not fair. The terms Micah uses have one purpose: to get the attention of the ones he is accusing, to make them listen. Yahweh uses the same tactics in dealing with Pharaoh. It is not fair. It is not intended to be fair.

Which is not to say that God acts, or wants us to act, arbitrarily.

The lack of fairness is one of the main objections to the kind of advocacy that Micah practiced—and to the advocacy on behalf of Palestinians and other such marginalized groups, especially when the oppressors are states, the system of domination, imperial rule. The state always demands the right to be heard, usually in its own court of law, and assumes the prerogative of truth. But in Israel God begins to be seen, for the first time in history, as identified with the *victims* of violence.

When my rabbi friend objected that the actions we took as advocates for Palestinians shamed him and other Jews, he mistook the issue and the object of our witness. Advocacy is always about the system of domination, the imperial rule, which persists through what Walter Wink calls the "myth of redemptive violence." That is to say, the object of advocacy is institutions, which carry out policies of oppression because, left alone, that is their nature. The work of faithful advocacy is to make sure that the institutions that make up the system of domination are not left alone. What we do when we advocate for justice is not about someone like my rabbi friend. It is about institutions that oppress us both.

The tradition of the prophetic word is carried forward in the ministry of Jesus. We can read all of the Gospels as advocacy narratives, but during this time of reflection on my friend's stinging remarks, I was reading the Gospel of Mark. Of all of the Gospel narratives, Mark's is the most like Micah's style of prophecy. Jesus speaks uncompromisingly out of his experience of truth as the lived expression of relationship with God. And he acts with certainty in that context. The characteristic act of Jesus in Mark is healing. In personal terms, he frees individuals of oppression in the form of illness (which in Mark is always related to the social and political): he casts out demons, releasing both the one inhabited and the demons themselves. But he does not give the demons an opportunity to defend themselves. He advocates always for the one who has been invaded by the demon.

In Mark, Jesus is always uncompromising. He says to the twelve, when he sends them out to claim authority "over the unclean spirits": "Wherever you enter a house, stay there until you leave the place. If any place will not welcome you and they refuse to hear you, shake off the dust that is on your feet as a testimony against them" (Mark 6:7, 10–11, NRSV). This is advocacy directed against unclean spirits, and the disciples are to take no prisoners. Jesus does not advocate violence, however, in this work of cleansing the culture. What he says is that we must oppose evil, but (in Walter Wink's words) "refuse to oppose it on its own terms. We are not to let the opponent dictate the methods of our opposition. [Jesus] urges us to transcend both passivity and violence by finding a third way, one that is at once assertive and yet nonviolent" (Wink 100–101). This strategy, which I would define as advocacy, is the same as that of the prophets in the Hebrew Scriptures.

The Gospel of Mark portrays Jesus, the early church, and the disciples, as a community of resistance. Jesus resists not just the oppressiveness of the Roman Empire but the puppet government it established in Palestine. Most importantly, he accuses the religious leaders associated with the Temple in Jerusalem of collaborating with the oppressors. It is difficult to practice resistance to the empire from within the empire (and we in our time live in the empire, just as Jesus did and the prophets of Israel did.) The extent of the difficulty can be seen in the fate of Jesus, whose advocacy results in his death. The nature of his critique cannot be answered by the system of domination because it refuses to engage in any dialogue at all. Its only mode of response is violence. What the system tells its people is that violence against resistance makes them strong because the empire remains strong. There can be no question of fairness in such an environment.

How do we practice Gospel resistance? How do we recover our moral and political imagination in the empire to confront the empire? Because we are socialized into its very being, it is difficult for us to do it. The Gospel frees us to be advocates because through the life, death, and resurrection of Jesus we are made a new people who, like Jesus, are liberated to be advocates for victims and the marginalized, wherever they may be. When Jesus acts against the institutional structures of Judaism or denounces the Pharisees and Scribes, he is not attacking the *faith* of the Jews, to its shame, as is often taught. In fact, he is holding up to the Jews the tradition of the Mosaic Covenant, calling them back to the prophetic faith of the Exodus. He is attacking the collusion of institutional leaders with imperial power and therefore with oppression. And the church has not been immune to such collusion in its own history.

The lay theologian and lawyer William Stringfellow wrote that the church of Christ is called to advocate for every victim of oppression, not because the victim is right (we cannot know how any of us will be judged by God) but "because the victim is a victim. Advocacy is how the church puts into practice its own experience of the victory of the word of God over the power of death" (Stringfellow 94). In other words, advocacy is not advocacy when it advances my agenda or the program of my cause. It is only advocacy in the Gospel sense when it is truth-telling on behalf of God and when the truth is about the system of domination ultimately embodied in the power of death.

This truth telling is also sanctioned because it is not about personal truth. Conscience is not, as we often imagine, a privately-owned organ that produces morally superior opinions held by an individual disconnected from and pronouncing judgment on the community. Christian conscience is liberating; it frees us to transcend our selves, to share in suffering. It leads us not to smugness but to the risk of death for the sake of others and on behalf of the world. Conscience, for Christians, expresses itself most fully in the church's corporate and corporal witness of advocacy (Stringfellow 102).

The advocate claims to tell the truth, but it is clear from the example of the prophets, Jesus, and the church as community of resistance that the truth we tell when we advocate for others against the system of domination is not our own. The question is how we come to know this truth. How can we speak with the certainty of Micah, using such outrageous language, and continue to live in God's favor?

Although fairness may not be required of prophecy, prayer is. Prayer calls us to the place of suffering and also gives us ears and eyes for discernment, to see where God is or is not. It gives us access to truth by cutting through the veneer of culture, the untruth of apparent reality. The lens of faith is as valid as the daily news. As Christians we need not be captive to a particular government or position. We are without boundaries in the world and that gives us the right to speak to all situations of oppression, especially when we are party to it as members of this state (the United States) and its empire, which includes the state of Israel. Our nation's support for Israel, for example, with weapons and money gives us not only a right but a duty to speak.

Prayer is more than the asking of favors from God or wishing that things might be better. The Ignatian tradition of "discerning the spirits," which the founder of the Jesuits designed as a spiritual discipline for conscious living, is one that I have followed in my own prayer life. Although there is a formal process in which such discernment is engaged, usually with an experienced director, the principles of Ignatian discernment can help us understand how advocates might come to a place of truth that is more than individual desire. (For an excellent, nontechnical explanation of Ignation discernment, see Tad Dunne, *Spiritual Mentoring*.)

Discernment of spirits is not the same thing as the discernment of God's will. In fact, when we talk about knowing God's will, we are on potentially dangerous ground. What we are up to in discerning truth is not the discovery of esoteric information God has and wants me to have so that I can do what God wants. Such an understanding of truth actually absolves me of the responsibility to think about what I am doing in the face of uncertainties.

Discernment begins with our paying close attention to what is going on around us. That is where prayer begins, with the concrete situation in which we find ourselves—which might be something in ourselves or something in the world. The habit of paying attention allows us to notice the biases, the obstructions in ourselves, that prevent our acting on behalf of others or out of some other impulse than our own needs. In prayer, we develop the habit of seeing in the concrete events of our lives the presence of God and asking ourselves how God is speaking to us through these events.

Once we understand that God is speaking to us, we need to test the nature of the message through reflection and meditation on scripture, on the stories of our faith tradition in which God has spoken in the past. How does a particular text help me understand what feels like a call to be an advocate on behalf of one group or another? How does the Gospel help me interpret an invitation to stand on the street in front of the Israeli Consulate on behalf of Palestinians? As I said earlier, my experience of political murder in Israel during the first *intifada* led me to pray daily for peace in Jerusalem. My daily prayer included reflection on scripture and contemplating the meaning of what I read in light of my concern for the conflict between Israelis and Palestinians. What was the truth of that situation for me as a monk, a priest, a bishop? What was I to do about something that affected me so deeply?

As it happened, the fruits of that discernment were fourteen years in coming. The judgment to be an advocate for the Palestinians was not my own, even though the actions I took and continue to take have been criticized as being out of step with my own church community and the city and nation in which I live. But discernment is not a process of finding a way to accept inherited wisdom. It is a way of questioning tradition, testing it against new information and revelation. But most of all, this discernment is undertaken in love. Whatever action my prayer leads me to take, the goal should not be efficiency or even "being right." The goal is to come to a place of rest in God that allows us to speak with authority and without fear.

This process is also one that continues. Having noticed and reflected on the circumstances of my life, and then having acted out of love to advocate for justice, I am once again in the place of paying attention to what is happening now. What has been the result of my advocacy? How is God speaking to me and to us now through the actions we have taken? And what are we called through community, scripture, and love to do next?

The result of this process of prayer, which is also the fabric of our life in God, is what Ignatius called "consolation." When we have joined God in advocating for justice, we are affirmed in a peacefulness of spirit that we see over and over in the lives of God's prophets. The prophet Elijah, for example, condemned the royally-sanctioned worship of Baal, defeating the prophets of Baal on Mount Carmel. But when his life was threatened by Jezebel, he fled to the wilderness, where for forty days and nights he was tended and fed by the angel of the Lord. In a cave, he was visited by the word of the Lord which, famously, came not in a fierce wind or earthquake or fire but in "sheer silence." It was in this silence, this consolation, that Elijah's prophetic witness was affirmed (1 Kings 19:4–18). And so it has been with others. Desmond Tutu has spoken of the deep peace and consolation he experienced in the midst of terrifying situations of advocacy in South Africa. Martin Luther King wrote of similar moments.

I have outlined my own approach to discerning through prayer and meditation not to hold up myself in some special way—I am not a prophet—but to recommend to others who feel called to be advocates a way of testing motive and action against a measure greater than our own desires. Indeed, the way of discernment is the way of Christian life and witness. When we promise in our Baptismal Covenant to seek justice and peace in all people, we are also promising to pay attention, meditate on God's work, contemplate our call to action, and to act in the name of love.

Nonviolent action is the Christian's response to the empire. Although that message seems to me essential to the Gospel, it has not always been one that Christians have followed or even believe possible. Certainly, in our own history as Americans, we have regularly heard the Christian God invoked on behalf of war or, more recently, violent retaliation against the agents of terror. There are numerous examples in our history of Christian violence on behalf of what the empire has declared to be truth, beginning with the Emperor Constantine. The church's alliance with empire led to Augustine's Just War argument, based on the perception that the Gospel forbids us to use violence to defend ourselves but permits it in defense of others. Whatever else one might say of the argument, its origins as apology for the actions of the state make it suspect as an instrument of prophecy. The early church was clearly pacifist. Once it became allied with the state, its stance on violence changed.

Carter Heyward reclaims the vision of the Christian faith as one that preaches compassion and nonviolence. The way to God, she asserts in her book *Saving Jesus*, is one in which compassion replaces honor and even self-respect as the highest good, and nonviolence becomes a way of life, "a liberating response to the ongoing savaging of ourselves and one another." The compassion she proclaims is not passivity; it is not a "spiritualized state of being." It is "a shared—communal—commitment to do everything in our power to struggle toward the well-being of all people and creatures, including our adversaries....Nonviolence is a first fruit of compassion. It is also a collective, public force, seldom an option for individuals who are in harm's way." Nonviolence, Heyward says, is "a shared way of life that invites a dialogue" (Heyward 194–197).

Founder of the Palestinian Independent Commission for Citizens' Rights and a former spokesperson for the leadership of the Palestinians in Occupied Territories, Hanan Ashrawi described the first *intifada* in a way that evokes this understanding of nonviolent advocacy as, paradoxically, an invitation to dialogue. The *intifada* brought seemingly irreconcilable factions of Palestinian society together and charged them with "creating an alternative social, political, and national order, free of the distortions of the Israeli Occupation. We had a simple message: let there be freedom!...It was only when we refused dehumanization that we placed the occupiers on a course of recognition. We hoped that ultimately it [the Israeli military machine] would understood that its freedom lay in affording us ours" (Ashrawi 43).

The question for our time, raised by such situations as the conflict in the Middle East, is this: Can the church be the advocate for compassion and nonviolence in the twenty-first century that it was as a first-century community of resistance?

The Christian Church as the Advocate for Non-Violence

The Church is the Body of Christ; it is also an institution that, like all institutions, can act as part of the empire. We regard the church-community as the locus of the Christian and of Christ. If the truth we advocate is not personal, then it must thrive in a community whose prayer is a constant process of discernment of the spirits, in light of tradition, scripture, and reason (as we Anglicans like to say). Dietrich Bonhoeffer speaks of the church community as having a real impact on the life of the world because "it gains space for Christ. For whatever is 'in Christ' is no longer under the dominion of the world, of sin, or of the law. Within the newly created community, all the laws of this world have lost their binding force....The church-community can never consent to any restrictions of its service of love and compassion toward other human beings. For wherever there is a brother or sister, there Christ's own body is present; and wherever Christ's body is present, his church-community is also always present, which means that I must also be present there" (Bonhoeffer, 236).

This perspective led Bonhoeffer to return to Germany to be present with the suffering of the people under Hitler (and to die in a concentration camp) when he could have stayed comfortably at Union Theological Seminary. Although we are seldom asked to be advocates in the dangerous situation that called Bonhoeffer to die, the decision to go to Palestine and witness for peace on behalf of Palestinians or the decision to march for peace in the city of Boston is motivated by the same impulse that Bonhoeffer describes in his classic book on discipleship. As he writes in one place there, when Jesus calls us to follow him, "he bids us come and die." The death we experience in discipleship is the death of self, whether physical or not, that is necessary to Christian advocacy.

When I went to Palestine and Israel in the Spring of 2002 with a group of Episcopalians, our goal was to be with the Christians in the West Bank who had suffered and were suffering terribly from incursions by the Israeli forces that had resulted in the destruction of so many homes and businesses, the imprisonment of so many young men, the deaths of so many men, women, and children. Our going to that place was part of our prayer of intercession, part of our discernment of the spirits. What are we to do as Christians in Boston when we hear of the plight of our brothers and sisters in Ramallah or Jenin? Although we were a small band of pilgrims, we spoke in the prophetic voice of the church by our very presence.

We did not go as mediators. We went as nonviolent advocates. But our hope as Christians, even when we are advocates, is for reconciliation. Having identified the work of the empire as destructive to the spirit of God in human community, we need to reach out as followers of Christ to those "on the other side" who are also victims of the empire. Our brothers and sisters in the Jewish community are as oppressed by the situation in the Middle East as the Palestinians. The demon that possesses the region must be expelled so that everyone can be free.

Following the terrorist attacks of September 11, the bishops of the Episcopal Church issued a statement entitled "Waging Reconciliation." The statement contained the following paragraph:

> We are called to self-examination and repentance: the willingness to change direction, to open our hearts and give room to God's compassion as it seeks to bind up, to heal, and to make all things new and whole. God's project, in which we participate by virtue of our baptism, is the ongoing work of reordering and transforming the patterns of our common life so they may reveal God's justness—not as an abstraction—but in bread for the hungry and clothing for the naked. The mission of the church is to participate in God's work in the world. We claim that mission.
>
> *(Douglas xi)*

It has been argued that the presence of the Church—the witness of Christianity—is central to the resolution of the Israeli-Palestinian conflict. It has not been a strong advocate for peace, in part because the Christian community in the region, divided among different denominations with different agendas and comprised of people who are simply struggling to survive, has been unable to formulate a coherent response. And when there has been a "Christian" response to the power of the state of Israel, the results have been mixed, to say the least.

In the spring of 2002, the Episcopal Diocese of Massachusetts sponsored a series of three evenings, at which we heard three perspectives on the conflict in the Middle East, from a Muslim, a Christian, and a Jew. The Christian speaker, Charles Sennott, recounted his travels around the Holy Land (recorded in his compelling book, *The Body and the Blood*) seeking to read in present events the story of Jesus as he walked in that same place. What he was looking for was the contemporary presence of Christianity. What role are Christians playing in the conflict? And how might we read the Gospel in current events?

One of the stories Sennott tells is about the West Bank village of Beit Sahour, which is the setting of the biblical story of the appearance of angels to shepherds at the birth of Jesus. About seventy-five percent of the 12,000 people living in the village are Christians, and they played an important role in the first *intifada*, which began in the winter of 1987. As members of an educated and relatively affluent community, Beit Sahour's residents wanted to participate in the resistance to Israeli power structures but did not want to engage in a violent response. What resulted was what Sennott calls "the most effective and perhaps [the *intifada*'s] only sustained campaign of nonviolent resistance" (Sennott 136).

The powerful potential of such nonviolent response led to a determined Israeli effort to crush the movement in Beit Sahour and even to efforts by the Palestine Liberation Organization to undercut the movement's gains. The nonviolent resistance in Beit Sahour took the form of a tax revolt in which village businesses refused to pay taxes to Israel because "under international law it is illegal to collect taxes on occupied land" (144). The taxes collected were being spent, village leaders had determined, to fund the Israeli military administration. In other words, they were paying for the very Occupation that oppressed them.

Furthermore, the village leaders rejected the primary instrument of Israeli control, identity cards, which (with their associated database) governed the daily lives of Palestinians. Without identity cards, Palestinians were literally unable to function. More than five hundred residents turned in their identity cards during July 1988. The act was a classic example of non-violent resistance, and the Israeli authorities reacted strongly. The local military governor announced that the whole town would be punished. Heavily armed soldiers arrived at the Roman Catholic Church across from city hall to confront a gathering of protesting townspeople. The protestors sat down. And then the soldiers opened fire with rubber bullets. Some were injured; many were arrested. A curfew was imposed on the town.

The nonviolent resistance movement was gathering force, and Israelis had been cautioned by U.S. advisers not to permit, under any circumstances, a nonviolent resistance movement to gain strength. It is easier for a military regime to respond to violence. And so the Israelis crushed the movement by seizing the assets of local business leaders, imposing exorbitant fines, and arresting local merchants, many of whom were jailed for months. Homes were stripped of furniture and personal belongings. Beit Sahour was placed under siege. At the same time, the PLO leadership (under Yasser Arafat) wanted to discredit the village resistance movement to bolster its own claim to authority over Palestinians.

By early 1990, the Beit Sahour tax revolt and the nonviolent movement it generated were over. The example of this act of resistance appears to be negative in its effect, as indeed many such actions across history have seemed at first to be futile. The wonder is that the story has not been told, that all we hear of Palestinian resistance is the actions of suicide bombers and terrorists. Nor do we hear about the brutal repression suffered by the residents of Beit Sahour when they attempted to respond to Israeli Occupation nonviolently.

The relationship between Palestinians and Christianity is complex, and I am not in a position to explore it fully here. The people of Beit Sahour were not Christian pacifists. Theirs was strategic nonviolence. Many of the participants in the revolt decline to describe it as "Christian" nonviolence, even though they might affirm that the movement took hold in a Christian community because of the Christian message of nonviolence. But as one community leader said, it was only a small part of the movement. And to be Christian in the Palestinian struggle to end the Occupation is not necessarily a good thing in the eyes of the Palestinian leadership. In fact, the church and its leaders are often viewed as part of the problem: the Orthodox, the Catholics, and the Anglicans are seen as colonizers. Many Arab Christians are reluctant to assert their Christian beliefs. Sennott notes: "Politicized Christian Arabs were consciously just as much part of an Islamic culture as they were of a Christian culture; and to embrace a Christian identity in too strenuous a manner would offend the Islamic and Arab part of their identity" (Sennott, 154). (The preceding information is based on Sennott, 135–165.)

The Beit Sahour resistance did invite the participation of the Israeli left and of Palestinian Christian women, who came together under the banner of nonviolence in a way that had not been possible before. And perhaps the rise of this cooperative movement for peace is the result of the Beit Sahour experience that has kept alive in the region the idea of nonviolence in a Christian mode.

Our role as Western Christians is to work to keep such witnesses alive, even when we are regarded by some Palestinians as merely colonizers. That is part of the legacy of our having been agents of the empire in the past. Our calling now is to cease to be agents of anyone but God and the Gospel truth of nonviolent resistance to the system of domination that holds all of us in thrall. Even when we hear, as we always do, that nonviolence does not work and that we are naïve to continue to strive for justice and peace among all people, we have to return to our Gospel roots and to our prayer to reassert the power of God's reign. In the spring of 2003, another group of us from the Boston area will return to Palestine to be with those living under oppression and to witness to the truth of the spirit.

Perhaps the most stunning example of the power of this truth in our own times is to be found in the example of South Africa. Desmond Tutu's book, *No Future Without Forgiveness*, tells the story of the Truth and Reconciliation Commission that called former enemies—the oppressed and the oppressor—into new community through a public process of confession, forgiveness, and reconciliation. There has been almost nothing like it in human experience, and the success of the Commission, which Archbishop Tutu chaired, is a model for Christian advocacy.

The assumption behind the Commission, as Tutu put it, was that we inhabit a moral universe in which injustice and oppression cannot have the last word. The life, death, and resurrection of Jesus Christ are all the proof we need that love is stronger than hate, that compassion and gentleness and truth are stronger than their "ghastly counterparts"(Tutu 86). The Commission dared to demonstrate that truth in the political arena.

In the struggle against *apartheid*, advocacy on behalf of the oppressed was based on faith—and so was the Truth and Reconciliation Commission that followed the end of *apartheid*. The white oppressors were not punished if they agreed to acknowledge their actions and join the new society. Blacks who engaged in terrorist or violent activities were also called to acknowledge their crimes. No one was permitted to walk away from the requirements of a community in dialogue.

The end of advocacy is reconciliation, and in that it differs from merely political action. The people of Beit Sahour wanted to pursue their lives in peace and would have preferred to be reconciled to the Israelis and live with them in a just order—just as the African-Americans who fought for civil rights in the 1960s sought reconciliation under the leadership of Martin Luther King, Jr. It is what Christian advocates must always seek.

Tutu recounts in his book traveling to Israel and suggesting that the model of reconciliation that worked in South Africa might work there too. But when he suggested that forgiveness offered a way out of the cycle of vengeance that gripped both Israelis and Palestinians, he was rebuffed. When he pointed out that the Israeli treatment of Palestinians was a variance with the teachings of Jewish prophets, he was charged with being an Anti-Semite. Graffiti appeared on the walls of St. George's Anglican Cathedral in Jerusalem, in whose close he was staying, that read: "Tutu is a black Nazi pig" (Tutu 268).

What then can we do? The problems we face in places like the Middle East do not admit easy solutions, as the experiences of people in Beit Sahour and South Africa attest. The Gospel, however, is not a roadmap for success in the ordinary sense of the word. It is profoundly countercultural in all times and in all places. We are called to be advocates for God's truth when we have prayed deeply on its meaning for our lives and actions. We are also called to do works of mercy as a faithful community in support of the suffering, whoever they are and wherever they are, by supporting hospitals, schools, and agencies that provide food, shelter, and clothing. The church acts to co-create the future in such ways. Our advocacy is in our acts of love, as Matthew 25 tells us: when we have done it unto the least among us we have done it to our Lord. Our advocacy is always on behalf of that model of the just reign of God.

The church is an advocate, a community of resistance, or it is helpless or even useless in places like the Middle East. The danger we face as a faith community is not from taking positions on behalf of the oppressed. It is from continuing to hide in the power of our place within the empire and to feed off of the flesh of those over whom our system of domination holds power. The Gospel calls us to be in relationship with creation, and we cannot do that from a position of armed power.

When we speak on behalf of the oppressed, it is not to shame the other, not to bring the marginalized into power over the other. Our advocacy is on behalf of something greater than the singular grievance. In the Christian tradition, we are called especially to announce the just reign of God, which begins in forgiveness. The prophet church speaks to every situation in which violence prevents compassion and hurt trumps forgiveness. It is into such situations that we are called to put ourselves as Christian advocates. True forgiveness, as Tutu writes, makes the future possible (Tutu 279).

We are agents of resurrection. The Risen One has gone before us into the future, calling us to follow, as he called the disciples to meet him in Galilee. To make that journey is to affirm that the future is about hope and that the just reign of God lies within our reach. The power of evil over us has been definitively broken by Jesus Christ, whose life, death, and resurrection have changed everything and all things. That reality is right in front of us. As Christians we are set free of the constraints of power and politics to point to that reality and to name it both as God's and as redeemed by God. And our calling as the church is to live that reality.

I am grateful to the Reverend Deacon Ken Arnold, Director of Communications for the Episcopal Diocese of Massachusetts, for research and editorial assistance.

---

* The following text of a resolution passed by the Executive Council in June 2002 summarizes the church's position. Texts of previous resolutions can be found on the web site of the Episcopal Church: www.episcopalchurch.org.

Peace for Palestinians and Israelis
Resolution
June 18, 2002
Resolved, that the Executive Council, meeting in Durham, New Hampshire, June 10–14, 2002, mindful of the Church's longstanding commitment to a just peace for Palestinians and Israelis, condemns the violence of suicide bombers and the violence of the Occupation and pleads with both sides to pursue all avenues of negotiation based on United Nations Security Council Resolutions 242 and 338, and be it

Resolved, that Council reiterates the Church's position in support of a just peace that guarantees Israel's security and Palestinian aspirations for a viable sovereign state with Jerusalem as the shared capital of both Israel and Palestine, and be it

Resolved, that the Council commends President Bush's repeated call for a Palestinian State and urges Congress not to initiate legislation that undermines the President's efforts to broker a just peace, and be it

Resolved, that Council recognizes that the Israeli policy of building settlements in the Occupied Territories thwarts the peace process and thus Council restates the Church's position that all settlement activity should cease immediately, and be it

Resolved, that appropriate copies of this resolution be distributed by the Office of Government Relations.

Explanation: The Episcopal Church has supported a just peace for Israel and Palestine and an end to Israeli Occupation for many years. Last October, Council called for a peace process as a 'direct action against terrorism.' While the violence from both sides is undermining efforts for peace, the Council insists that those responsible for the violence must not be allowed to dictate the course of events. The mandate must be for a defined peace process to be pursued immediately by the two parties and supported by the international community. It is urgent that the Occupation of the Palestinian people is ended after decades of unbearable collective suffering. The outcome must result in a viable, sovereign Palestinian state along with the guarantee of an Israel secure and at peace with her neighbors.

The Occupation of the West Bank, including East Jerusalem, and Gaza, has been the single most aggravating source of tension in this long conflict and has resulted in the general humiliation of the Palestinian people. The decades old policy of Israel to build settlements on this land for Israelis greatly exacerbates the Occupation, taking prime land from Palestinians and populating them with Israelis protected by Israeli Defense Forces. Roads built for settlers connecting them to Israel sever ties between Palestinian villages and towns, resulting in severe travel restrictions on the Palestinian people and isolation of local communities into virtual cantons. The consequence is further humiliation and dislocation of the Palestinian people.

Works Cited

Ashrawi, Hanan. *This Side of Peace: A Personal Account*. New York: Simon and Schuster, 1995.

Bonhoeffer, Dietrich. *Discipleship*. Translated Barbara Green and Reinhard Krauss.

Dietrich Bonhoeffer Works, Volume 4. Minneapolis: Fortress Press, 2001.

Brueggemann, Walter. *Theology of the Old Testament: Testimony, Dispute, Advocacy*. Minneapolis: Fortress Press, 1997.

Douglas, Ian T. *Waging Reconciliation: God's Mission in a Time of Globalization and Crisis.* New York: Church Publishing Incorporated, 2002.

Dunne, Tad. *Spiritual Mentoring: Guiding People through Spiritual Exercises to Life Decisions.* San Francisco: Harper San Francisco, 1991.

Fiorenza, Elisabeth Schussler. *Jesus, Miriam's Child, Sophia's Prophet: Critical Issues in Feminist Christology.* New York: The Continuum Publishing Company, 1995.

Heyward, Carter. *Saving Jesus from Those Who Are Right: Rethinking What It Means to Be Christian.* Minneapolis: Fortress Press, 1999.

Leech, Kenneth. *Experiencing God: Theology as Spirituality.* San Francisco: Harper & Row, Publishers, 1985.

Sennott, Charles M. *The Body and the Blood: The Holy Land's Christians at the Turn of a New Millennium.* New York: Public Affairs, 2001.

Stringfellow, William. *Conscience & Obedience: The Politics of Romans 13 in the Light of the Second Coming.* Waco, Texas: Word Books, Publisher, 1978.

Tutu, Desmond. *No Future Without Forgiveness.* New York: Doubleday (Image Books), 1999.

Wink, Walter. *The Powers That Be: Theology for a New Millennium.* New York: Doubleday (A Galilee Book), 1998.

CHAPTER TWELVE

Healing and Love for Israel and Palestine

Michael Lerner

Jews did not return to Palestine in order to be oppressors or representatives of Western colonialism or cultural imperialism. Although it is true that some early Zionist leaders sought to portray their movement as a way to serve the interests of various Western states, and although many Jews who came brought with them a Western arrogance that made it possible for them to see Palestine as "a land without a people for a people without a land" and hence virtually to ignore the Palestinian people and their own cultural and historical rights, the vast majority of those who came were seeking refuge from the murderous ravages of Western anti-Semitism or from the oppressive discrimination that they experienced in Arab countries. The Ashkenazic Jews who shaped Israel in its early years were jumping from the burning buildings of Europe—and when they landed on the backs of Palestinians, unintentionally causing a great deal of pain to the people who already lived there—but were so transfixed with their own (much greater and more acute) pain that they couldn't be bothered to notice that they were displacing and hurting others in the process of creating their own state.

Their insensitivity to the pain that they caused and their subsequent denial of the fact that in creating Israel they had simultaneously helped create for the Palestinian people a life in which most were forced to live as refugees, leaving their many descendants still living as exiles and dreaming of "return" just as we Jews did for some 1800 plus years, helped produce today's crisis. They were aided by the arrogance, stupidity and anti-Semitism of Palestinian leaders and their Arab allies in neighboring states who dreamt of ridding the area of its Jews and who, much like the Herut "revisionists" who eventually came to run Israel over the past twenty years, consistently resorted to violence and intimidation to pursue their maximalist fantasies. By failing to recognize the Jews as refugees, by seeing them entirely as extensions of European colonialism and refusing to allow them refuge when Jews were being mass murdered in Europe, the Palestinian people created enmity which gave credibility to those ultra-nationalist Jews who felt that there was "no alternative" but to displace Arabs in order to provide safety for Jews.

By the time Palestinians had come to their senses and acknowledged the reality of Israel and the necessity of accommodating to that reality if they were ever to find a way to establish even the most minimal self-determination in the land that had once belonged to their parents and grandparents, it was too late to undermine the powerful misperception of reality held by most Jews and Israelis that their state was likely to be wiped out any moment if they did not exercise the most powerful vigilance. Drenched in the memories of the Holocaust and in the internalized vision of themselves as inevitably powerless, filled with righteous anger at the way Arabs had refused them refuge when Jews were powerless and facing genocide, outraged at continuing acts of violence and terror which Jews interpreted as proof that the Palestinian people were like European Christians in irrationally hating them, Jews were unable to recognize that they had become the most powerful state in the region and among the top 20% of powerful countries in the world—and they have used this sense of imminent potential doom to justify the continuation of the Occupation of the West Bank and Gaza for over thirty years.

The Occupation could only be maintained by what become an international scandal: the violation of basic human rights of the Occupied, the documented and widespread use of torture, the systematic destruction of Palestinian homes, the grabbing of Palestinian lands to allow expansion of West Bank settlements that had been created for the sole purpose of ensuring that no future accommodation with Palestinians could ever allow for a viable Palestinian state in the West Bank (since, as many settlers argued, the land had been given to the Jewish people by God, thereby precluding any rights to Palestinians), and the transformation of Israeli politics from a robust democracy into a system replete with verbal violence that sometimes spilled over into real violence (most notably, the assassination of Prime Minister Rabin because of his pursuit of peace and reconciliation with the Palestinian people).

The distortions in Israeli society required to enable the Occupation to continue have produced yet another dimension of the problem: first, the pervasive racism towards Arabs, manifested not only in the willingness to blame all Palestinians for the terrorist actions of a small minority but also in the willingness to treat all Israeli citizens of Palestinian descent as second class citizens (e.g. in giving lesser amounts of financial assistance to East Jerusalem or to Israeli Palestinian towns than to Jewish towns); second, in the refusal to allocate adequate funds to rectify the social inequalities between Ashkenazic and Sephardic/Mizrachi Jews; third in the willingness of both the Labor and Likud Parties to make electoral deals with ultra-orthodox parties intent on using state power to enforce religious control over Israelis' personal lives and to grab disproportionate state revenues in order that they could count on these religious parties to back whatever their engagement or disengagement plans in the West Bank might be.

Perhaps the greatest victim of all these distortions has been Judaism itself. Judaism has always had within it two competing strands, one that affirmed the possibility of healing the world and transcending its violence and cruelty, the other that saw "the Other" (be that the original inhabitants of the land, who were to be subject to genocidal extermination, or later Greeks, Romans, Christians, or now Arab) as inherently evil, beyond redemption, and hence deserving of cruelty and violence. The latter strand, which I call "settler Judaism" because it reflects the ideology of settling the land that reaches its fulfillment as much in the Book of Joshua (and in some passages in Torah) as in the reckless acts of Ariel Sharon and the current manifestations of the National Religious Party in Israel, was actually a very necessary part of keeping psychologically healthy in the long period of Jewish history when we were the oppressed and we were being psychologically brutalized by imperial occupiers or by our most immoral "hosts" in European societies. But today, when Jews are the rulers over an Occupied people or living in Western societies and sharing the upper crust of income and political power with our non-Jewish neighbors, the supremacist ideas of Settler Judaism create a religious ideology that can only appeal to those stuck in the sense that we are eternally vulnerable. For a new generation of Jews, bred in circumstances of power and success, a Judaism based on fear and demeaning of others, a Judaism used as a justification for every nuance of Israeli power and Occupation, becomes a Judaism that has very little spiritual appeal. Ironically, the need to be a handmaiden to Israel distorts Judaism and causes a "crisis of continuity" as younger Jews seek spiritual insight outside their inherited tradition.

Yet Judaism has another strand, what I and others call "Renewal Judaism," which started with the Prophets and has reasserted itself in every major age of Jewish life, insisting that the God of Torah is really the Force of Healing and Transformation, and that our task is not to sanctify existing power relations but to challenge them in the name of a vision of a world of peace and justice. Perhaps the greatest danger that Israel poses to the Jewish people is the extent to which it has helped Jews become cynical about their central task: to proclaim to the world the possibility of possibility, to affirm the God of the universe as the Force that makes possible the breaking of the tendency of people to do to others the violence and cruelty that was done to them, the Force that makes possible the transcendence of "reality" as it is so that a new world can be shaped. If Israel is ever to be healed, it will only be when it is able to reject this slavish subordination to political realism and once again embrace the transformative spiritual message of renewal.

In the years following the attacks on the World Trade Center, those who hear the voice of God as a voice of love and compassion are being drowned out by the "realists" and their cynical view of humanity and of the inevitable triumph of Evil. To stand for love today is perhaps as intense a challenge as it was for Jesus and others of my Jewish brothers and sisters during the days when Rome oppressed the world. To maintain one's faith that there really is a Force of Healing and Transformation (God, YHVH, Adonie, Allah) is to refuse to be a "realist," to refuse to allow what is to define for ourselves what can be.

So it is as faithful servant of God and inheritor of the prophetic tradition that I say to you that the world can, in fact, be healed and that that healing must start in the Holy Land.

And, yes, there are political steps that need to be taken. It would be wonderful if the Israeli people would elect a peace oriented government, but that won't happen as long as there is Palestinian violence against Israeli civilians. It would be nice if the Palestinian people were to embrace non-violence. But that won't happen as long as so many Palestinians experience daily humiliation and violence. If Palestinians were to build mass support for a totally non-violent movement, arrest those who helped support terrorists, and consistently respond to the hateful acts of settlers and the repressive acts of the Israeli army with massive non-violent, non rock-throwing, demonstrations, they would make huge progress. Five years of total non-violence and a discourse that publicly affirmed the humanity of the Jewish people and their right to a Jewish state within the pre-67 borders, and Palestinians would find themselves in a whole new political situation, one in which a majority of Jews both in Israel and around the world would be wanting to give peace a chance.

Some people argue that it's not fair to ask the Palestinians to have to engage in non-violence when they are facing the violence of the Occupation every day. The same argument could have been made by African American facing the violence of segregationist states in the South. But the issue for Martin Luther King, Jr. was not "Is it fair?" but "What will actually break through to the consciousness of American whites so that they feel less threatened, more affirmed in their own humanity, and thus more able to see that civil rights for us is in accord with their own highest sense of who they are as a people?" It is this kind of smarts that is needed by the Palestinians, not the whiney voice of "what's fair" but the intelligent voice of "what will make us win." Winning will never come from violence, and it is unlikely to come from the good will of American elites prodded by Arab elites. But it could come if the Palestinian people themselves convey to the Jewish people that the Jews have little to fear from Palestinian national self-determination. This was the brilliance of Gandhi, King, and Mandela—they all realized that the most important issue was to reassure the oppressors that they were seen *not only* as oppressors but also as fellow human beings whose lives deserve to be preserved. The secret underbelly of all oppressors is that they are scared that if they stop, those who are oppressed will rise up in anger and revenge, doing to their oppressors precisely what has been done to them. So the smartest thing that the oppressed can do in these circumstances is to affirm the humanity of the oppressor and, through that act, allow the oppressor to reconnect to the highest elements within themselves. When they do that, they will feel safe to end the Occupation.

It is precisely because it is hard to see signs of such a transformation happening in the near future that many Arabs and Jews in the peace forces in Israel have turned to *Tikkun* and the *Tikkun* Community and asked us to play a central role in changing the public understanding about Israel/Palestine in the United States and then to mobilize people to push their government to support a more balanced perspective.

We've done that by forming The *Tikkun* Community, an international organization of Christians, Jews, Muslims, Hindus, Buddhists and secular humanist atheists who are working together to educate the American public about the need to End the Occupation of the West Bank and Gaza. Our co-chair Cornel West often talks of the importance for radical democrats like himself of putting the fight for Middle East peace at the center of our agenda. We are doing that by creating local chapters of the *Tikkun* Community, organizing house parties to educate our neighbors, bringing people from every Congressional district in the US once a year to educate Congress about the need for a new approach, organizing people to challenge the media for its one-sided reporting, organizing a national *Tikkun* Campus Network to provide a "middle path" on campus between those who are rabidly anti-Israel and those who mistakenly have identified being "pro-Israel" with being "pro-Sharon, pro-Netanyahu, pro-hard line politics in the West Bank and Gaza."

We need Christians to join us, yet this connection has been very difficult to achieve because the most sensitive Christians have in their consciousness that the Christian past is filled with anti-Semitism. Thus, they feel uncomfortable critiquing anything Jewish. This feeling is manipulated by the Israeli Right and their domestic apologists who label as "anti-Semitic" anyone who dares question the wisdom or morality of contemporary policies of the most right-wing government Israel has ever had.

We in the Jewish world who are fighting for a progressive and love-oriented Judaism, very much need the help of our non-Jewish allies. You are not helping the Jewish people by allowing the Jewish Right to discourage you from speaking the deepest truths you know about Palestine. On the contrary: Israel's current policies are self-destructive and immoral. Those who give Israel a bit of "tough love" by pushing her to end the Occupation are Israel's true friends, while those who follow the path of giving a blank check to the current Israeli government will end up having actually weakened and potentially undermined the Israel which they wish to protect. On behalf of the hundreds of thousands of Israelis who are seeking peace, I implore you to not be silent, not to allow the fear of being labeled "anti-Semitic" (as you will be by the Jewish Right) to stop you from giving your money, your time, your energies to the struggle to bring peace to the Middle East.

Part of the way to do that is to join the *Tikkun* Community and help us by getting your local church, union, professional group, civic activities group, or anyone else you can find to endorse the resolution below. *Tikkun*'s intent is to place this perspective on ballots throughout the U.S. and eventually to have it endorsed by the US Congress, as far away as that date seems today in 2002 when I write.

Resolution

Whereas we recognize the humanity and fundamental decency of both the Israeli and Palestinian people, and wish to see them living in peace with each other, side by side in a safe Israel and a safe Palestine, and

Whereas we abhor acts of terror and violence against Israeli civilians, and reject the notion that these attacks on civilians can ever be justified (no matter how justified the anger at the Occupation), and whereas we abhor acts of terror and violence against Palestinian civilians, destruction of Palestinian homes, confiscation of Palestinian land and property, and other violations of their human rights, and whereas we reject any notion of moral equivalence because we see each act of terror and violence as uniquely awful and a violation of the sanctity of human life, and

Whereas we see all attempts to put the blame primarily on one side or the other of this conflict as yet another way to keep the conflict going and as fundamentally obscuring the way that both sides participate in co-creating the struggle, and

Whereas the continuation of this conflict is destructive to the people of the Middle East, counter to the best interests and values of the United States, and might contribute to an increase in anti-Semitism and anti-Arab sentiments both worldwide and in our own community,

Be It HEREBY RESOLVED THAT THE CITY OF _____ SHALL

1. Call upon its representatives in Congress to ask the U.S. government to support an international intervention (either through the UN or through some other appropriate multinational force) to separate the two sides, provide protection for each, and impose a settlement on both sides which includes:

> a. return of Israel to its pre-67 borders, with minor border changes mutually agreed upon (including Israeli control of the Western Wall and Palestinian control of the Temple Mount);
> b. creation of an economically and politically viable Palestinian state in all of the pre-67 West Bank and Gaza with small border changes mutually agreed upon, and with its capital in East Jerusalem;

c. an international fund to provide reparations for Palestinians and generous resettlement opportunities in the new Palestinian state;

d. recognition of Israel by Arab states and peaceful relations with all surrounding Arab and Islamic states;

e. sharing of the water and other resources of the area and joint ecological cooperation to preserve the ecological balance;

f. security cooperation by both Israel and Palestine with international participation and supervision to empower both sides to take decisive action to curb extremist elements that seek to block a peaceful resolution by resorting to provocation or violence against the citizens and/or territory of the other;

g. international guarantees of the military safety and security of Israel and Palestine, either through inclusion in NATO, a bilateral mutual defense agreement with the U.S., or some similar arrangement guaranteed to protect Israel and Palestine from other states which may have hostile intention.

2. Assist in the collection of voluntary contributions from the citizens of This City and those who study or work here, such funds to be allocated to non-profit organizations for the following purposes:

a. to provide aid for families of victims of terror, violence and military actions in both Israel and Palestine;

b. to create an Office of Middle East Peace in Washington D.C. which will provide public education to our elected representatives in support of peace in the Middle East consistent with the ideas in this proposition. The Office of Middle East Peace will be administered by and responsible to the City;

c. to provide education to our own citizens about the complexities of the Middle East situation, education which reflects the perspectives of those who are committed to points listed under 1 above;

Organizations receiving these funds shall prove that they genuinely support the right of the Jewish people to their own homeland in Israel and genuinely support the right of the Palestinian people to their own homeland in the West Bank and Gaza, reject violence as a means to achieve ends (including both Palestinian violence and Israeli violence) and demonstrate that they will clearly and unambiguously include this kind of even-handedness as well as support for an end to the Occupation in their public educational activities.

3. Publicly honor those in our community who have been working to create mutual understanding, peaceful reconciliation, and recognition of the need for a Palestinian state and an end to terror and an end to all forms of discourse which seem to blame one side or the other rather than acknowledge mutual responsibility for the Middle East tragedy.

If enough American communities were to pass this resolution, it would push our own government to begin to address this issue more even-handedly. But no amount of policy change will ultimately be sufficient. We are deeply committed to a world of love, and that can only begin when there is a reconciliation of the heart on both sides. *Both sides* must recognize that the world needs us to forgive each other and to take acts of repentance and atonement, acknowledging the way each of us has inflicted pain and cruelty on the other. It is only with this kind of generosity of spirit that we can hope to reach the generosity on the material level to share the land in a way that is truly sensitive to the needs of both sides.

When that happens, we will probably need a few generations of healing and therapy (both individual and social/spiritual) and a few generations in which the loving wisdom of our religious traditions can once again be heard. And that will happen. The children of Isaac and the children of Ishmael will reconcile and live in peace. They will be aligned in the same way that former enemies Germany and France are now aligned.

And when the new time does come, people will look back to this period and ask, "What could those people have been thinking back in the early 21st century when they allowed the carnage to continue daily, watched it, but then uttered a few words of quiet condemnation and shifted their focus back to increasing their own private lives?" Let our answer be: we were doing everything we could to use our religious community, our national and local organizations and religious institutions, to break through the circle of denial and moral deep sleep and reengage humanity in the quest for a world based not only on justice and peace, but also on love and generosity and open-heartedness and a response of awe and wonder to the grandeur of creation and the miracle of each and every human being on this planet.

CHAPTER THIRTEEN

Holistic Peace Process for the Middle East

Yehezkel Landau

With the Oslo peace process in shambles, and Israelis and Palestinians feeling demoralized after more than two years of war and terror, it is time to explore other ways of healing this seemingly intractable conflict. It is clear that military force, from either side, cannot prevail, for it can not make the opposing side accept the terms dictated by the perpetrators of violence. Both sides are exhausted by the ongoing cycle of violence and retaliation, but neither has a vision of an alternative way toward peace and security.

The architects of the Oslo framework were well-meaning political leaders who tried to strike a deal that would bring about the establishment of a Palestinian state in the West Bank, Gaza, and East Jerusalem in return for guarantees ensuring Israel's security and acceptance by the Arab world. That exchange sounds reasonable, but something got distorted in the translation from vision to reality. Partly it was a breakdown of trust between the two sides. But there was, in my view, a more fundamental problem, a "congenital defect" in the Oslo concept: its rationalist assumption of how the conflict could be resolved. The negotiators were secular nationalists who tried to impose a "secular" peace plan on a holy land whose inhabitants include many people motivated by religious passions. Since the religious militants on both sides were effectively shut out of the negotiating process, they have done their best to sabotage the outcome. In order to overcome this serious obstacle to any mutually acceptable agreement, we need to adopt what I would call a more holistic approach to peacemaking, involving a broader spectrum of

Israelis and Palestinians than just the politicians and diplomats. A genuine peace process for Israel/Palestine has to address the following four aspects simultaneously:

On the *political level*, both Jews and Palestinians need to compromise on the tangible issues in dispute, including territory, sovereignty in Jerusalem, water resources, arsenals of weapons, and the repatriation or rehabilitation of refugees. Painful concessions need to be made by both sides, forcing them to undergo what is tantamount to an amputation of the collective body, so that the State of Israel will be smaller than the Land of Israel and the State of Palestine will be smaller than the Land of Palestine. Political leaders must acknowledge the painful sacrifices this renunciation entails for the other side as well as their own, and they have to find appropriate symbolic expressions of the collective grief. Economic incentives for both parties, especially the much poorer Palestinians, are a key element in the peacemaking agenda. Commercial interdependence based on equity, in a regional framework involving Israel, Palestine, Jordan, Egypt, Saudi Arabia, Syria, and Lebanon has to be established. For this political transformation from hostility to partnership, courageous political leadership will be required from all sides, including outside powers like the Americans and Europeans.

On the *cognitive level*, new understandings of identity—who I am in relation to the "Other"—have to be nurtured. It is much more challenging than simply changing the notion of "enemy" into "peaceful neighbor." Both Israelis and Palestinians have cultivated "victim scripts" over many years. The interior landscape requires a brutal adversary in order to justify an existential struggle that gives meaning to life, with a deep sense of belonging and loyalty. One of the chapter titles in Menachem Begin's book *The Revolt* is "We Fight, Therefore We Are." Who do we become when the war is over? How do we justify what we have done, or what others have done in our name, when we no longer have the other side to blame for all the horrors of war? How can we move from partisan scripts to more inclusive renderings of history? The Oslo process began with declarations of "mutual recognition" but neither side was ready back in 1993 to re-cognize the other side, to perceive and conceive the "enemy" and one's own self and community in non-dualistic terms. To transform the dualistic worldviews pitting "us" against "them" and to inculcate a more inclusive humanistic vision will require the diligent labor of many professional educators over the coming years. At OPEN HOUSE in Ramle, Israel, a site that has been home to a Muslim

Palestinian family before 1948 and a Jewish Israeli family since then, our peace education for children and adults is based on a candid retelling of the tragic events of the 1948 war, including the Arab world's rejection of Jewish statehood and expulsions of Palestinian civilians by the Israeli army.

On the *emotional level*, we need to address and transform intense feelings that keep both peoples locked in antagonistic inter-dependence. The most obvious one is *fear*. Transforming fear to mutual trust requires re-humanizing encounters with the "enemy" at all levels, from the political echelon down to the classroom, ideally at kindergarten age. To prepare people to actually meet their dreaded counterparts, video representations of the positive qualities in the demonized "Other" should be broadcast on both national television networks, replacing the negative accounts we are fed daily. The media are a serious problem in this regard, and we have to challenge communications professionals to change the "script". The messages we receive every day not only perpetuate our cognitive dualism; they also keep us trapped in "visceral inertia," preventing us from taking responsibility for our conditioned feelings and response patterns. Fear, in particular, is a powerful irrational force driving much of the destructive behavior in Israel/Palestine, as it does in so many other places. And both peoples have legitimate reasons for feeling afraid. But if we want to overcome our fears, we need to organize widespread encounters between Arabs and Jews of all ages. Our experience at OPEN HOUSE has taught us that joint activities which focus on common interests and provide practical skills have a much greater chance of success than amorphous "Jewish-Arab dialogues."

Another strong feeling that keeps us trapped is *anger*. To transform anger to acceptance, perhaps even forgiveness, requires a capacity for empathy that is sadly lacking among both Palestinians and Israelis. The challenge for educators and mental health professionals is to help people see that they have been a real threat to the well-being of the other side. In other words, we are victimizers as well as victims. We need to grasp that the other side has understandable reasons to be angry, too, and that had we been born among "them," we would probably be fighting "us" instead of the reverse. To deal with our anger constructively, we need to take at least two practical steps:

- *listening with empathy* to the grievances on the other side, so that our own are put into a broader perspective. There is a U.S.-based project called "Compassionate Listening" which trains Israelis, Palestinians, and Americans in this discipline.

- *deciding* together with our adversaries *how to make amends* for the respective experiences of injustice. Apologies can be expressed by individuals and by governments. But to be sincere, the expressions of remorse have to be matched by acts of moral rectification, what in Jewish tradition is called *tikkun*. For example, if refugees are not able to return to their homes (Palestinians from what is today Israel, or Jews from Arab countries), then fair compensation must be offered to the families that suffered.

The third and last major emotion that has to be transformed is *grief*. Everyone has lost a loved one, a friend, or a neighbor during the course of this conflict. How can we help each other to embrace with compassion the suffering on the other side, too? We have to open our hearts to *their* stories of loss and grief, the stories we have filtered out by our own pain and denial. The Bereaved Parents Forum, comprised of Israelis and Palestinians who have lost loved ones to the conflict, offers an inspiring example of shared grief transformed into compassion. Educators, social workers, and psychologists, reinforced by the media, have to find ways to replicate this example by communicating the poignant stories of suffering across the barriers of willful ignorance.

Finally, on the *spiritual level*, a different understanding of holiness has to be taught by religious leaders and educators. Jews, Christians, Muslims, Druse, and others in the Holy Land are hungry for an experience of true holiness, based in an awareness of the all-loving and inclusively just God. Partisan interpretations of the sacred, especially regarding territory and history, need to be supplanted by a different theological paradigm whose essence can be summarized as "pluralistic monotheism." The One God not only suffers or tolerates difference; that God has created individuals and nations with such striking differences in order to create a variegated human community that can celebrate diversity instead of feeling threatened by it. If both Jews and Palestinians can be brought to see, and to know deeply, that the Land belongs to God alone, and that by the grace of God both peoples belong to the Land (see Exodus 19:5–6), then a new political vision can be generated on this spiritual foundation. Within this practical vision, all the children of Abraham can be partners in consecration, rather than rivals competing for divine favor on the basis of a scarcity principle. In regard to truth, holiness, and divine love, the principle of abundance, of gracious generosity, has to take over. For this to happen, religious educators have to assume responsibility for developing and teaching an inclusive under-standing of holiness. They must learn from one another, pray for one another, and work together to support the political agenda of reconciliation. Without a shared spiritual commitment to genuine sacrifice—humility and renunciation for the sake of God—all the peace plans advanced by diplomats will fail. Peace in the outer society can not come about so long as people's hearts are steeped in bitter resentment. God's Holy Land is meant to be a laboratory for practicing justice and compassion towards all. As privileged inhabitants of that land, we are called to transcend the bloody, divisive past and create a common future. If we rise to the challenge, we will all be blessed by the holiness of Shalom, Salaam, Peace. And then life will prevail, not death and destruction.

With such a holistic peace agenda, enlisting the services of a broad spectrum of people within society, not only the political leaders, we have a chance to redeem our tragic situation. The hour is late, the suffering on all sides heart-breaking. But if we commit ourselves to a new beginning, we can, with God's help, make the Holy Land a land of genuine holiness for all.

To visit OPEN HOUSE on the Web, go to www.openhouse.org.il

CHAPTER FOURTEEN

A Just Peace

Edward W. Said

A just peace is a subject that requires a series of reflections rather than a string of assertions or affirmations. I don't, therefore, believe that we can or should even try to produce a formula for just peace in the form of the sentence: "A just peace is so and so." What I propose instead is a method for thinking about just peace as a way of getting beyond the usually bipolar oppositions that lock collective antagonists together in conflicts that may or not be actual war. I shall assume that conflict and/or war between at least two such antagonists is what we must start with in order to think about just peace. At the same time, and perhaps paradoxically, I shall assume that if the conflict is profound and long enough in time—the Palestinian-Israeli one proposes itself immediately but there are others that have offered partition as the solution—one should concentrate on those elements in the antagonism that are irreconcilable, basic, irremediably concrete. In other words, I think it is futile to look for a just peace in transcendence, synthesis, and ultimate reconciliation. Finally, a most important disclaimer on my part: I write these things not as a practical politician in search of results nor as a policy expert looking for new proposals to present to the parties nor as a philosopher trying to define the terms analytically, but rather as a cultural and literary historian concerned with secular ways of articulating and re-presenting experience that defy ordinary patchwork solutions because that experience by its nature is so extreme, intractable, and intransigent at its core. Most of my work has been concerned both with the history of conquest and dispossession, generally through imperialism, and the various strategies for national, as well as cultural, emancipation and liberation that opposed empire and successfully brought about re-possession and the enfranchisement of the peoples who had been the objects of empire. In particular I have been interested in the kind of knowledge and cultural forms that arise in these struggles, both for and against conquest.

This concern, I believe, requires a particular care with the rhetoric and style one uses when trying to come to terms with these subjects, which because they stretch out well beyond the here and now, well beyond so-called pragmatic frameworks that underpin discussions of the what-is-to-be-done kind, well beyond the highly limited histories of the sort that create convenient narratives for action and choice based on simple binary oppositions (us–versus–them), require more deliberation, more care in rendering different views together. Elsewhere, in *Culture and Imperialism* mainly, I have discussed this style and called it contrapuntal, that is, trying to render some sense both of a longer and wider view and also of the reality of simultaneous voices.

This is not so much a matter of hesitation and qualification as it is of trying to break out of the mold of maintaining the classic oppositions that provoke war and, alas, have underwritten notions of what peace is possible, notions in which a just peace is simply the mirror image of what "we" think a just war is. Can one break out of that instrumental style of thought which, in my opinion, was one of the flaws in the America-Israeli vision of peace via the Oslo process? Justice and peace are inherently, indeed irreducibly, positive in what they suggest separately and, of course, even more so when they are used together. It would be hard to imagine anyone for whom the notion of just peace in a world where injustice and conflict are so prevalent is not in itself desirable. And yet the questions how and in what circumstances a just peace could take hold surround the notion forbiddingly with such a number of qualifications and circumstances as to make the phrase "just peace" nearly impossible to use with any kind of universal consistency.

At closer range, however, there is no doubt, for instance, that a people whose basic rights to self-determination have not been realized because they are under military or imperial occupation and who have struggled to achieve self-determination for years and years, have a right in principle to the peace that comes as a result of liberation. It's hard to fault that as a statement of what a just peace might entail. But what is also entailed is perhaps greater suffering, more destruction, more distortion and a whole host of problems associated with an aggrieved nationalism ready to exact a very high price from its enemy and its internal opponents in order to achieve justice and peace.

The cases of Algeria and the Congo are stark evidence of what I mean, the colonial distortion giving rise to later post-colonial distortions that multiply the horror of the initial situation. These too must be figured in.

Still, concrete circumstances, and the historical setting are very important here, especially since, as I use the word secular, I am referring neither to an ultimate condition that develops redemptively or because of revelation, nor to miraculous conversions of swords into ploughshares. These may be wonderfully attractive to long for, but they pertain to another realm entirely, that of revelation, divine or sacred truth against which, following Vico, the historical, secular world made by human labor is set. It is this historical world that I am talking about, not the mysterious or inaccessible (to me, at least) one of religion or of nature. To try to establish an order in which, as Blake put it, the lion and the lamb shall lie down together, and to try to impose it on a real conflict, seems to me a form of what Adorno sarcastically once called a kind of extorted reconciliation that is very much what religious politics (Judaic, Christian, Islamic, Sikh, Hindu, or whatever) has always been propagating. For all sorts of reasons, many of them obvious enough now, my inclination is to shun the blandishments of religious solutions, particularly in cases where religion already plays a role in fomenting and deepening conflict. I don't say that religion isn't important, but I do say that it must be treated as a special exacerbated aspect of the secular.

On the other hand it must be underlined that, as Edward Thompson once argued when in the late 1920's he set about describing why Indians took offense at the tone and content of such monuments of scholarship as the Oxford History of India, great and disproportionate power inflects, imprints, conditions any thought about peace and justice usually in very insidious and sometimes invisible ways. Contrast for example writings about the Irish troubles in 19th century British prose and that of Irish writers. There is in the former instance a loftiness, even an Olympian quality to the tone that derives from a history of holding power so that the prose of Lloyd George during the negotiations of 1921–2 prompted a sense in his Irish antagonists of an outraged feeling that he was "playing with phrases" while they were desperately pressing their case for liberation.

A just peace must necessarily reflect these differences, all of them based on actual but widely divergent experiences, and this is one reason why a just peace, which in its meaning suggests the stability of something finally achieved, is a contradictory or at least a very fluid, rather than a stable, concept. A just peace doesn't bring quiet and the end of history at all, but rather a new dynamic which I want to discuss later. For the time being I'd like to stress that all modern wars are fought over territory, not ideas or values or civilizational projects, as has been quite incredibly argued by recent policymakers in the US and Europe. So I want to suggest that the geographical element is basic in that claims for sovereignty, ownership, dominance, and hegemony made by one side against another run through the conflicts that concern me here, even though it is also true that such claims are not always pressed in those terms alone, and second, that in many instances (Ireland's being one) imperial partition postpones peace as the ownership of land remains unsettled.

To recapitulate, a just peace pertains to the secular historical domain, i.e., it is the result of human labor. Second, the process for peace takes place on and over the ownership and disposition of territory which—and this is very important—is imagined in different ways by the antagonists. Why? Because territory is depicted as the culmination or the stage for the enactment of collective histories. During the era of high imperialism, for instance, Britain's destiny as a nation was imagined as the result of a native genius for overseas colonial expansion, in which education, trade, administration and even scholarship were seen as taking place in distant locations, over and above the wishes of the native inhabitants—hence the colonization of South and Southeast Asia, India, West and South Africa, the Middle East, North America, Australia, and Ireland. This in turn produces counter-narratives of nationalist resistance that I have described in my book *Culture and Imperialism*, narratives whose logic was intended to dislodge one presence with another. The various processes of handing power from the British to the local nationalist authority, as in India on August 14, 1947, don't necessarily fall into the category of a just peace because the partition of India, the subsequent disturbances, and the feelings of loss and betrayal all round detracted from universal feelings of satisfaction and fulfillment. Retrospectively, however, the emergence of a multi-cultural Indian society and the emergence also of new discourses in revisionary historiographies of Britain and India seems to have mitigated the damage of partition and colonial failure and produced currents of thought that have escaped the old binary oppositions, but at the same time introduced new ones. This may be inevitable.

In all sorts of ways, the Palestinian-Israeli impasse is in part a confirmation, in part an exception to what I have been saying. I might as well begin with my own experience of 1948, and what it meant for many of the people around me, since the actual experience of real Palestinians is at the very core of what I am trying to discuss here. I talk about this at some length in my memoir *Out of Place* (1999). My own immediate family was spared the worst ravages of the catastrophe: we had a house and my father a business in Cairo, so even though we were in Palestine during most of 1947, when we left in December of that year, the wrenching, cataclysmic quality of the collective experience (when 780,000 civilian Palestinians, literally 2/3 of the country's population were driven out by Zionist troops and design) was not one we had to go through. I was 12 at the time so had only a somewhat attenuated and certainly no more than a semi-conscious awareness of what was happening; only this narrow awareness was available to me, but I do distinctly recall some things with special lucidity. One was that every member of my family on both sides became a refugee during the period; no one remained in our Palestine, that is, that part of the territory (controlled by the British Mandate) that did not include the West Bank, which was annexed to Jordan. Therefore, those of my relatives who lived in Jaffa, Safad, Haifa and West Jerusalem were suddenly made homeless, in many instances penniless, disoriented, and scarred forever.

I saw most of them again after the fall of Palestine but all were greatly reduced in circumstances, their faces stark with worry, ill-health, despair. My extended family lost all its property and residences, and like so many Palestinians of the time bore the travail not so much as a political but as a natural tragedy. This etched itself on my memory with lasting results, mostly because of the faces which I had once remembered as content and at ease, but which were now lined with the cares of exile and homelessness. Many families and individuals had their lives broken, their spirits drained, their composure destroyed forever in the context of seemingly unending, serial dislocation: this was and still is for me of the greatest poignancy. One of my maternal uncles went from Palestine to Alexandria to Cairo to Baghdad to Beirut and now, in his 80's, lives a sad, silent man, in Seattle. Neither he nor his immediate family ever fully recovered. This is emblematic of the larger story of loss and dispossession, which continues today.

The second thing I recall was that for the one person in my family who somehow managed to pull herself together in the aftermath of the *nakba*, my paternal aunt, a middle-aged widow with some financial means, Palestine meant service to the unfortunate refugees, many thousands of whom ended up penniless, jobless, destitute and disoriented in Egypt. She devoted her life to them in the face of government obduracy and sadistic indifference. I have described her more fully in my memoir *Out of Place* (1999). From her I learned that whereas everyone was willing to pay lip service to the cause, only a very few people were willing to do anything about it. As a Palestinian, therefore, she took it as her lifelong duty to set about helping the refugees—getting their children into schools, cajoling doctors and pharmacists into giving them treatment and medicine, finding the men jobs, and above all, being there for them, a willing, sympathetic and, above all, selfless presence. Without administrative or financial assistance of any kind, she remains an exemplary figure for me from my early adolescence, a person against whom my own terribly modest efforts are always measured and, alas, always found wanting. The job for us in my lifetime was to be literally unending, and because it derived from a human tragedy so profound, so unacknowledged, so extraordinary in saturating both the formal as well as the informal life of its people down to the smallest detail, it has been and will continue to need to be recalled, testified to, remedied.

For Palestinians, a vast collective feeling of injustice continues to hang over our lives with undiminished weight. If there has been one thing, one particular delinquency committed by the present group of Palestinian leaders for me, it is their supernally gifted power of forgetting: when one of them was asked recently what he felt about Ariel Sharon's accession to Israel's Foreign Ministry (well before he became Prime Minister), given that he was responsible for the shedding of so much Palestinian blood, this leader said blithely, "We are prepared to forget history." This is a sentiment I neither can share nor, I hasten to add, easily forgive.

One needs to recall by comparison Moshe Dayan's statement in 1969:

> We came to this country which was already populated by Arabs, and we are establishing a Hebrew, that is a Jewish state here. In considerable areas of the country [the total area was about 6 percent] we bought the lands from the Arabs. Jewish villages were built in the place of Arab villages, and I do not even know the names of these Arab villages, and I do not blame you, because these geography books no longer exist; not

only do the books not exist, the Arab villages are not there
either. Nahalal [Dayan's own village] arose in the place of
Mahalul, Gevat in the place of Jibta, [Kibbutz] Sarid in the place
of Haneifs and Kefar Yehoshua in the place of Tel Shaman.
There is not one place built in this country that did not have
a former Arab population.

[*Ha'aretz,* April 4, 1969]

What also strikes me about these early Palestinian reactions is how
largely unpolitical they were. For twenty years after 1948, Palestinians were immersed in the problems of everyday life with little
time left over for organizing, analyzing and planning, although there
were some attempts to infiltrate Israel, try some military action,
write and agitate. With the exception of the kind of work produced
in Mohammed Hassanein Haykal' s Ahram Strategic Institute, Israel
to most Arabs and even to Palestinians was a cipher, its language
unknown, its society unexplored, its people and the history of their
movement largely confined to slogans, catch-all phrases, negation.
We saw and experienced its behavior towards us, but it took us a
long while to understand what we saw or what we experienced.

The overall tendency throughout the Arab world was to think of
military solutions to that scarcely imaginable country, with the result
that a vast militarization overtook every society, almost without
exception in the Arab world; coups succeeded each other more or less
unceasingly and, worse yet, every advance in militarism brought an
equal and opposite diminution in social, political and economic
democracy. Looking back on it now, the rise to hegemony of Arab
nationalism allowed for very little in the way of democratic civil
institutions, mainly because the language and concepts of that
nationalism itself devoted little attention to the role of democracy in
the evolution of those societies. Until now, the presence of a putative
danger to the Arab world has engendered a permanent deferral of
such things as an open press, or unpoliticized universities, or
freedoms to research, travel in, and explore new realms of knowledge.
No massive investment was ever made in the quality of education,
despite largely successful attempts on the part of the Nasser
government in Egypt as well as other Arab governments to lower the
rate of illiteracy. It was thought that given the perpetual state of
emergency caused by Israel, such matters, which could only be the
result of long-range planning and reflection, were ill-afforded
luxuries. Instead, arms procurement on a huge scale took the place of
genuine human development with negative results that we live with

until today. Thirty per cent of the world's arms are still bought by Arab countries today.

Along with the militarization went the wholesale persecution of communities, preeminently but not exclusively the Jewish ones, whose presence in our midst for generations was suddenly thought to be dangerous. Similar abuses were visited on Palestinians inside Israel, who until 1996 were ruled by the Emergency Defense Regulations first codified and applied by the British; they remain a discriminated against community, without even the status of a national minority (They exist juridically as "non-Jews.") even though they constitute twenty of Israel's citizenry. In terms of land, budgetary support, and social status, they are woefully under-privileged and underrepresented. I know that there was an active Zionist role in stimulating unrest between the Jews of Iraq, Egypt, and elsewhere on the one hand, and the scarcely democratic govern-ments of those Arab countries on the other, but it seems to me to be incontestable that there was a xenophobic enthusiasm officially decreeing that these and other designated "alien" communities had to be extracted by force from our midst. Nor was this all. In the name of military security in countries like Egypt, there was a bloody minded, imponderably wasteful campaign against dissenters, mostly on the Left, but also against independent-minded people whose vocation as critics was brutally terminated in prisons, by fatal torture and summary executions. As one looks back at these things in the context of today, it is the immense panorama of waste and cruelty that stands out as the immediate result of the war of 1948 itself.

Along with those went a scandalously poor treatment of the refugees themselves. It is the case, for example, that the thousands of Palestinian refugees still resident in Egypt must report to a local police station every month; vocational, educational and social opportunities for them are curtailed, and the general sense of not belonging adheres to them despite their Arab nationality and language. In Lebanon the situation is direr still. Almost 400,000 Palestinian refugees have had to endure not only the massacres of Sabra, Shatila, Tell el Zaatar, Dbaye and elsewhere, but have remained confined in hideous quarantine for almost two generations. They have no legal right to work in at least 60 occupations, they are not adequately covered by medical insurance, they cannot travel and return, they are objects of suspicion and dislike. In part—and I shall return to this later—they have inherited the mantle of opprobrium draped around them by the PLO's presence (and since 1982 its unlamented absence) there, and thus they remain in the eyes of many ordinary Lebanese a sort of house enemy to be warded off and/or punished from time to time.

A similar situation in kind, if not in degree, exists in Syria; as for Jordan, though it was, to its credit, the only country where Palestinians were given naturalized status, a visible fault line exists between the disadvantaged majority of that very large community and the Jordanian establishment. I might add, however, that for most of these situations where Palestinian refugees exist in large groups within one or another Arab country—all of them as a direct consequence of 1948—no simple, much less elegant or just, solution exists in the foreseeable future. It is also worth asking, why it is that a destiny of confinement and isolation has been imposed on a people who quite naturally flocked to neighboring countries when driven out of theirs, countries which everyone thought would welcome and sustain them. More or less the opposite took place: no welcome was given them (except in Jordan), another unpleasant consequence of the original dispossession in 1948.

This now brings me to a especially significant point, namely the emergence since 1948 in both Israel and the Arab countries of a new rhetoric and political culture. For the Arabs this was heralded in such landmark books as Constantine Zurayk's *Ma 'nat ai-Nakba*, the idea that because of 1948 an entirely unprecedented situation had arisen for which an unprecedented state of alertness and revival was to be necessary. What I find more interesting than the emergence of a new political rhetoric or discourse—with all its formulas, prohibitions, circumlocutions, euphemisms, and sometimes empty blasts—is its total water-tightness (to coin a phrase) with regard to its opposite number. Perhaps it is true to say that this occlusion of the other has its origin in the fundamental irreconcilability of Zionist conquest with Palestinian dispossession, two antithetically opposed secular experiences related to each other, however, as cause and effect. The developments out of that fundamental antinomy led to a separation between the two on the official level that was never absolutely real even though on a popular level there was a great deal of enthusiasm for it.

Thus we now know that Nasser, whose rhetoric was next to none in implacability and determination, was in contact with Israel through various intermediaries, as was Sadat, and of course Mubarak. This was even truer of Jordan's rulers and somewhat less so (but nevertheless the case) with Syria. I am not advancing a simple value judgment here since such disparities between rhetoric and reality are common enough in all politics, although they were cruelly wide between the negotiating and the actual on-the-ground environments of the Oslo peace process. But what I am suggesting is that a sort of orthodoxy of hypocrisy developed inside the Arab and Israeli camps that in effect fueled and capitalized the worst aspect of each society. The tendency towards orthodoxy, uncritical repetition of received ideas, fear of innovation, one or more types of double-speak, etc. has had an extremely rich life.

I mean, in the general Arab case, that the rhetorical and military hostility towards Israel led to more, not less ignorance about it, and ultimately to the disastrous politico-military performances of the 60s and 70s. The cult of the army which implied that there were only military solutions to political problems was so prevalent that it overshadowed the axiom that successful military action had to derive from a motivated, bravely led, and politically integrated and educated force, and this could only issue from a citizens' society. Such a *desideratum* was never the case in the Arab world, and it was rarely practiced or articulated. In addition, there was consolidated a nationalist culture that encouraged rather than mitigated Arab isolation from the rest of the modern world. Israel was soon perceived not only as a Jewish but as a Western state, and as such was completely rejected even as a suitable intellectual pursuit for those who were interested in finding out about the enemy.

From that premise a number of horrendous mistakes flowed. Among those was the proposition that Israel was not a real society but a makeshift quasi-state; its citizens were there only long enough to be scared into leaving; Israel was a total chimera, a "presumed" or "alleged" entity, not a real state. Propaganda to this effect was crude, uninformed, ineffective. The rhetorical and cultural conflict—a real one—was displaced from the field so to speak to the world stage, and there too with the exception of the Third World, we were routed. We never mastered (or were permitted) the art of putting our case against Israel in human terms, no effective narrative was fashioned, no statistics were marshaled and employed, no spokespersons trained and refined in their work emerged. We never learned to speak one, as opposed to several contradictory languages. Consider the very early days before and after the 1948 debacle when people like Musa al-Alami, Charles Issawi, Walid Khalidi, Albert and Cecil Hourani, and others like them undertook a campaign to inform the Western world, which is where Israel's main support derived from, about the

Palestinian case. Now contrast those early efforts, which were soon dissipated by infighting and jealousy, with the official rhetoric of the Arab League or of any one or combination of Arab countries. These were (and alas continue to be) primitive, badly organized and diffused, insufficiently thought through. In short, embarrassingly clumsy, especially since the human content itself, the Palestinian tragedy, was so potent, and the Zionist argument and plan vis-a-vis the Palestinians so outrageous. I don't want to waste any time here giving examples of what those from my generation already know too well.

By impressive contrast, the Israeli system of information was for the most part successful, professional, and in the West, more or less all-conquering. It was buttressed in parts of the world like Africa and Asia with the export of agricultural, technological and academic expertise, something the Arabs never really got into. That what the Israelis put out was a tissue of ideological, incomplete, or half-truths is less important than that as a confection it served the purpose of promoting a cause, an image, and an idea about Israel that both shut out the Arabs and in many ways disgraced them.

Looking back on it now, the rhetorical conflict that derived from and was a consequence of 1948 was amplified well beyond anything like it anywhere else in the world. To forget or ban it from consideration of what a just peace might be is a mistake, because even in 2002, most of the developed world sees Arabs through Israel's eyes. For part of the time, the rhetorical conflict took on some of the vehemence and prominence of the Cold War, which framed it for almost thirty years. What was strange about it is that like the events of 1948 themselves, there was no real Palestinian representation at all until 1967, and the subsequent emergence and prominence of the PLO. Until then we were simply known as the Arab refugees who fled because their leaders told them to. Even after the research of Erskine Childers and Walid Khalidi utterly disputed the validity of those claims and proved the existence of Plan Dalet thirty-eight years ago, we were not to be believed. Worse yet, those Palestinians who remained in Israel after 1948 acquired a singularly solitary status as Israeli Arabs, shunned by other Arabs, treated by Israeli Jews under a whip by the military administration and, until 1966, by stringent emergency laws applied and assigned to them as non-Jews. The lopsidedness of this rhetorical conflict in comparison, say, with the war between American and Japanese propagandists during World War II as chronicled by John Dower in his book *War Without Mercy* is that Israeli misinformation, like the Zionist movement itself, allowed no room for an indigenous opponent, someone on the ground whose land, society and history were simply taken from him/her. We were largely invisible, except occasionally as *fedayin* and terrorists or as part of the menacing Arab hordes who wanted to throttle the young Jewish state, as the expression had it.

One of the most unfortunate aspects of this state of affairs (and this brings me back to what I said earlier about rhetoric) is that even the word "peace" acquired a sinister, uncomfortable meaning for many Arabs, at just the time that Israeli publicists used it at every opportunity. We want peace with the Arabs, they would say, and, sure enough, the echo went around that Israel fervently desired peace, while the Arabs—who were represented as ferocious, vengeful, gratuitously bent on violence—did not. In fact, what was at issue between Israelis and Palestinians was never a real or a just peace but the possibility for Palestinians of restitution of property, nationhood, identity—all of them blotted out by the new Jewish state, and this was never even talked about. Moreover, it appeared to Palestinians that peace with Israel was a form of exterminism that left us without political existence: it meant accepting as definitive and unappealable the events of 1948, the loss of our society and homeland. So even more alienated from Israel and everything it stood for, the whole idea of separation between the two peoples acquired a life of its own, though it meant different things for each. Israelis wanted it in order to live in a purely Jewish state, freed from its non-Jewish residents both in memory and in actuality. Palestinians wanted it as a method for getting back to their original existence as the Arab possessors of Palestine. The logic of separation has operated since 1948 as a persistent motif and has now reached its apogee and its logical conclusion in the hopelessly skewed, unworkable and, since September 29, 2000, terminated Oslo accords. At only the very rarest of moments did either Palestinians or Israelis try to think their histories and cultures—inextricably linked for better or for worse—together, contrapuntally, in symbiotic, rather than mutually exclusive terms. The sheer distortion in views both of history and of the future that has resulted is breathtaking and requires some example and analysis here.

I don't think that anyone can honestly disagree that since 1948 the Palestinians have been the victims, Israelis the victors. No matter how much one tries to dress up or prettify this rather bleak formulation, its truth shines through the murk just the same. The general argument from Israel and its supporters has been that the Palestinians brought it on themselves: Why did they leave? Why did the Arabs declare war? Why did they not accept the 1947 plan of partition? And so on and on. None of this, it should be clear, justifies Israel's subsequent official behavior both towards itself and its Palestinian victims, where a hard cruelty, a dehumanizing attitude, and an almost sadistic severity in putting down the Palestinians has prevailed over all the years, rarely more so than in recent months. The frequently expressed Israeli and general Jewish feeling, that Israel is in serious peril and that Jews will always be targets of anti-Semitic opportunity, is often buttressed by appeals to the Holocaust, to centuries of Christian anti-Semitism, and to Jewish exile. This is a potent and in many ways justifiable sentiment.

I have gone on record in the Arab world as saying that it is justified for Jews—even for American Jews whose experiences have been nowhere nearly as traumatic as their European counterparts—to feel the agonies of the Holocaust as their own, even unto the present, but I keep asking myself whether the use of that feeling to keep Palestinians in more or less permanent submission can repeatedly be justified on those grounds alone. Are the official and intemperate (to say the least) harangues about Israeli security justified, given what a miserable lot has been that of the Palestinians? Are the huge numbers of soldiers, the obsessive, excessive measures about terrorism (the meandering and profligate significations of which require a treatise of their own), the endless fencing in, the interrogations, the legal justification of torture, the nuclear, biological and chemical options, the discriminations against Israeli Palestinians, the fear and contempt, the bellicosity—one could go on and on—are all these things not a sort of massive distortion in perception and mode of life, all of them premised on and fueled by the extreme separatist, not to say xenophobic sentiment that Israel must be, must remain at all costs an endangered, isolated, unloved Jewish state? And that its strength is derived falsely from its unwillingness to examine or reflect candidly on its past and to accord Palestinians the right to remember their catastrophe as the essential feature of their collective experience. Doesn't one have the impression that the language and discourse of Israel—there are exceptions of course—generally signify a refusal to engage with the common regional history except on these extreme separatist terms?

Here is Adorno discussing in the *Minima Moralia* distortions of language in the dominated and the dominating:

"The language of the dominant turns against the masters, who misuse it to command, by seeking to command them, and refuses to serve their interests. The language of the subjected, on the other hand, domination alone has stamped, so robbing them further of the justice promised by the unmutilated, autonomous word to all those free enough to pronounce it without rancor. Proletarian language is dictated by hunger. The poor chew words to fill their bellies. From the objective spirit of language they expect the sustenance refused them by society; those whose mouths are full of words have nothing else between their teeth. So they take revenge on language. Being forbidden to love it, they maim the body of language, and so repeat in impotent strength the disfigurement inflicted on them."(65)

The compelling quality of this passage is the imagery of distortion inflicted on language, repeated, reproduced, turning inward, unable to provide sustenance. And so it seems to me has been the interplay since 1948 between the official discourses of Zionism and Palestinian nationalism, the former dominating but in the process twisting language to serve an endless series of misrepresentations organized around the basic binary opposition which does not serve their interests (Israel is more insecure today, less accepted by Arabs, more disliked and resented.), the latter using language as a compensatory medium for the unfulfillment of a desperate political self-realization. For, fifty-four years after 1948, the Palestinians are still an absence, a desired and willed negativity in Israeli discourse, on whom various images of absence have been heaped: the nomad, the terrorist, the *fellah*, the Arab, the Islamic fanatic, the killer, and so forth. For Palestinians their official discourse has been full of the affirmation of presence, yet a presence mostly dialectically annulled in the terms of power politics and hence affirmed in a language like that of Darwish's poem "Sajjil Ana 'Arabi,"—"I am here, take note of me"—or in the ludicrous trappings including honor guard and bagpipes of a head of state allowed himself by Yasser Arafat. Over time it is the distortions that are increased, not the amount of reality in the language.

This is a difficult point but, for my argument, central to try to express, so let me give it another formulation. The modern history of the struggle for Palestinian self-determination can be regarded as an attempt to set right the distortions in life and language inscribed so traumatically as a consequence of 1948. Certainly in religious terms, this is what Hamas and Islamic Jihad promise. There has never been any shortage of secular Palestinian resistance, and while it is true that there have been some advances here and there in Palestinian struggle —the first *intifada* and the invigorations provided by the PLO before 1991 being two of the most notable—the general movement either has been much slower than that of Zionism, or it has been regressive. Where the struggle over land has been concerned, there has been a net loss, as Israel through belligerent as well as pacific means has asserted its actual hold on more and more of Palestinian land. I speak here, of course, of sovereignty, military power, actual settlement. I contrast that with what I shall call Palestinian symptoms of response, such as the multiple rhetorical attempts to assert the existence of a Palestinian state, to bargain with Israel over conditions of Israeli (and not Palestinian) security, and the general untidiness, sloppiness, and carelessness—absence of preparations, maps, files, facts and figures among Palestinian negotiators in the Oslo process—that have characterized what can only be called a lack of ultimate seriousness in dealing with the real, as opposed to the rhetorical, conditions of dispossession. These, as I said earlier, multiply the distortions stemming from the original condition of loss and dispossession: rather than rectifications they offer additional dislocations and the reproduction of distortions whose widening effects extend the whole range, from war to increasing numbers of refugees, more property abandoned and taken, more frustration, more anger, more humiliation, more corruption and cruelty, and so on. From all this derives the force of Rosemary Sayigh's startlingly appropriate, and even shattering phrase, "too many enemies." The poignancy is that Palestinians, by a further dialectical transformation, have even become their own enemies through unsuccessful and self-inflicted violence.

For Israel and its supporters—especially its Western liberal supporters—none of this has mattered very much, even though the encomia to Israel, and/or a generalized embarrassed silence when Israel has indulged itself in ways normally not permitted any other country, have been unrelenting. One of the main consequences of 1948 is an ironic one: as the effects of that highly productive dispossession have increased, so too the tendency has been to overlook their source, to concentrate on pragmatic, realistic, tactical responses to "the problem" in the present. The recent peace process is unthinkable without an amnesiac official abandonment, which I deplore, by the Palestinian leaders of what happened to them in 1948 and thereafter. And yet they could not be in the position they are in without that entirely concrete and minutely, intensely lived experience of loss and dispossession for which 1948 is both origin and enduring symbol. So there is an eerie dynamic by which the reliving of our mistakes and disasters comes forward collectively without the force or the lessons or even the recollection of our past. We are perpetually at the starting-point, looking for a solution now, even as that "now" itself bears all the marks of our historical diminishment and human suffering.

In both the Israeli and Palestinian cases there is, I think, a constitutive break between the individual and the whole, which is quite striking, especially insofar as the whole is, as Adorno once put it, the false. Zeev Sternhell has shown in his historical analysis of Israel's founding narratives (*The Founding Myths of Israel,* 1998) that an idea of the collective overriding every instance of the particular was at the very heart of what he calls Israel's nationalist socialism. The Zionist enterprise, he says, was one of conquest and redemption of something referred to almost mystically as "the land." Humanly the result was a total subordination of the individual to a corporate self, presumed to be the new Jewish body, a sort of super-collective whole in which the constituent parts were insignificant compared to that whole. Many of the institutions of the state, especially the Histadrut and the land agency, overrode anything that might smack of individualism, or of individual agency since what was always of the utmost importance was the presumed good of the whole. Thus, according to Ben Gurion, nationhood mattered more than anything else: consequently, frugality of lifestyle, self sacrifice, pioneer values were the essence of the Israeli mission. Sternhell traces out with more detail than anyone I know what sorts of complications and contradictions were entailed by this vision—how, for example, Histadrut leaders and military men got higher pay than the laborers who were, in the going phrase, conquering the wasteland, even though an ideology of complete egalitarianism (often referred to abroad as "socialism") prevailed.

Yet this did not evolve once Israel became an independent state. "The pioneering ideology, with its central principles—the conquest of land, the reformation of the individual, and self-realization—was not an ideology of social change; it was not an ideology that could establish a secular, liberal state and put an end to the war with the Arabs"(Sternhell, 46). Nor, it must be added, could it develop a notion of citizenship since it was meant to inform a state of the Jewish people, not of its individual citizens. The project of Zionism therefore was not only this entirely new modern state but, as

Sternhell puts it, "the very negation of the diaspora." It would be extremely difficult to find within the parallel Arab dominant ideology or practice of the period after 1948 anything like a concerned attention paid to the notion of citizenship.

Quite the contrary, there was if anything a mirror image of Zionist corporatism except that most of the ethnic and religious exclusivity of Jewish nationalism is not there. In its basic form Arab nationalism is inclusive and pluralistic generally, though like Zionism there is a quasi-messianic, quasi-apocalyptic air about the descriptions in its major texts of revival, the new Arab individual, the emergence and birth of the new polity, etc.

Even in the emphasis on Arab unity in Nasserism, one feels that a core of human individualism and agency is missing, just as in practice it is simply not part of the national program in a time of emergency. Now the Arab security state already well described by many scholars, political scientists, sociologists, and intellectuals, is a nasty or sorry thing in its aggregate, repressive, and monopolistic in its notions of state power, coercive when it comes to issues of collective well-being. But, once again, it is thunderingly silent on the whole matter of what being a citizen, and what citizenship itself entails beyond serving the motherland and being willing to sacrifice for the greater good. On the issue of national minorities there are some scraps here and there of thought, but nothing in practice given the fantastic mosaic of identities, sects, and ethnicities in the Arab world. Most of the scholarly, scientific literature that I have read on the Arab world—the best and most recent of which is critical and highly advanced—speaks about clientelism, bureaucracies, patriarchal hierarchies, notables, and so on, but spends depressingly little time talking about *muwatana* (citizenship) as a key to the socio-political and economic morass of recession and de-development that is now taking place. Certainly accountability is left out of the critical picture more or less totally.

I am not the only one to have said, though, that one of the least discouraging consequences of 1948 is the emergence of new critical voices, here and there, in the Israeli and Arab worlds (including diasporas) whose vision is both critical and integrative. By that I mean such schools as the Israeli new historians, their Arab counterparts and, among many of the younger area studies specialists in the West, those whose work is openly revisionist and politically engaged. Perhaps it is now possible to speak of a new cycle opening up in which the dialectic of separation and separatism has reached a sort of point of exhaustion, and a new process might be beginning, glimpsed here and there within the anguished repertoire of communitarianism which by now every reflecting Arab and every Jew somehow feels as the home of last resort. This communitarianism is likely to be exacerbated for a while by the terrible events of September 11 and their political and military aftermath. It is of course true and even a truism that the system of states in the region has done what it can do as a consequence of 1948, that is, provide what purports to be a sort of homogenized political space for like people, for Syrians, Jordanians, Israelis, Egyptians and so on. Palestinians have aspired and continue to aspire to a similar consolidation of self-hood with geography, some unity of the nation, now dispersed, with its home territory. Yet the problem of the Other remains, for Zionism, for Palestinian nationalism, for Arab and/or Islamic nationalism. There is, to put it simply, an irreducible, heterogeneous presence always to be taken account of which, since and because of 1948, has become intractable, unwishable away, there. September 11 has brought this out with alarming intensity, as Ariel Sharon justifies his policies of collective punishment against the Palestinians by associating himself and Israel with the US campaign in Afghanistan.

Conclusion and Proposals

How then to look to the future? How to see it, and how to work towards it, if all the schemes either of separatism or exterminism, or of going back either to the Old Testament or the Golden Age of Islam or to the pre-1948 period, simply will not do, will not work, so far as any peace, much less a just peace, is concerned? What I want to propose is an attempt to flesh out the emergence of a political and intellectual strategy based on just peace and just coexistence based on secular equality. This strategy is based on a full consciousness of what 1948 was for Palestinians and for Israelis, the point being that no bowdlerization of the past, no diminishment of its effects can possibly serve any sort of decent future. I want to suggest here the need for a new kind of grouping, one that provides a critique of ideological narratives as well as a form that is compatible with real citizenship and a real democratic politics. In the context of my opening remarks about just peace, what I want to discuss now is the dynamic, developing nature of just peace at the point where precisely most peace-making efforts normally stop.

- We need to think about two histories not simply separated ideologically, but together, contrapuntally. Neither Palestinian nor Israeli history at this point is a thing in itself, without the other. In so doing we will necessarily come up against the basic irreconcilability between the Zionist claim and Palestinian dispossession. The injustice done to the Palestinians is constitutive to these two histories, as is also the crucial effect of Western anti-Semitism and the Holocaust.

- The construction of what Raymond Williams termed an emergent composite identity based on that shared or common history, irreconcilabilities, antinomies and all. What we will then have is an overlapping and necessarily unresolved consciousness of Palestine/Israel throughout its history, not despite it, an acknowledgement—as yet unknown in Israeli mainstream discourse—of the injustice committed against the Palestinians. Since no comparable injustice was committed against Israel by the Palestinians, none should be sought.

- A demand for rights and institutions of common secular citizenship, not of ethnic or religious exclusivity, with culmination first in two equal states, then in a unitary state, as well as rethinking the Law of Return and Palestinian Return together. Citizenship should be based on the just solidarities of coexistence and the gradual dissolving of ethnic lines.

- The crucial role of education with special emphasis on the Other. This is an extremely long term project in which the diaspora/exilic and research communities must play a central role. There are now at least two or perhaps more warring research paradigms based on the lamentable clash of civilizations model, which is so misleading and constitutively bellicose: to their credit, this series of interventions acknowledges the transitional state of research on Israel/Palestine, its precarious, rapidly evolving, and yet fragmentary and uneven character. They need to focus on equality and coexistence.

Ideally, of course, the goal is to achieve consensus by scholars and activist intellectuals that a new, synthetic paradigm might slowly emerge which would re-orient the combative and divisive energies we've all had to contend with into more productive and collaborative channels. This cannot occur, I believe, without some basic agreement, a compact or entente whose outlines would have to include first, regarding the Other's history as valid but incomplete as usually presented, and second, admitting that despite the antinomy, these histories can only continue to flow together, not apart, within a broader framework based on the notion of equality for all. This, of course, is a secular and, by no means, a religious goal, and I believe it needs to start life by virtue of entirely secular, not religious or exclusivist, needs. Secularization requires demystification, it requires courage, it requires an irrevocably critical attitude towards self, society, and Other, at the same time, keeping in mind the imperatives or principles of justice and peace. But it also requires a narrative of emancipation and enlightenment for all, not just for one's own community.

For those who challenge all this and call it utopian or unrealistic, my answer is a simple one: show me what else is available today as a way of thinking about and moving towards a just peace. Show me a scheme for separation that isn't based on abridged memory, continued injustice, unmitigated conflict, *apartheid*. There just isn't one—hence the value of what I've tried to outline here.

CHAPTER FIFTEEN

A Clarion Call

Desmond Tutu

*from his keynote address on April 13, 2002, Old South Church, Boston, MA USA
for Friends of Sabeel North America's Conference, from a transcription
prepared by Allison B. Hodgkins, Friends of Sabeel, New England*

God weeps over what God sees in the Middle East and other places and says: "Gee Whiz! What ever got into me to create that lot?" And then God sees those who are working for justice. God looks down and God smiles and says: "Hey! Don't they justify the risk that I took?" And God says to them: "Thank you—thank you for proving me right in creating humanity." Because you see, actually God has no one except ourselves—absolutely no one. God is extraordinary because God is omnipotent and you know what that means—omnipotent, all powerful—but, God is also utterly impotent. God does not dispatch lighting bolts to remove tyrants as we might have hoped he would. God waits for you, for you, for you, for you, for me. Because God says to each of us: "You are my partner, and I am as weak as the weakest of my partners."

That's just a small preamble. God thanks us, but I would actually like to say in return, "Thank you, God, for me. Thank you, God, that you made me myself so that I can celebrate who you are." Because, for God, each of us is the best thing that God ever created, a masterpiece in the making. And so, let's give ourselves a warm cheer for being God's partners in the task before us.

That task is giving peace a chance—for peace is possible even though the events of these days do not suggest that is true. You see, we are bearers of hope for God's children in the Holy Land—for God's people the Israeli Jews and God's people the Palestinian Arabs. We want to say to them: our hearts go out to all who have suffered as a result of the violence of suicide bombers and the violence of military incursions and reprisals and we want to express our deepest sympathies to all who have been injured and bereaved in the horrendous events of recent times. We want to say to all involved in the events of these past years—peace is possible. Israeli Jew, Palestinian Arab can live amicably side by side in a secure peace, a secure peace built on justice and equity. These two peoples are God's chosen and beloved, looking back to a common ancestor Abraham and confessing belief in the one creator God of *salaam* and *shalom*.

As Christians, we give thanks for all that we have learned from the teachings of God's people, the Jews. When we were opposing the vicious South African system of *apartheid*, which claimed that what invested people with worth was a biological irrelevance—skin color —we turned to the Jewish Torah, which asserted that what gave people their infinite worth was the fact that they were created in the image of God. Thus, on this score, *apartheid* was evil, unbiblical, and therefore, unchristian.

And when our people groaned under the burden of racist oppression, we invoked the God who addressed Moses in the burning bush. We told our people that our God had heard their cry, had seen their anguish and knew their suffering, and would come down, this great God of exodus, this liberator God, as in the past, to deliver us as God had delivered Israel from bondage. We told them that God was notoriously biased in favor of those without clout: the poor, the weak, the hungry, the voiceless, as God had shown when God intervened through the Prophet Nathan against King David on behalf of Uriah, Bathsheba's husband. Or, as God intervened through Elijah on behalf of Naboth against King Ahab and Jezebel when they confiscated Naboth's vineyard and caused Naboth to be killed.

This same God did not abandon us in South Africa. For when we were thrown into the fiery furnace of tribulation and suffering caused by *apartheid*, this God was there with us as Emanuel, 'God with us,' just as God had been there with Daniel and his companions. We reminded those enduring suffering that this God rejects worship which does not change the lives and conduct of the worshippers to make them care especially for the widow, the orphan and the alien, those in most societies who are among the most vulnerable and least influential. This God prefers obedience to sacrifice, prefers acting upon the truth to sacrifice, prefers showing mercy to sacrifice, prefers making justice flow like a river, walking humbly with God. And this God calls on God's people always to remember that their ancestors had been aliens and slaves so that this memory would galvanize them and inspire them to be in their turn compassionate and generous with the alien in their midst.

We invoked the Jewish scriptures, which have always asserted that this is God's world and that, despite all appearances to the contrary, God is in charge and this is, therefore, a moral universe. There is no way in which might can ever be right. Injustice, lies, oppression can never have the last word in the universe of this God. Oppressors and dictators and those who flout the laws of this moral universe will, in the end, bite the dust.

And in our struggle against *apartheid*, some of the most outstanding stalwarts were Jews: the Helen Suzmans, the Joe Slovos, the Alvie Saches. As in the United States during the Civil Rights movement, Jews almost instinctively, as a matter of course, had to be on the side of the disenfranchised, of the discriminated against, of the voiceless ones fighting injustice, oppression and evil, given their religious traditions, their history.

I have continued to feel a strong bond with the Jews, along with many other Nobel Peace Laureates. After taking counsel with the then Bishop of Jerusalem, I became a member of the Board of the Shimon Peres Peace Center in Tel Aviv. I am a patron of the Holocaust Center in Capetown. I believe that Israel has a right to secure borders, internationally recognized, in a land assured of territorial integrity and with acknowledged sovereignty as an independent country. I believe that the Arab nations made a bad mistake in initially refusing to recognize the existence of sovereign Israel and in pledging to work for her destruction. It was a short sighted policy that led to Israel's nervousness, her high state of alert and military preparedness to guarantee her continued existence. This was understandable.

What was not so understandable, what was not justifiable was what Israel did to another people to guarantee her existence. I have been very deeply distressed in all my visits to the Holy Land because so much of what has been taking place there reminded me so much of what used to happen to us Blacks in *apartheid* South Africa. I have seen the humiliation of the Palestinians at the checkpoints and recall what used to happen to us in our motherland when arrogant young white police officers would hector and bully us and demean us when we ran the gauntlet of their unpredictable whims as to whether they would let us through or not. Often the police seemed to derive great fun out of our sullen humiliation. I have seen such scenes or heard of them being played out in the Holy Land. Rough and discourteous demands for IDs from the Palestinians were uncannily reminiscent of the infamous Pass Law raids of the vicious *apartheid* regime.

Moreover, I saw on those visits to the Holy Land or read about things that did not happen even in *apartheid* South Africa. The demolition of homes because of a suspicion that one or other family member was a terrorist meant all paid a price in these acts of collective punishment. Such attacks have been repeated more often recently in the attacks on Arab refugee camps. We don't know the exact truth of the attacks on innocent civilians because the Israelis won't let the media in. What are they hiding?

But perhaps even more seriously we must ask, why there is no outcry in the United States at the censorship by their media. For you see, what now happens is that we are frequently being shown the harrowing images of what suicide bombers have done, which is something we all condemn unequivocally, but we don't see what those tanks are doing to the homes of just ordinary people.

On one of my visits to the Holy Land, I drove one Sunday to a church service with the Anglican Bishop. We went past Ramallah. I could hear the tears in his voice as he pointed to the Jewish settlements, and I thought of the desires of the Israelis for security and of the anguish of the Palestinians at the land they have lost. The occupying settlers and military seem to have said of the Palestinians, "They are nothing, they count for nothing." And the pain of the dispossessed and the many humiliations that have been suffered are fertile soil for the desperation of suicide bombers.

I have heard Palestinians describing a confiscated residence. I once was walking with Canon [Naim] Ateek, whose father was a jeweler. And as we walked in Jerusalem, he pointed and said, "Our home was over there. We were driven out of our home. It is now occupied by Israeli Jews." Then I recalled how many times people of color would point in much the same way to their former homes in South Africa from which they had been expelled and which were now inhabited by whites.

My heart aches. I say why are our memories so short? Have our Jewish sisters and brothers forgotten the humiliation of wearing arm bands with the yellow Star of David? Have our Jewish sisters and brothers forgotten the collective punishment, the home demolitions and confiscations? Have they forgotten their own history so soon? And have they turned their back on their profound noble and religious traditions? Have they forgotten that their God, our God, is a God who sides with the poor, the despised, the downtrodden? That this is a moral universe? That they will never, never get true security and safety from the barrel of a gun? That true peace can ultimately be built only on justice and equity?

We condemn the violence of suicide bombers. If Arab children are taught to hate Jews, we condemn the corruption of young minds, too. But we condemn equally and unequivocally the violence of military incursions and reprisals that won't let ambulances and medical personnel reach the injured and that wreak an unparalleled and totally imbalanced revenge. Such revenge is totally out of balance even with the Torah's law of "an eye for an eye," which was actually designed to **restrict** revenge to the perpetrator and perhaps those supporting him. It is the humiliation and desperation of an occupied and hapless people which are the root causes of the suicide bombing.

The military action of recent months—I want to predict with almost absolute certainty—will not provide the security and the peace the Israelis want. All it is doing is intensifying hatred and resentment and guaranteeing that one day more suicide bombers will arise to wreak revenge.

Israel has three options: 1) to revert to the stalemate of the recent status-quo, one bristling with tension, hatred and violence; 2) to perpetrate genocide and exterminate all Palestinians; or 3) the option I hope they will chose, to strive for peace based on justice, based on withdrawal from all the Occupied Territory. This option requires Palestinians to be committed to such a peace—and to say so loudly and clearly at every opportunity.

We in South Africa had a situation where everyone thought we would be overwhelmed by a blood bath. The blood bath did not happen. We had a relatively peaceful transition. Instead of revenge and retribution, we had a remarkable process of forgiveness and reconciliation via the Truth and Reconciliation Commission. If our madness, if our intractable problem could have ended as it did, then we believe it must be possible everywhere else in the world to find peaceful solutions. For South Africa was, yes, an unlikely candidate, but South Africa has become a beacon of hope, a true beacon of hope for the rest of the world. If it could happen in South Africa it can happen anywhere else. If peace could come in South Africa, then surely it can come in the Holy Land.

Sometimes people ask: "Does this mean you are pro-Palestinian?" Many must say what we used to say, too: I am not pro this or that people, I am *pro-justice*. I am *pro- freedom*. I am *anti-injustice, anti-oppression* any and everywhere that they occur. But you know as well as I do that somehow the Israeli government is placed on a pedestal so that to criticize it is immediately to be dubbed anti-Semitic—as if the Palestinians themselves were not Semitic!

I have not even been anti-white despite all the suffering that that crazy group inflicted on our people. *No!* How could I, if I wasn't even anti-those who did such harm to us, be anti-Jewish? That is actually the term that ought to be used, anti-Jewish, not anti-Semitic. If anti-Jewish were the term, you would have to say the same thing to the biblical prophets—because they were some of the most scathing critics of the Jewish leadership of their day.

We don't, however, criticize Jewish people. We have criticized and we will criticize the government of Israel when it needs to be criticized. The government of Israel charged us with being anti-Semitic when we asked them during the *apartheid* era, "Can you explain to us why you are willing to collaborate with the South African government on security matters and thus prolong *our* oppression?" To that charge of anti-Semitism, I said then, "Tough luck. Really tough luck."

When I raised similar questions about the government's mistreatment of Palestinians that we observed while visiting the Holy Land, people painted graffiti just outside St. George's Cathedral in Jerusalem: 'Tutu is a black Nazi Pig.' We've been in that position before and know we cannot be silenced.

People in the United States are scared to say *wrong* is *wrong* because the Jewish lobby is powerful, very powerful. So what? So what! This is God's world! For goodness sake, this is God's world! The *apartheid* government was very powerful, but we said to them: "Watch it! If you flout the laws of this universe, you're going to bite the dust! Hitler was powerful. Mussolini was powerful. Stalin was powerful. Idi Amin was powerful. Pinochet was powerful. The *apartheid* government of South Africa was powerful. Milosevic was powerful. But, this is God's world. A lie, injustice, oppression, those will never prevail in the world of this God."

That is what we told our people as we struggled against *apartheid*. We said over and over: "Those ones in power, they have already lost! They are going to bite the dust one day. We may not be around, but they will fall." Now we affirm that an unjust Israeli government, however powerful, will fall in the world of this kind of God.

We don't want the Israeli government to collapse, but those who are powerful have to remember the litmus test that God gives to the powerful—what is your treatment of the poor, the hungry? What is your treatment of the vulnerable, the voiceless? And on the basis of that litmus test, God passes God's judgment.

We should put out a clarion call. Let's make a clarion call to the government and the people of Israel, a clarion call to the government and the Palestinian people. Let's say, "Peace is possible! Peace based on justice is possible!" We will continue to go on, to call for this just peace for your own sakes, Israeli Jews, for your own sakes, Palestinian Arabs. Peace is possible and we will do all we can to assist you in achieving this peace which is within your grasp because it is God's dream that you will be able to live amicably together as sisters and brothers, side by side because you belong in God's family. Peace! Peace! Peace!

Glossary

Items in bold type appear as entries in the glossary.

Abrahamic religions: Judaism, Christianity, and **Islam**, the three monotheistic faiths that trace their origins to the Patriarch Abraham, Jews and Christians via Isaac, his son by Sarah and **Muslims** via Ishmael, his son by Hagar

ADL (acronym): Anti-Defamation League, a Jewish organization that monitors statements or actions that it views as anti-Semitic

AIPAC (acronym): American-Israeli Public Affairs Committee, a lobbying organization dedicated to promoting the interests of **Israel** in the United States Congress and media

al Aqsa Mosque: mosque located on the **Haram al-Sharif/Temple Mount**, Jerusalem, near the **Dome of the Rock**; Ariel **Sharon**'s visit to the site in September 2000 with 1000 soldiers was alleged to have initiated the second *intifada*, also known as the al Aqsa *intifada*

al Nakba (Arabic): "the catastrophe"; the term used by Palestinians to describe the destruction of Palestinian society resulting from the declaration of Israeli statehood (May 14, 1948), and the subsequent **Arab-Israeli war** resulting in 750,000-800,000 Palestinians forced to flee their homes and property—200,000 of whom were expelled before the war—and more than 420 Palestinian villages destroyed.

al Quds (Arabic): Jerusalem in Arabic, one of three cities sacred to **Muslims,** the other two being Mecca and Medina, as well as the holiest city to Jews and Christians

Allah (Arabic): "God"; is the Arabic language name for God by which **Muslims** and Arab Christians refer to the One God of Judaism, Christianity and Islam

Aliyah (Hebrew): "an ascent"; commonly refers to migration from the Diaspora to the State of **Israel**

apartheid (Afrikaans): "separateness"; racial segregation as previously sanctioned by law in South Africa and now used to describe the segregation of Palestinians both within Israeli proper and especially within the Occupied Territories by civil and military means

Arab: member of a group of Semitic origin that shares language and culture but not necessarily religion

Arab-Israeli War of 1948–49: known to Israelis as the War for Independence; in this war, the young state of Israel expanded its territory from the approximately 55% allocated to Jews in the November 1947 U.N. partition plan of British Mandate Palestine to 78% of that territory; Jordan occupied and later annexed the West Bank and East Jerusalem, while Egypt took control of, and administered Gaza.

Arab Israelis: Palestinians who are citizens of Israel but with fewer legal rights and services than Jewish Israelis; they comprise approximately 20% of the Israeli population; their identification cards list them by their ethnic nationality as "Arabs", while their passports list them as citizens of Israel, thus recognizing that Israel is the state of the Jewish nation rather than all of its citizens. Also Israeli Arabs.

Arab League: a loose and non-binding union of 22 Arab states founded in 1945 with headquarters in Egypt of which Palestine became a member in 1976

Arafat, Yasser: President of the Palestinian Authority (elected 1996) and long time Chairman of the Palestinian Liberation Organization (PLO); has governmental offices in Gaza and Ramallah, West Bank, where he has been under siege since March 2002.

Areas A, B, and C: Under the terms of the Oslo Accords, "temporary" designation of areas within the Occupied Territory of the West Bank to indicate areas under Palestinian control (A, 17%), under shared Palestinian/Israeli control (B, 24%), and under total Israeli control (C, 59%). Since the Israeli incursions in 2002 these designations do not apply.

Ashkenazi (plural Ashkenazim) (Hebrew): Jews of Northern and Middle European origin who comprise the majority of Israelis and dominate the political and economic life of the country in contrast to the **Sephardim,** Jews of Spanish, North African, Middle Eastern, or Asian origin.

Glossary

Balfour Declaration (1917): letter written by British Foreign Secretary Arthur James Balfour to Lord Rothschild assuring the **Zionist** Federation of Britain's "sympathy with Jewish Zionist aspirations...: His Majesty's Government view with favour the establishment in Palestine of a national home for the Jewish People, and will use their best endeavours to facilitate the achievement of this object, it being clearly understood that nothing shall be done which may prejudice the civil and religious rights of existing non-Jewish communities in Palestine or the rights and political status enjoyed by Jews in any other country." This became policy of the **British Mandate** for Palestine and fueled the Zionist goal of a Jewish state.

Bantustan (Afrikaans): originally used in South Africa to identify homelands set apart for the native populations; now used to describe the rapidly diminishing, noncontiguous Palestinian areas surrounded by illegal Israeli settlements, protected by the Israeli Army, and bisected with **by-pass** roads

Barak's "Generous Offers": The proposals by Israeli Prime Minister Ehud **Barak** in December 2000 which would have transferred approximately 10% of the most fertile areas in the West Bank, where 85% of Israeli settlers reside, to Israel; would have designated another 10% to remain under Israeli military and civil control for an indefinite period; and would have created a "Palestinian state" lacking territorial contiguity, with all border crossings subject to Israeli supervision, along with other restrictions.

British Mandate (1917–48): British control of Palestine began 9 December 1917 near the end of World War I when Jerusalem surrendered to the British forces under Gen. Allenby, ending four centuries of rule by the **Ottoman Turks**. In July 1920, Palestine was placed under the British Colonial office and civil administration replaced the military; the British Mandate over Palestine was officially implemented on September 29, 1923 (proposed in 1922) and remained in power until the establishment of the State of **Israel** on May 15, 1948.

by-pass roads: network of paved roads and highways within the West Bank and Gaza, begun after the initiation of the Oslo peace process and funded by $3 billion from the US, which are for the exclusive use of Israelis and forbidden to Palestinians; they further isolate Palestinians in one area from those in another.

Biblical Zionism: the belief that God chose the Jewish people and bequeathed to them as an everlasting possession the Land of Canaan, so that they should give to the world God's Word, his prophets, and the Messiah.

CAMERA (acronym): "Committee for Accuracy in Middle East Reporting in America," a Jewish watchdog group that monitors print and broadcast journalism in order to stifle voices perceived to be critical of Israeli policy, including accounts of Palestinian suffering

Camp David Accords (1979): framework for peace signed by US President Jimmy Carter, Egyptian President Anwar al-Sadat, and Israeli Prime Minister Menachem Begin, the latter two of whom received the Nobel Prize for Peace as a result. The Accords led to a peace treaty between Israel and Egypt which included the return to Egypt of the Sinai, which Israel had captured in 1967, but did not resolve Israel's conflicts with other Arab states nor address the issues of Palestinian lands occupied by Israel in 1967.

checkpoint: Israeli barrier, either at crossing points between the Occupied Territories and Israel or within the Occupied Territories, at which Palestinians and internationals must submit documentation and comply with other Israeli military demands before being granted passage to their destination.

Christian Zionist: a Christian who believes that the Lord's Covenant tying the Land of **Israel** to the People of Israel remains in force and that when all Jews have returned to the Land of Israel, the Messiah will come again and Armageddon, the final battle between good and evil will usher in the end time; those Jews who accept the Messiah will be among the chosen 144,000 and those who do not will be damned. The Rev. Jerry Falwell and the Rev. Pat Robertson are prominent examples.

CIPAC (acronym): Christian-Israeli Public Affairs Committee, a sister organization to **AIPAC**, lobbies the US Congress on behalf of the government of Israel and has successfully supported $10 billion in US government loan guarantees to Israel as well as raising millions of dollars from churches and televangelism to support Israeli **settlements.**

closure: the shutting off of entry from the **Occupied Territories** into **Israel,** thereby preventing Palestinian workers from reaching their jobs, farmers from delivering produce to their markets, students from reaching schools and colleges, and the sick and pregnant women from reaching hospitals in **Jerusalem**. The effect of closures is widespread unemployment and rapidly increasing numbers of Palestinians living below the poverty line.

corpus separatum: Under the 1947 **UN Resolution** calling for a Jewish state and an Arab state within the **British Mandate**, the city of **Jerusalem** was to be a "separate body" administered by an international organization.

curfew: the restriction of Palestinians in the **Occupied Territories** to their homes, often for extended periods, so that they cannot work, tend their farms, go to school, or go to the market except when granted permission by the Israeli military

Deir Yasin: Palestinian village near Jerusalem attacked on 9 April 1948 by the combined **Zionist** forces, resulting in the massacre of all 254 inhabitants; news of the massacre prompted tens of thousands of Palestinians to abandon their homes immediately

Diaspora: the communities of Jews dispersed by the Romans outside of Palestine in 70 CE; also now used for Palestinians in forced exile since 1948.

Dome of the Rock: crowned by the frequently-pictured golden dome, this shrine on the *Haram al-Sharif*/**Temple Mount** was built in 691 CE to mark the spot when Abraham offered his son to God in sacrifice (Ishmael to Muslims; Isaac to Jews and Christians) and to commemorate the Prophet Muhammad's mystical night journey to heaven from the same site

Eretz Israel (Hebrew): "Greater Israel" or "Land of Israel"; not the modern State of **Israel** but the Israel of Genesis 15:18: "To your descendants I give this land, from the river of Egypt [the Nile] to the great river, the river Euphrates..." and from the Sinai into Syria and Iraq. To some **Zionists**, this is the ultimate goal; to others, the concept of *Eretz Israel* validates the Occupation as reclamation of Judea and Samaria.

Fatah: founded in 1959, a major guerrilla group founded in 1959 and headed by Yasser Arafat while in exile, which became the leading force in the larger Palestine Liberation Organization when Arafat became its Chairman in 1969, and now a strong, if somewhat split, political organization among the Palestinian population, especially in the Occupied Territories *fatwa* (Arabic): a formal legal opinion by a religious scholar on matters of Islamic law

fedayin (Arabic): freedom fighters

First Zionist Congress (1897): held in Basel, Switzerland, under the leadership of Theodore **Herzl**, the Congress asserted the following: "The aim of Zionism is to create for the Jewish people a home in Palestine secured by public law. The congress contemplates the following means to the attainment of this end:

> 1. The promotion, on suitable lines, of the colonization of Palestine by Jewish agricultural and industrial workers.
> 2. The organization and binding together of the whole of Jewry by means of appropriate Institutions, local and international, in accordance with the laws of each country.
> 3. The strengthening and fostering of Jewish national sentiment and consciousness.
> 4. Preparatory steps towards obtaining Government consent, where necessary to the attainment of the aim of Zionism.

Five Pillars of Islam: the primary duties of every **Muslim**: profession of faith in **Allah** as the One God and **Muhammad** as his prophet; prayer five times each day; almsgiving to the poor and to the mosque; fasting during daylight hours during the month of **Ramadan**; and pilgrimage to Mecca at least once during one's lifetime if possible.

Geneva Conventions: four international agreements, the Fourth being most often cited, drawn up at the end of World War II to protect inhabitants of territories under occupation from both individual and collective punishment. Israel contends that the Fourth Geneva Convention does not apply to its occupation of Gaza and the West Bank.

Great Arab Rebellion (1936–39): a series of Arab uprisings in response to increasing Jewish migration to Palestine and to the 1937 Peel Commission, which recommended the partition of Palestine into a Jewish State, an Arab State, and a British enclave. The Jews, who at the time owned 5.6% of Palestine, were to be given 33% of the country, from which Peel suggested that the Palestinians be expelled.

Green Line: line drawn in 1949 as part of the Rhodes agreement ending the 1948 **Arab Israeli War** and giving Israel control of 78% of historic Palestine. The Green Line included a buffer zone or "no man's land" until 1967, when Israel occupied the West Bank and Gaza; the

Green Line is the approximate route of the "security fence" (actually a concrete wall) currently being constructed between **Israel** and the **Occupied Territories**.

Haganah (Hebrew): "defense"; para-military group commanded by later Prime Minister David **Ben Gurion**, one of three Zionist military units that fought the British forces in Palestine in pursuit of establishing the modern State of **Israel**

Hamas (Arabic): acronym for Islamic Resistance Movement, a group which provides significant social and communal support for Palestinians and whose military arm carries out armed struggle against the Occupation.

Hajj (Arabic): the pilgrimage to Mecca required of all **Muslims** able to make the journey; one of the **Five Pillars of Islam**

Haram al-Sharif (Arabic): "the noble sanctuary"; the platform in Jerusalem that includes the **Dome of the Rock** and the **Al Aqsa Mosque**; known to Jews as the **Temple Mount**

Herzl, Theodore (1860–1904): hailed as the "father of political Zionism," Herzl was a Viennese journalist who shifted from espousing Jewish assimilation into European society to becoming the spokesperson of the Zionist movement and author of declarations issued at the **First Zionist Congress** of 1897. His conversion to **Zionism** resulted from the wave of anti-Semitism that swept over Europe from the 1880's and culminated in the 1894 Dreyfus Affair when a Jewish officer was unjustly court-martialed by the French.

Hijrah (Arabic): "migration"; journey of the Prophet Muhammad and his disciples from Mecca to Medina in 622, the first year of the Islamic calendar.

home demolitions: the practice of removing Palestinian families and destroying their homes under the supervision of the Israeli army, sometimes because the house was built without a usually denied Israeli permit, sometimes to confiscate the land, and sometimes to punish family members of suspected terrorists; such actions are illegal under the **Fourth Geneva Convention**.

Hussein-McMahon Correspondence of Agreement: a 1915 agreement in which the British promised independent statehood to the Arab people after the end of the **Ottoman Empire** contrary to the promises made in 1917 to the **Zionists** in the **Balfour Declaration**.

IDF (acronym): the Israeli Defense Force, the official army formed by combining the various independent para-military groups that fought against the British to attain independence; most Jewish Israelis, male and female, must commit two years to serving in the military and function as reserves thereafter although the Ultra Orthodox are exempt and Palestinian Israelis are excluded.

Imam (Arabic): teacher and leader of prayers at a mosque

incursion: invasion of **Palestinian Authority** controlled areas begun during March–April 2002 by the Israeli army using tanks, helicopters, and other assault weapons; as a result, Palestinian homes have been demolished, Palestinian infrastructure, olive groves and agricultural lands destroyed, and Palestinians killed, wounded, held under curfew, and denied individual and collective rights.

Intifada (Arabic): from root meaning "to shake off, to recover"; uprising against the Israeli Occupation. The first *intifada* (1987–93) quickly became a movement that incorporated all segments of Palestinian society in opposition to Israeli policies, gained international sympathy for the Palestinian cause, and helped to initiate the various peace efforts of the 1990's at **Madrid** and **Oslo**. The second *intifada* (the *al Aqsa intifada*) began in September 2000 when Arial Sharon and a large military force descended upon the **Haram al-Sharif**/Temple Mount and continues to the present time.

Irgun (Hebrew): Jewish underground para-military unit formed in 1931 for the purpose of establishing a Jewish state in the entire Mandated Palestine, including the Transjordan; Menachim **Begin**, later to be Prime Minister was a member of the group.

Iron Wall: term coined by Zionist Vladimir Jabotinsky, active in the 1920's and 30's, in his public declaration that "Zionist colonization... must either be terminated or carried out in defiance of the will of the native population." To secure dominance over the natives, he argued, they must be dispossessed of the land by military means, leading to the creation of "an iron wall which they cannot break through..."

Islam (Arabic): literally "surrender"; a religion which declares God (*Allah* in Arabic) to be the One God, **Muhammad** his true and final prophet in a long line of prophets beginning with Adam, including Moses and all the prophets of Hebrew scripture as well as Jesus. Adherents of Islam are **Muslims**.

Glossary

Islamic *Jihad*: militant Palestinian organization formed in the 1980's and advocating armed struggle against Israeli Occupation.

Israel: the UN General Assembly Partition Plan Resolution 181 passed on November 29, 1947, with 33 votes in favor, 13 opposed, and 10 abstentions called for a Jewish State and an Arab State in Palestine. The modern Jewish State of Israel was formally established on May 14, 1948 by declaration of the Zionist Council in Palestine, but Israel never accepted 181 in full, especially the call for an Arab State, fixed borders, and the internationalization of Jerusalem.

Israeli Arabs: See **Arab Israelis**.

Israeli Prime Ministers: This is not a complete list but includes those whose names frequently arise in the context of the Israeli/Palestinian conflict:

- Barak, Ehud: protégé of Yitzak Rabin and, like him, a soldier who declared his determination to pursue peace, elected PM in 1999; under his leadership, Israel withdrew from its 17 year occupation of southern Lebanon and the final efforts at peace with Palestinians failed despite what is often called "**Barak's Generous Offer.**" The failure culminated in his defeat by **Sharon** in Feb. 2001

- Begin, Menachem: PM (1977–83) awarded the Nobel Peace Prize in 1978 for his role in the **Camp David Accords**, the first treaty between Israel and an Arab country (Egypt); Begin also authorized the Israeli invasion of Lebanon in 1982 and expanded **settlements** in the **Occupied Territories**.

- Ben-Gurion, David: first PM of Israel, leader of **Haganah** and known as the "George Washington" of his country who was dedicated to forging sense of national identity for the immigrants flooding into the new State of Israel

- Meir, Golda: third PM (1969–1974) in office when crucial decisions were made about the disposition of the territories acquired in the 1967 War; while General Moshe Dayan advocated colonization and annexation into the State of Israel, Meir opted to retain the land under Israeli control.

- Netanyahu, Benyamin: PM (1996–99) during the period of Oslo II when illegal Israeli settlers in "greater Jerusalem" and the Occupied Territories increased from a few thousand to approximately 400,000; on record as opposing a Palestinian state; failed in his challenge of Sharon for leadership of Likud Party in fall of 2002

- Peres, Shimon: PM (1984–86 and 95–96), he was a member of **Haganah** and later a founder of the Israeli Labor Party, has been a proponent of peace with Palestinians and other Arab countries, and was from 2001 to late 2002 part of the coalition government.
- Rabin, Yitzak (1992–95): participant in the famous handshake with Yasser **Arafat** on the White House lawn 13 September 1993, inaugurating the efforts toward peace during the **Oslo** era; assassinated at a Peace Rally 4 November 1995 by a Jewish settler claiming to be acting in God's name
- Shamir, Yitzak: head of the **Stern Gang**, became PM in 1986
- Sharon, Ariel: became PM in 2001 after his visit with armed troops to the *Haram al Sharif*; under his leadership, Israeli **incursions** into Palestinian cities have produced widespread unemployment, destruction and death as well as increasing numbers of suicide bombings; coalition government dissolved when Labor withdrew in late 2002; elections scheduled for January 2003.

Jerusalem: both a modern city and the location of ancient sites holy to Jews, Christians, and Muslims. The "old city" is surrounded by stone walls built by **Suleiman the Magnificent** in the mid-16th century and is divided into 4 Quarters: the Arab, the Armenian, the Christian, and the Jewish Quarters. Proposed to be under international control in the original 1947 **UN Resolution** that called for Jewish and Arab states, the metropolitan area is divided into East (Arab) and West (Jewish) Jerusalem. The Israeli government has unilaterally declared a "greater Jerusalem" that incorporates much of the Palestinian area, including expansion into the West Bank, as its eternal Capital and is rapidly building settlements to squeeze out the Palestinian residents.

Jihad (Arabic): "striving, effort, struggle"; refers in **Islam** to the struggle within the self to obey the will of God (the greater *jihad*) and the struggle with the external world (the lesser *jihad*). War in Islamic law can only be undertaken in defense, and civilian life and property are off limits as purposeful targets.

Jordan, the Hashemite Kingdom: Originally called **Transjordan**; established at the end of WWII, the Kingdom occupied and later annexed the West Bank of the Jordan River and East Jerusalem after the 1948 war; it then changed its name to the Hashemite Kingdom of Jordan; Israel conquered and occupied those territories in 1967.

Ka'aba (Arabic): the ancient shrine in Mecca, holiest site of pilgrimage (the *Hajj*) for Muslims

King David Hotel: site of 1946 Jerusalem bombing by the **Irgun** in which 91 civilians were killed; one of the first acts of terrorism in which civilians were purposefully targeted

Knesset: the 120 seat Israeli Parliament in which any party gaining 1.5% of the national vote gains representation; hence the Knesset is comprised of MK's (Members of the Knesset) from a wide array of political parties who often control the balance in forming coalition governments.

Labor Party: one of the two major Israeli political parties, known historically to be the party left of center, more open to negotiation and compromise with Palestinians but from 2001 to late 2002 part of the coalition government of Prime Minister Ariel **Sharon**.

Law of Return: declaration by the Israeli Knesset in 1950 giving any Jew in the world the right to move to and settle in Israel as a citizen; also see **Right of Return for Palestinians**

Likud Party: one of the two major Israeli political parties, known historically as the party to the right of center, aggressive in opposition to Palestinian statehood and rights

Madrid Peace Conference (1991–92): Organized by the US and the Soviet Union, the Conference included Israel, Syria, Lebanon, **Jordan**, and Palestinians and sought to pursue a peace process between Israel and Palestinians in the territories, as well as with Syria and other Arab countries on issues such as the future of the people under occupation, water rights, Jerusalem, settlements, refugees, and security matters. It failed.

matrix of control: term coined by Dr. Jeff Halper, founder of the Israeli Committee against House Demolitions, to summarize the military, political, geographic—especially the placement of illegal Israeli settlements in the territories—and economic methods by which Palestinian lands have systematically been diminished to an "archipelago of 190 islands" without contiguity and viable state boundaries.

Muhammad (570–632 CE): the "seal of the prophets" to whom the Holy *Qu'ran* was revealed, producing the Islamic "people of the book." In 622 Muhammad and his followers made the *hijrah* (emigration) from Mecca to Medina

Muslim: literally "one who surrenders"; as adherents of **Islam**, Muslims are committed to surrender their will to **God (Allah)** by following the **Five Pillars**. There are about 5.5 million adherents of Islam in the United States and 1.2 billion worldwide.

Occupation: The term commonly used to describe Israeli military, civil, and economic control of lands conquered in the 1967 War. Israel denies that it is bound by the conditions of the Fourth **Geneva Convention** for forces occupying the territory of another people since it does not admit to being an occupying power.

Occupied Territories: In the 1967 War, Israel took control of the West Bank from Jordan, the Sinai Peninsula and Gaza from Egypt, and the Golan Heights from Syria. With 1978 **Camp David Accords**, the Sinai reverted to Egypt. While the Golan Heights remain under Israeli control, the term Occupied Territories is popularly understood to refer to the West Bank and Gaza, the site of a potential Palestinian state.

Oslo/Oslo Accords: Following secret negotiations in Oslo, Norway, **Israel** and the **PLO** signed the "Declaration of Principles on Interim Self-Government [for Palestine]" on 13 September 1993 and initiated a series of partial interim agreements thereafter; final status talks in July 2000 at Camp David failed, bringing the process to a halt.

Ottoman Empire: For approximately four centuries (1517–1917), the Ottoman Turks governed the entire Middle East, along with the Balkans and other portions of Eastern Europe. Under Suleiman the Magnificent, the current walls of the Old City of Jerusalem were constructed. Allied with Germany in WWI, the Empire, which had been in decline for many decades, finally collapsed at the end of the war. The victorious forces, especially England and France, took control of the former Ottoman territories, leading to a set of French and British mandates over most of the area including the **British Mandate** of Palestine.

Palestinian Authority (PA) or Palestinian National Authority (PNA): the designation for the elected government officials and agencies authorized by the **Oslo Accords**. Yasser **Arafat** was elected President of the Palestinian Authority on 20 January 1996.

Palestinian Legislative Council: a group of 88 members elected on 20 January 1996 from 16 districts in the Palestinian territories to create a civil government but lacking responsibility for foreign affairs

Palestine Liberation Organization (PLO): established in May 1964 when the **Arab League** designated the group to represent the stateless Palestinians. Yasser **Arafat** became Chairman of the PLO in 1969; the UN recognized the PLO in 1974 as the representative of Palestinians with an observer at the UN General Assembly. **Israel** recognized the body in 1993, and it is the official signatory to the Oslo Accords.

Palestine National Council (PNC): the Parliament in exile of the **PLO** with 669 members representing Palestinians worldwide; it signed the Palestinian National Charter in 1964, the Palestinian Declaration of Independence in 1988, and in agreement with the Oslo Declaration of Principles in 1996 recognized the State of Israel.

Peel Commission (1936–37): British commission that recommended the partition of **British Mandate** Palestine into a Jewish state, a Palestinian state, and a British enclave. The Jews, who then owned 5.6% of the land, were to be given 33% of the land from which the Palestinians were to be expelled, according to the Commission's recommendations. This report fueled the 1936–39 **Great Arab Rebellion**.

Present-Absentee Law (1950): This 1950 Israeli law declares that Palestinians who fled their homes during the 1948–49 War but remained in Israeli-held territory were "present-absentees" who lost their rights to land and citizenship. Another component of the Law allows the Israeli government to declare any land area a "closed military zone," preventing its cultivation; then when the land has lain fallow, it is claimed by the state of Israel as "heir of the Sultan," following an **Ottoman** law that declared that fallow land reverted to the Sultan, *i.e.*, became state lands

Qur'an or Holy Qur'an (spelling preferred over Koran): literally "recitation," the scriptures of Islam in 114 *suras* (chapters). The prophet **Muhammad** received the scriptures in a series of revelations from God via the angel Gabriel.

Ramadan: a month-long period of purification and fasting from sun up to sundown; one of the **Five Pillars of Islam**

Reconstructionism: a modern movement, founded by Professor Mordecai M. Kaplan, attempting to unify the Jewish community and treating Judaism as a civilization.

Right of Return: Based on the **UN General Assembly Resolution 194**, Palestinian refugees were guaranteed the right to return along with to their original homes and compensation for losses, or to fair compensation if they chose not to return. Because there are now more than four million Palestinian refugees worldwide, Israel rejects this right while holding to the **Law of Return** for anyone born of a Jewish mother anywhere in the world.

Rosh Hashanah (Hebrew): the Jewish New Year, a "Day of Memorial" in which humanity remembers Creation and the Creator; the *shofar* (ram's horn) is sounded and special hymns and poems are recited. The observation begins the Ten Days of Penitence, ending with **Yom Kippur**.

Sabra and *Shatila:* Palestinian refugee camps in Lebanon, sites of infamous massacres by Israeli forces under the command of Gen. Arial **Sharon** after Israel invaded and occupied southern Lebanon in 1982.

Saudi Peace Proposal (2001): Saudi Crown Prince Abdullah proposed in summer 2001 during the *Al Aqsa* **intifada** and the Israeli **incursions** into **Palestinian Authority** areas that peace talks resume; key proposals were the recognition and establishment of normal relations between all Arab countries and Israel and the establishment of a viable Palestinian state. The proposal has not been enacted.

Sephardic Jews: Jews originally of Spanish origin and subsequently all Jews of North African, Middle Eastern and Asian heritage who have less economic and political clout in Israel than the *Ashkenazic* Jews of Northern and Middle European origin.

settlement: a colony of Israelis living in the Occupied Territories. Although new settlements were outlawed by the **Oslo Accords**, the number of settlers has increased from a few thousand at the time of Oslo I to more than 200,000 in the West Bank and Gaza, with an additional 200,000 established in "neighborhoods" of the Israeli-defined "greater **Jerusalem**" and an estimated growth rate of 8% a year. While many settlers are Ultra-Orthodox who believe that they are living on land promised to them since Biblical times, others are immigrants who have found homes in inexpensive, government-subsidized housing. The settlements are often located on hilltops; their red-tiled roofs, green lawns, and highly visible security systems differ dramatically from the Palestinian villages nearby.

Shahid (Arabic): "martyr"; anyone who dies for his/her faith or more broadly for political freedom; used for but not limited to **suicide bombers**

Shaftesbury, Lord: British nobleman who in the 1830's coined the phrase, "a country without a nation for a nation without a country" to describe Palestine. Later Zionist **Israel Zangwill** revised the phrase to the well-known "land without a people for a people without a land."

Sharia (Arabic): the body of Islamic sacred law derived from the Qur'an, custom, and commentary (*hadith*).

Shii Islam (Arabic): the smaller of the two major branches of Islam, Shiites do not differ in belief from **Sunni Islam** but believe that the succession of leadership after the death of Muhammad had to come through Muhammad's son-in-law, Ali.

Shoah: the Jewish Holocaust in which six million Jews were killed, evoking worldwide sympathy and support for the founding of the State of **Israel**

Six Day War (June, 1967): A series of provocative actions between Israel and the bordering Arab States built up tensions that resulted in the 1967 war. Israel struck first, quickly destroying the Egyptian air capacity on the ground and the alerted Arab armies, and took control of Gaza and the Sinai (from Egypt), the West Bank (from Jordan), and the Golan Heights (from Syria). Israel returned the Sinai to Egypt in the **Camp David Accords**, but continues to occupy the other territories.

Stern Gang: a para-military force supporting the creation of the State of Israel of which Itzak Shamir, later Prime Minister, was a member; it broke from the **Irgun** in 1940 and advocated the compulsory expulsion of the entire Arab population of Palestine in exchange for Jews living in Arab lands.

suicide bomber: term used by the Western media to describe a Palestinian who detonates explosives strapped to his or her body. Although suicide is prohibited by Islam, the purposeful targeting of civilians or military is seen by some Palestinians as a legitimate means of resistance on the part of an occupied people and, therefore, as martyrdom.

Sunni Islam (Arabic): the majority branch (80%) of Islam, Sunnis do not differ significantly in belief from Shii Muslims but accept a succession of leadership not traced to Muhammad's son-in-law, Ali.

Temples, First and Second: the holiest sites in ancient Israel, the temple structures followed a plan established in the Bible and were located on the **Temple Mount**, the First, Solomon's Temple, was destroyed in 587 BCE at the time of Babylonian Captivity; Herod's Temple, on the same site, was destroyed in 70 CE by the Romans.

Temple Mount: the site of the First and Second Temples of ancient Israel, now the site of the **Dome of the Rock** and the *Al Aqsa* **Mosque**. The Western or **Wailing Wall**, the one remaining wall of the platform of the Temple Mount is a holy site to Jews Ariel Sharon's visit to the Temple Mount with a large company of soldiers in September 2000 was a spark that contributed to igniting the *Al Aqsa Intifada.*

Torah (Hebrew): literally "instruction, teachings" given by God to the people; while *Torah* may refer specifically to the five Books of Moses, the term is also used for the entire Hebrew Bible

transfer: a euphemism for ethnic cleansing. Although transfer was included in Zionist ideology from its inception, reference is often made to the Zionist master plan, Plan Dalet (Plan D), the name given by the Zionist High Command to military operations in April–May 1948 that was a main plan in the expulsion of some 750,000–800,000 Palestinians and the destruction of over 420 villages. A February 2002 poll by the Israeli newspaper *Ma'ariv*, indicated that more than a third of Israelis surveyed said they supported the idea of "transfer" of Palestinians out of the West Bank and the Gaza Strip to Arab countries.

Transjordan: See **Jordan.**

United Nations Resolutions pertinent to Israel/Palestine: hundreds of resolutions have been presented by both the General Assembly and the Security Council, many vetoed by the United States. The crucial ones include:

- 1947: UN Gen. Assembly Resolution 181 called for the partition of the **British Mandate** into "independent Arab and Jewish States" and the "establishment of The City of Jerusalem as a *corpus separatum* under a special international regime...to be administered by the United Nations." After the **Arab-Israeli War,** the land that Israel did not occupy became part of the Hashemite Kingdom of **Jordan**, not a Palestinian State; Jerusalem never became an international city. *This resolution is the basis of the two-state solution.*

- 1948: UN General Assembly Resolution 194 came after the dispossession of some 750,000–800,000 Palestinians from their homes during the **Arab-Israeli War** and provides the legal basis, along with the international refugee conventions to which it is tied, for their **right to return**: Paragraph 11 "Resolves that the refugees wishing to return to their homes and live at peace with their neighbours should be permitted to do so at the earliest practicable date, and that compensation should be paid for the property of those choosing not to return and for loss of or damage to property which, under principles of international law or in equity, should be made good by the Governments or authorities responsible."

- 1967: UN Security Council Resolution 242 affirmed "(i) the withdrawal of Israel armed forces from territories occupied in the recent conflict; (ii) termination of all claims or states of belligerency and respect for and acknowledgement of the sovereignty, territorial integrity and political independence of every State in the area and their right to live in peace within secure and recognized boundaries free from threats or acts of force" and affirmed further "the necessity: (a) for guaranteeing freedom of navigation through international waterways in the area; (b) for achieving a just settlement of the refugee problem; and (c) for guaranteeing the territorial inviolability and political independence of every State in the area, through measures including the establishment of demilitarized zones."

The Resolution also called for a UN Representation to work out a peace settlement with the representatives of the "States concerned." *Hence, it is the foundation for the peace process and makes clear that settlements by the occupying power are illegal.*

- 1973: UN Security Council Resolution 338: calls on all parties in the **Yom Kippur** War to cease hostilities and to implement SC Resolution 242 in all its parts, with negotiations for peace to start at once.

wadi: a valley or deep ditch in the desert, dry except during the rainy season when floods of water can pass through very rapidly

Wailing Wall or Western Wall: a towering wall of massive stones that served as the western wall of the large platform on which the First and Second Temples stood. Divided into separate sides for men and women, it is a place of prayer and pilgrimage for Jews from around the world, who traditionally insert prayers on small slips of paper into the crevices between the stones.

Yom Kippur (Hebrew): Day of Atonement, the holiest day in the Jewish year, observed as a fast day and characterized as a "Sabbath of solemn rest" during which all manner of work is forbidden. Emphasis is placed upon confession of sin, repentance, and whole-hearted reconciliation with God and humanity.

Yom Kippur War (October 1973): Arab armies, led by Egypt and Syria, attacked the Israeli army on Yom Kippur, the holiest day in the Jewish calendar and quickly assumed control of some land taken by Israel in the Six Day War. Israel recovered and defeated the Arab forces but suffered casualties and destruction in a two-day period. (Also known as the Arab-Israeli War of 1973 or as the **Ramadan** War.)

Zangwill, Israel: changed Lord **Shaftesbury**'s slogan, "A country without a nation for a nation without a country," to the more frequently quoted, "A land without a people for a people without a land."

Zion: a biblical name for Jerusalem, either in whole or in part. For Christian Zionists, it is the presumed site of God's future kingdom after the apocalypse.

Zionism/Zionist: a form of secular Jewish nationalism made popular by **Theodor Herzl** and his followers before and after the **First Zionist Congress** in 1897. It assumes all Jews worldwide are part of a national entity called "the Jewish people" who suffer from anti-Semitism and therefore need a country of their own. In 1975 the UN General Assembly passed resolution 3379 declaring Zionism "a form of racism and racial discrimination." In 1991, due to diplomatic lobbying by the United States, the 1975 resolution was repealed. Contemporary Zionists are those who have associated themselves with the goals of the modern state of Israel, some through cultural, economic, and political means, some through military and other strategies.

Chronology of the Historic Land of Palestine

from the Ottoman Empire to the Present

Please see the Glossary for details of specific events.

1517–1917
Ottoman Empire

1878
First Zionist settlement

1897
First Zionist Congress convened by
Theodore Herzl in Basel, Switzerland

1914–17
Britain makes conflicting promises: Balfour Declaration
promises a Jewish home in Palestine.Hussein-McMahon agreement
promises independence to the Arab peoples

1917–1947
British Mandate

1936–1939
Great Arab Rebellion in response to the Peel Commission
proposal for a Jewish state, an Arab state, and a British enclave

1947
UN Resolution 181 establishes the State of Israel (55%)
and State of Palestine (45%) with Jerusalem
to be a *corpus separatum* under international control

1947 (con't)
Arab-Israeli War: On May 15, 1948, Israel becomes an independent
state and the Green Line dividing Israel from Jordan is established,
giving Israel 78 of the land. More than 420 Palestinian villages
are destroyed and 800,000 Palestinians become refugees

1956
Israel, with Britain and France,
invades Egypt and occupies Sinai and Gaza,
but US President Eisenhower forces their withdrawal

1964
Palestine Liberation Organization (PLO)
recognized by the Arab League
as the representative of Palestinian people

1967
Israel makes a "preemptive strike" against Egypt and Syria
and in six days takes the West Bank from Jordan,
the Golan Heights from Syria, and the Sinai and Gaza from Egypt.
UN Resolution 242 calls for Israeli withdrawal from occupied
territories and for the right of all states in the area to live in peace
within secure and recognized borders. Palestinians and Arab states
reject the resolution because it recognizes Israel but not a
Palestinian state. PLO becomes a commando organization
committed to establishing a "secure democratic, secular state
in which all Palestinians including Jews can live together."
Spiral of violence increases PLO attacks; Israel retaliates
against Palestinian refugee camps in Jordan and Lebanon;
about 3000 Palestinians are killed. PLO moves to Lebanon.

1978
Israel invades Lebanon and sets up a security zone

1979
Camp David Accord signed between Israel and Egypt;
Sinai is returned to Egypt

1981
Ceasefire agreement, sponsored by US and Saudi Arabia,
signed between Palestinians and the Israeli government

Chronology

1982
Israel breaks ceasefire and invades Lebanon; PLO agrees
to another ceasefire and withdrawal from Lebanon.
Israeli troops enter Beirut; the massacre at Sabra and
Shatila Refugee camps and the slaughter of thousands
of Palestinian Christians by Phalangists follow.

1987–93
The first *Intifada*

1988
Palestinian National Council declares an independent state
in the West Bank, East Jerusalem and Gaza and accepts
UN Resolution 242; US begins talks with the PLO.

1990
US breaks off talks with PLO

1991
Madrid Conference establishes issues for
a negotiated settlement

1993
Oslo I Agreement; handshake between PM Rabin and Chairman
Arafat on White House lawn confirms PLO as legitimate
representative of Palestinian people. PLO confirms its
acceptance of the State of Israel, laid out in UN Resolution 242,
and originally accepted by PLO in 1988.

1995–1997
Oslo II Accords; Israeli settlements increase rapidly despite being
outlawed by the Accords and "greater" Jerusalem expands to
incorporate much Palestinian territory under Israeli control.

2000 (Sept)
Ariel Sharon's visit to the Haram al Sharif/Temple Mount
ignites the Al Aqsa *Intifada*

2000 (Dec)
PM Barak's "Generous Offer" rejected by Palestinians
as not creating a viable and contiguous state

2001 (Feb)
Ariel Sharon defeats Barak and becomes Prime Minister,
forming a coalition government with the Labor Party.

2002 (Nov)
Labor Party withdraws from coalition government;
Sharon calls elections for January 2003;
Palestinian elections also slated for January 2003.

Contributors

Dr. Haidar Abdel-Shafi, Founder and Director of the Red Crescent Society of Gaza, an organization which provides medical care and serves as a forum for cultural activities there, has been a longtime activist for Palestinian rights. Dr. Abdel-Shafi was leader of the Palestinian delegation to the Madrid Peace Conference and to the Washington peace negotiations and was elected to the Palestinian Legislative Council but resigned in 1996.

The Rt. Rev. Riah Abu El-Assal, Episcopal Bishop of the Diocese of Jerusalem, is the author of *Caught in Between,* the story of his life and the lives of his people, Arab Palestinian Christian Israelis. Bishop Riah not only administers a diocese that includes much of the Middle East but serves as eloquent spokesman for the suffering of his people and the rapidly diminishing Palestinian Christian community.

Andrea L. Anderson, Associate Director of the Middle East Initiative at the John F. Kennedy School of Government of Harvard University, received her M.A. in Theological Studies at the Harvard Divinity School where she specialized in the intersection of policy and religion in the Middle East. Her research includes the role of religion and religious rhetoric in terrorism and the role of justice in post-conflict studies.

The Rev. Dr. Naim Ateek, Founder and President of the Sabeel Center in Jerusalem, an ecumenical grassroots liberation theology movement among Palestinian Christians, is the author of *Justice and Only Justice.* He travels worldwide as an advocate for a spirituality based on justice, peace, non-violence, liberation, and reconciliation for the different national and faith communities.

Dr. Henry R. Carse, Director of Special Programs at St. George's College in East Jerusalem, teaches theology and the practice of authentic pilgrimage in a contemporary context. He has lived in the Middle East for over thirty years, has degrees from Hebrew University and General Theological Seminary, is completing a doctorate at the

University of Kent, England, and holds American, Israeli, and Irish citizenship.

Martin Federman, Jewish educator, has worked in a several Jewish educational and communal groups and was Hillel Director and Jewish Chaplain at Northeastern University. Since participating in a fact-finding delegation in Israel/Palestine in 2001, he has worked primarily on Middle East issues and is currently co-chair of Visions of Peace with Justice in Israel/Palestine and an Operating Committee member of the Greater Boston Israel/Palestine Peace Network.

Dr. Elaine C. Hagopian, Professor Emerita of Sociology at Simmons College Boston, has received two Fulbright-Hays Grants and held visiting appointments at the American Universities of Beirut and Cairo. Author of several publications on Arab-Americans and the Israel/Palestine conflict, she was the major organizer of "Right of Return: Palestinian Refugees and a Durable Peace," a conference held at Boston University in 2000.

Dr. Jeff Halper, Professor of Anthropology at Israel's Ben Gurion University, immigrated to Israel from the US more than 30 years ago. Author of several articles on the "Matrix of Control," he is Coordinator of the Israeli Committee against House Demolitions (www.icahd.org), a direct-action Israeli group that opposes Israel's expanding control of Palestinian territory via land confiscation, house demolition, and settlement development.

Yehezkel Landau, Co-director of Open House (www.openhouse.org.il), a center for Jewish-Arab reconciliation and co-existence in Ramle, Israel, lectures internationally on issues of religion and politics and Middle East peacemaking. He and his wife, Dalia, the daughter of Jewish Holocaust survivors, knowing that the house she inherited had been taken from a Muslim family 1948, dedicated it and themselves to the creation of an interfaith youth community there.

Rabbi Michael Lerner, Founder of the Tikkun Community (www.tikkun.org) and editor of *Tikkun* Magazine, is author of *Spirit Matters: Global Healing and the Wisdom of the Soul; Jewish Renewal: a Path to Healing and Transformation,* and *Healing Israel/Palestine.* He lectures widely on the concept of TIKKUN, the healing and transformation of the planet through the building of a worldwide community.

Dr. Sara Roy, Senior Research Scholar at the Center for Middle Eastern Studies at Harvard University, is the author of *The Gaza Strip: The Political Economy of De-Development* and other scholarly works. In addition to her academic contributions, Dr. Roy speaks and writes evocatively of the ways in which her Jewish social conscience was shaped by her parents, both of whom were Holocaust survivors.

Dr. Edward Said, University Professor Emeritus of English and Comparative Literature at Columbia University, is the author of more than twenty books, including *Orientalism*, which was nominated for a National Book Critics Circle Award, *Culture and Imperialism*, *The Edward Said Reader*, and *Out of Place*, a memoir that details his life in Egypt and the United States after his family became refugees from Palestine in 1947.

The Rt. Rev. M. Thomas Shaw SSJE is a member of the Society of Saint John the Evangelist, an Anglican religious community for men in Cambridge, Massachusetts. In 1995 he became the fifteenth bishop of the Episcopal Diocese of Massachusetts. He is a member of the Episcopal Church's Committee on International and National Concerns.

Gila Svirsky, Founding member of Israel's Women in Black (1988) and Co-founder of the nine organization Israeli Coalition of Women for a Just Peace, has staged a number of dramatic acts of resistance to the Occupation. With Samaya Farhat-Naser, a Palestinian woman, she received two peace prizes in 2002, the Hermann Kesten Medal from the PEN Associate of Germany and the Solidarity Prize of Bremen.

The Rt. Rev. Desmond Tutu, Nobel Peace Laureate and Retired Anglican Archbishop of Capetown, was long a courageous spokesman against South African *apartheid* and leader of the internal protests and international sanctions that brought about its demise. In 1996 he retired as Archbishop to serve as Chair of South Africa's Truth and Reconciliation commission; he continues to be an advocate for justice and to argue that ultimately interracial and interpersonal harmony must prevail around the globe.